The Workshop of Being

The Workshop of Being

Religious Affections and Their Pragmatic Valuein the Thought of Jonathan Edwards and William James

S. T. Campagna-Pinto

LEXINGTON BOOKS
Lanham • Boulder • New York • Toronto • Plymouth, UK

Published by Lexington Books
A wholly owned subsidiary of The Rowman & Littlefield Publishing Group, Inc.
4501 Forbes Boulevard, Suite 200, Lanham, Maryland 20706
http://www.lexingtonbooks.com

Estover Road, Plymouth PL6 7PY, United Kingdom

Copyright © 2011 by Lexington Books

All rights reserved. No part of this book may be reproduced in any form or by any electronic or mechanical means, including information storage and retrieval systems, without written permission from the publisher, except by a reviewer who may quote passages in a review.

British Library Cataloguing in Publication Information Available

Library of Congress Cataloging-in-Publication Data
Campagna-Pinto, S. T.
 The workshop of being : religious affections and their pragmatic results in the thought of Jonathan Edwards and William James / S.T. Campagna-Pinto.
   p. cm.
 Includes bibliographical references (p.   ).
 ISBN 978-0-7391-4143-4 (cloth : alk. paper) -- ISBN 978-0-7391-4145-8 (electronic)
 1. Experience (Religion) 2. Edwards, Jonathan, 1703-1758. 3. James, William, 1842-1910. I. Title.
 BL53.C255 2011
 204'.2--dc23
                    2011031984

⊖™ The paper used in this publication meets the minimum requirements of American National Standard for Information Sciences—Permanence of Paper for Printed Library Materials, ANSI/NISO Z39.48-1992.

Printed in the United States of America

For my brother Fred

Contents

List of Abbreviations	viii
Acknowledgments	xi
Chapter 1 The Sacred Trace	1
Chapter 2 A New Reach of Freedom	24
Chapter 3 Heart Religion and the Pragmatist Imagination	52
Chapter 4 The Art of Expansiveness	76
Chapter 5 Strenuous Democracy and the Workshop of Being	110
Notes	144
Bibliography	160
Index	166
About the Author	171

List of Abbreviations

The following works have been abbreviated in endnotes for convenience.

AW Jonathan Edwards, *Apocalyptic Writings, The Works of Jonathan Edwards*, vol. 5. Edited by Stephen J. Stein. New Haven and London: Yale University Press, 1978.
EP William James, *Essays in Philosophy*. Edited by Frederick Burkhardt and Fredson Bowers. Cambridge, Massachusetts: Harvard University Press, 1978.
ERE William James, *Essays in Radical Empiricism*. Edited by Frederick Burkhardt and Fredson Bowers. Cambridge, Massachusetts, and London, England: Harvard University Press, 1976.
ERM William James, *Essays in Religion and Morality*. Edited by Frederick Burkhardt and Fredson Bowers. Cambridge, Massachusetts, and London, England: Harvard University Press, 1982.
EW Jonathan Edwards, *Ethical Writings, The Works of Jonathan Edwards*, vol. 8. Edited by Paul Ramsey. New Haven and London: Yale University Press, 1988.
GA Jonathan Edwards, *The Great Awakening, The Works of Jonathan Edwards*, vol. 4. Edited by C.C. Goen. New Haven and London: Yale University Press, 1972.
ISDT Jonathan Edwards, *Images and Shadows of Divine Things*. Edited by Perry Miller. New Haven and London: Yale University Press, 1948.
LWJ William James, *Letters*, vol. 1 and 2. Boston: The Atlantic Monthly Press, 1920.
MA Jonathan Edwards, *The Miscellanies, a-500, The Works of Jonathan Edwards*, vol. 13. Edited by Thomas A. Schafer. New Haven and London: Yale University Press, 1994.
MA2 Jonathan Edwards, *The Miscellanies, 500-832, The Works of Jonathan Edwards*, vol. 18. Edited by Ava Chamberlain. New Haven and London: Yale University Press, 1994.
MEN William James, *Manuscript Essays and Notes*. Edited by Frederick Burkhardt and Fredson Bowers. Cambridge, Massachusetts, and London, England: Harvard University Press, 1988.
MT William James, *The Meaning of Truth*. Edited by Frederick Burkhardt and Fredson Bowers. Cambridge, Massachusetts, and London, England: Harvard University Press, 1975.
NS Jonathan Edwards, *Notes on Scripture, The Works of Jonathan Edwards*, vol. 15 . Edited by Stephen J. Stein. New Haven: Yale University Press, 1998.

PBC William James, *Psychology: Briefer Course*. Edited by Frederick Burkhardt and Fredson Bowers. Cambridge, Massachusetts, and London, England: Harvard University Press, 1984.
PJE *The Philosophy of Jonathan Edwards from His Private Notebooks*. Edited by Harvey G. Townsend. Eugene: The University of Oregon, 1955.
PR William James, *Pragmatism*. Edited by Frederick Burkhardt and Fredson Bowers. Cambridge, Massachusetts, and London, England: Harvard University Press, 1988.
PU William James, *A Pluralistic Universe*. Edited by Frederick Burkhardt and Fredson Bowers. Cambridge, Massachusetts, and London, England: Harvard University Press, 1977.
PW Jonathan Edwards, *Letters and Personal Writings, The Works of Jonathan Edwards*, vol. 16. Edited by George S. Claghorn. New Haven and London: Yale University Press, 1998.
RA Jonathan Edwards, *Treatise Concerning Religious Affections* in *The Works of Jonathan Edwards*, vol. 2. Edited by John E. Smith. New Haven and London: Yale University Press, 1959.
SC Jonathan Edwards, *Scientific and Philosophical Writings, The Works of Jonathan Edwards,* vol. 6. Edited by Wallace E. Anderson. New Haven and London: Yale University Press, 1980.
SJE *The Sermons of Jonathan Edwards: A Reader*. Edited by Wilson H. Kimnach, Kenneth P Minkema, and Douglas A. Sweeney. New Haven: Yale University Press, 1999.
SPP William James, *Some Problems of Philosophy*. Edited by Frederick Burkhardt and Fredson Bowers. Cambridge, Massachusetts, and London, England: Harvard University Press, 1979.
SPW Jonathan Edwards, *Scientific and Philosophical Writings*, *The Works of Jonathan Edwards*. Edited by Wallace Anderson. New Haven and London: Yale University Press, 1980.
TCWJ Ralph Barton Perry, *The Thought and Character of William James*, vols. 1 and 2. New York: George Braziller, Publisher, 1954.
TT William James, *Talks to Teachers on Psychology*. Edited by Frederick Burkhardt and Fredson Bowers. Cambridge, Massachusetts and London, England: Harvard University Press, 1983.
TW Jonathan Edwards, *Typological Writings, The Works of Jonathan Edwards*, vol. 11. Edited by Wallace E. Anderson and Mason Lowance, Jr., with David Watters. New Haven and London: Yale University Press, 1993.
WTB William James, *The Will to Believe*. Edited by Frederick Burkhardt and Fredson Bowers. Cambridge, Massachusetts, and London, England: Harvard University Press, 1979.

VRE William James, *The Varieties of Religious Experience*. Edited by Frederick Burkhardt and Fredson Bowers. Cambridge, Massachusetts, and London, England: Harvard University Press, 1985.

Acknowledgments

My primary thanks for their support, encouragement, and kindness go to my advisers, Richard R. Niebuhr and James Engell, both of Harvard University. In his classes, Dick Niebuhr's love of Edwards and of James was contagious. As a mentor, he has always been generous to a fault, and his conception of beauty as a major category by which to understand religion has inspired me. His compassion, contemplative mind, and love of teaching exemplify Edwardsean excellence.

Jim Engell's deep insight into the complexities of the creative imagination inspired my thinking on the nature of religious experience and satisfied many of my questions about Coleridge's thought. His generosity and insight as a reader and teacher, his thoughtful comments on drafts, and his ongoing encouragement and confidence in my abilities helped me greatly to complete this work.

Prof. Gordon Kaufman of Harvard Divinity School challenged my mind in ways I never expected, and sometimes did not want to accept. But one of the greatest experiences of my education was walking from a class with Gordon to a class of Dick Niebuhr's, for these very different teachers together stretched the minds of students in ways creative of serious and deep reflection. Together, Dick and Gordon shared a true intellectual conversation with their students that shaped many of us.

My thanks go to fellow travelers in American religious thought, Alan Hodder and Bud Ruf. Early conversations with them on Edwards, Emerson, and James shaped my interests and encouraged my research and writing. I am also grateful to Dean William Graham of Harvard Divinity School for his support of this project.

Dick Niebuhr's wife, Nancy Niebuhr, has been a true and constant friend who taught me lessons of the heart by example. She has my gratitude for all she has done for me.

Chesley Herbert, M.D., has been an insightful and compassionate friend. Without his wise counsel, this project would never have seen print. He has my gratitude.

My love and gratitude go to my parents, Dante and Marjorie Campagna-Pinto. They have long been supporters of this project.

I have dedicated this book to my brother and childhood companion, Alfred Campagna-Pinto, who died long before this work came to fruition, but who appreciated the meaning and importance of building an inclusive and pluralistic universe.

Chapter 1
The Sacred Trace

As he began the Gifford Lectures on Natural Religion that were to be published as *The Varieties of Religious Experience,* William James expressed reverence for the European culture honoring him. "It seems the natural thing for the United States to listen whilst the Europeans talk," James wrote. "The contrary habit, of talking whilst the Europeans listen, we have not yet acquired; and in him who makes the first adventure it begets a certain sense of apology being due for so presumptuous an act." Casting himself as a "humble self promoted from my native wilderness" who has been "transmuted into a colleague of these illustrious names," James felt "a sense of dreamland as much as of reality."[1]

James's puckish wit was surely at play here. After all, in the year 1900 Edinburgh was no more a dreamland than Cambridge, Massachusetts, a wilderness. James's respect for his audience and his wry self-deprecation do reveal something about the Americanness of his project, however. The contrast of a European dreamland with the wilderness of America emphasizes the desire for transformation that deeply marks James's subject, religious experience. To make a wilderness into a dream reveals the American burden of self-justification, the demand that Americans validate the abandonment of home to the very Europe to whom James speaks. Caught between the excitement of the trail and the anxiety accompanying the onerous project of defending religious experience in an age of science, James feels a "heroic obligation" to carry out his task. He leaves "further deprecatory words" behind, and hopes to bring American philosophy to the world on an equal footing. His adventure in the wilderness makes of philosophy an act of trailblazing, marking the path with fragments of truth as he sought horizon after horizon. James's ironic celebration of the European dreamland advances his wilderness situation because, he proclaims, the dream is not real, not tested. This wilderness of America is native to him, a homeless home, a dream to be tracked and tested, an antinomianism altered by time rebelling against the laws and customs of a still burdensome past.

Tracing the sacred was vital to both Jonathan Edwards and William James. James's well-known commitment to witness "fact in the making" was also the method and measure of study when it came to religious experience. Some of Edwards's richest works—his diary entries, various youthful notes on nature and science, and especially his mass of "Miscellanies"—illustrate his love for the "fact of grace," as he crafted fragments that functioned like seeds of thought awaiting the germination of complex ideas and patterned relations. His homemade, hand-stitched notebook of *Images and Shadows of Divine Things* reveals thinking-in-action analogous to the quickening energy of divine presence in the natural world that prompted it. Edwards and James dig into the sedimentary layers of American history to examine the psychological dynamic of religious experience and, more importantly, the value of religious experience for the life of the community. Both men share a discourse that traces the tradition of Protestant heart piety, broadly interpreted, and its experimental or experiential quality, through an analysis of the awakenings and conversions of diverse persons. While arriving at similar views of America as a quest or experiment defined by prospect, advance, and affirmation of novel possibility, this is a thematic continuity altered by time. Thus for Edwards the purpose of America was its contribution to a global creation of the New Jerusalem; for James it was the building out of a universe that had the possibility of a cooperatively achieved salvation. For James, this represented a metamorphosis of an earlier theology of grace into a "protestant reformation in philosophy" that gave much worth to religious experience.[2] For both Edwards and James, a deep disappointment in aspects of the American experiment shaped distinctive prophetic styles within changed historical contexts.

Both men sought to transcribe an ever-vanishing horizon. One of the enduring images of Edwards is that of a man riding into the wilds of the Connecticut Valley only to return home wearing a coat now pinned with scraps of scribbled writing.[3] James, too, saw himself pursuing truth as a process of traveling with words, recalling Hanna Arendt's notion that "to think with an enlarged mentality one trains one's imagination to go visiting."[4] In "Philosophical Conceptions and Practical Results," James writes,

> I feel that there is a center in truth's forest where I have never been: to track it out and get there is the secret spring of all my poor life's efforts; at moments, I almost strike into the final valley, there is a gleam of the end, a sense of certainty, but always there comes still another ridge, so my blazes merely circle towards the true direction. . . . I cannot take you to the wondrous hidden spot to-day. To-morrow it must be, or to-morrow, or to-morrow; and pretty surely death will overtake me ere the promise is fulfilled.[5]

Both Edwards and James were situated in a cosmic wilderness liminally betwixt and between new religious, philosophical, scientific, and political concerns. And while Edwards sought to bring the glory of God to fruition as a means of fulfilling the promise of wilderness, James's view of wilderness speaks to the bold uncertainty resident within his philosophy of radical empiricism as the reinstatement of the vague that made for a malleable and flowing universe.

Edwards, well schooled in the Bible, the Cambridge Platonists, Newton, and Locke, among other influences, had a mind both theoretical and devotional. His daily role as pastor shaped the reflections of his personal notebooks and journals—notebooks preliminary to his formal works that functioned much like Emerson's journals—so as to suggest the practical lines drawing forth from pragmatically tested religious experience. Set within the turbulence of Connecticut River Valley revivalism, it is easy to witness the pained roots of Edwards's embryonic pragmatism.

Would-be artist, medical doctor, psychologist, philosopher, and profoundly insightful student and sometime practitioner of religious experiment, James presents a mind that entertained the combination of an artistic sensibility with the new psychology, Darwinian evolution, the emerging philosophy of pragmatism, and the religious demand that prioritized experience over institution. Both Edwards and James existed in times of changing intellectual currents and upheavals of moral and spiritual character. This locates their respective work as students of religion in an environment necessarily pragmatic because of the degeneration of spiritual values in an age of scientific and capitalist advance. Whether America would embrace the creativity requisite to a strenuous democracy or abandon the deeper feeling-tones of religious experience out of self-interest shaped the intellectual experiments and commitments of each man.

The Business of Religion

In some sense, the shadow of Antinomianism and Arminianism haunted their work, as both men recognized in personal struggles with theological and philosophical determinism. Edwards's criticism of false religious affections and their roots in a superficial and over-enthusiastic religiosity, and his distaste for rational Christianity, reveal his position, as does his privative notion of sin and fascination with grace. Amended by time, James's concern with grace finds expression in his assertion of the value and psychodynamics of first-hand religion, his processive notion of truth as a species of the good, and his desire to bring about a "protestant reformation in philosophy" that argued against the affective motives of system-building that suggest his use of a hermeneutics of suspicion. Caught between law and love, both men made concerted efforts and sophisticated arguments to support the fruits of charity and their roots in religious experience and the cognitive power of feeling or affection.

Situated in nostalgic longing for Europe and the wilderness situation attested to in James's opening lines of *The Varieties* is a continuity of ideas and themes. Edwards declared in his *Miscellanies*, "Religion [is] really the very business of men for which God made them," while James asserted in a letter to Frances Morse that religion is "mankind's most important function."[6] Both men swam against the tides of their times, and these remarks unsurprisingly reflect each man's magisterial work on religious experience, respectively *A Treatise Concerning Religious Affections* and *The Varieties of Religious Experience*. These books coincide with challenges to religion's value for the American community, and reflect the continuity of purpose, albeit altered by time, that runs between Edwards and James. As Andrew Delbanco has noted, *The Varieties* is "in some respects a self-conscious sequel to Edwards's *A Treatise Concerning Religious Affections*."[7]

Both Edwards and James see the true business of humanity as religious, though the ways in which the term evolves from Edwards to James are significant. James's oft-quoted remark that "religion is mankind's most important function" echoes Edwards's assertion that human beings "are concerned with nothing else" than excellence, or true religion. In some sense, Edwards and James worked to break from conventional assumptions to ask repeatedly about the nature of America's true calling, and to answer that the business of America is not business, but holiness, and the moral action that it inspired. This signals a concept of religion that dissents from the practices and habits of conventional institutions. The nouns with which each thinker describes religion—"business" and "function"—disclose the position of religion in intellectual contest with secularizing material values and scientific thinking. And though rational religion and market capitalism threatened to depose experiential religion from the beginning of the American project, science provided a wealth of ideas that deepened and sustained the defense of religion that Edwards and James each embraced. Edwards's "business" of religion sought, by pointing to the radical sovereignty of God, to displace enthusiastic hypocrites, rational religionists, and the worldly merchants of the Connecticut Valley who would themselves end up the strategists of his demise as town minister. Assured by bedrock faith in the sovereignty of God, Edwards's appeal to science, rather than dissipate religious faith, emboldened it. Newton and Locke supplied new ways of tracing the sacred and advancing greater understanding of God's glory, and humanity's dependence upon it.

Edwards's language anticipates James's metaphorical use of the term "cash-value" to assess religion's worth in the marketplace of ideas. James's functionalism, influenced by Darwinian evolution, led him to argue that religion's primary value for human advance lay in providing novel insights that fueled the strenuous mood that inspired historical change and human development in a singular way. When James speaks of building out a universe in which salvation is possible through social cooperation, he looks ahead to evolutionary interpretations of religion as a means to communal ritual and belief that fosters species survival. But he also looks historically to exemplary moments when religious experience ignited social change. In this, he particularly notes the power of Puritanism.

Religious experience, whether described in the terms of business or function, further suggests the experimental and pragmatic dimensions of the thought of Edwards and of James. Thinking was a radically creative act entering into a world of experience to be tried and tested for its value for building a social universe. The declension of the religious into the limited faiths of nationalism, capitalism, and individualism refashioned spiritual impulse into self-interested ends. Such degeneration revealed a rejection of the exploration of the religious wilderness that resulted from rational critiques of religion from without and the debilitating effect on religion's value from within, the result of enthusiastic extremism and fanciful faith. Entering this vacuum was the elevation of an exceptionalist concept of political power that has authorized imperial adventures and embraced self-interest to the point of narcissistic obsession. According to Delbanco, this American fixation is perhaps best witnessed as a nineteenth-century turn to tribal nationalism and a twentieth-century material overindulgence writ large as cultic self-pampering.[8] Both dismiss the true nature and value of the experience of religious affection. Certainly more recognizable than the rigors of spiritual transformation are the false affections that informed spiritual self-aggrandizement in the form of what James calls second-hand religion. One only need look to twenty-first century political rhetoric, religious fundamentalisms, and materialist indulgence to see the strained piety that shapes these American dreams. Experiment, diversity, enthusiasm, and deviance were of the fabric from America's advent, as the many extravagances of New England revivalism illustrate.

This was a fabric that cloaked the question of selfhood and identity. As migrants to an emerging world, Anglo-Americans faced a shifting reality imposing an unknown, rather than an imagined, orientation. What one expects and envisions on a flight from oppression is not equal to the reality one encounters. Michael Jackson writes,

> Behind the compliant and optimistic facade of the grateful migrant is a constant struggle with despair of themselves—since deep down they do not believe that their misfortune is a result of political events outside their control, but the result of some mysterious shortcoming in themselves, a defect in their personalities, an inability to maintain the social appearances to which they have for so long been accustomed.[9]

The founders of New England could not silence the discord of a new community striving to know and justify itself. The confrontation of religious belief with the burden of the past and the prospective wilderness was a desperate one. John Winthrop's ancestral charge to build the city on the hill was not at all akin to apostolic voices of exceptionalism like Ronald Reagan, whose clarion call to national self-interest and the celebration of power was grand political theatre that omitted cautionary counsel. Winthrop's utterance was both warning and threat that followed from the call for a community that was a "model of Christian charity" bound together as one body. Failure was as possible as virtue.

Failure was more than possible—it was inevitable. Winthrop's vision for America exemplified the anxiety from which experimental piety would flourish in New England because it embraced the tradition that interpreted the biblical tale of fall and redemption as historical reality. But the development of a new society also had worldly concerns such as a need for social order, economic survival, and the development of law and custom in relation to a novel environment that soon led to an inevitable rejection of Winthrop's directive that the new colony should be a community bound together by love. The generational declension of such a vision has been embedded within the tense counsel of jeremiads from Winthrop to the present day. And within several years of his oceanic sermon, Winthrop himself joined the company of the rulers of this unrealizable city on the hill.

Scholarly commentaries on the conflicts inherent in early New England are rich and diverse, but many agree that the themes to be found within the varieties of Puritan piety and its working out in the world have generated American culture in profound ways. Like any new religious movement—whether something as grand as Christianity or as humble as the latest product in the modern spiritual marketplace—there is a struggle for communal definition beyond that of the individual searching for a sense of authenticity. In early New England, the path to orthodoxy was complicated by the sense that the immigrant peoples knew themselves and their beliefs because they were arriving from someplace else. But part of the challenge of the wilderness was a persistently unraveling self-definition. As a result, claims to orthodox belief and practice developed out of the haunted emptiness defining fresh departure and new arrival.

The question for those advancing a particular vision as the defining characteristic of a society and a people here became that of the nature of religious experience as it shaped this new world. Winthrop's call for Christian charity would be construed in relation to survival in the face of disease and attack, and economic and political demands midst migratory and generational change. In *Orthodoxies in Massachusetts*, Janice Knight understands orthodoxy and its players in light of the necessary drive to forge "normative structures of faith and expression . . . the disputes of these years were less about discovering heresy than about establishing dominance."[10] These orthodoxies carried the names of the traditional Christian philosophies of Arminianism and Antinomianism that are described in the broadest way as the argument between salvation by works and salvation by grace. As John Cotton succinctly described the controversy in New England, "all the strife amongst us was about magnifying the grace of God; one party seeking to advance the grace of God within us, the other to advance the grace of God towards us."[11] In Cotton's words, the claims for the authentic self define a conflict between human methods of achieving grace that allayed the fear of loss of control and personal chaos, and the abandonment of the self to a power to which one belonged and from whom grace mysteriously emanated.

Delbanco, employing Mary Douglas's conception of religion as a visceral response to purity and pollution, adds to Cotton's observations. Delbanco sees in these two parties a response to fear and anxiety, and the pollution of sin, one in battle with active forces of evil, and the other affirming the good from which human beings have fallen. He writes,

> The idea of sin as entity leads directly to a very high valuation of social and political control . . . guarantees a shudder in the perception of deviance—and therefore is at the heart of middle-class culture, even perhaps as a constitutive element. The idea of sin as privation, on the other hand, can only exist simultaneously with (indeed is the same thing as) a felt conviction that a transcendent realm of plenitude exists by which human beings can, if they are open to its influence, transcend their moral limitations, or even their mortality.[12]

Knight's book suggests a genealogy of rational and affective expressions of American Puritanism and their evolutionary trajectory. Her interpretation of the Antinomian believers, who became heretical dissenters that threatened Arminian orthodoxy, surrounds the question of the nature of grace, and hence of divine sovereignty. The Antinomian group, which she calls the Spiritual Brethren, suggests currents of religious thinking that find resonance with the work of Edwards in his powerful emphasis on grace, or in James's greatly altered variation that resides in the distinction between primary and secondary religion, a metamorphosis attested to by the difference between unmediated and mediated spiritual experience found in *The Varieties*. The Spiritual Brethren inspired a tradition of passionate religious demand running throughout American history. Arguing for "significant differences and alternative voices within Puritan culture," Knight finds in this school of New England Puritanism "a passionate mysticism . . . an emphasis on charity . . . [and] an expansive communalism counter to tribal nationalism."[13]

Knight makes a compelling case that this strain of mystical piety flows from the Spiritual Brethren to Edwards and Ralph Waldo Emerson. The Brethren initiated a sermon style and religiosity that has marked the American literary tradition, Knight argues, with "a distinctive rhetoric of grace that valued affect over logic [and] sensibility over meaning."[14] While James's literary style when writing about religious experience suggests an evolution of the rhetoric of grace, illuminating the supernatural dynamics of sanctification in psychological and pragmatic ways, Edwards is famous for the rhetoric of sensation that sought to draw the listener towards an experience of the divine. The psychology of the affections informs an emphasis on a mystical sensibility at the heart of each man's thinking about religion. Rather than witnessing the voice of a prideful expression of exceptionalism or the prefiguration of a cult of narcissism, Knight's appreciative reading of the Brethren suggests an alternative vision of the religious wilderness, one to be explored rather than controlled.

According to Knight, the New England Puritan orthodoxy, notable for its claims to power and political theatre, whether in the form of show trials of visionaries like Anne Hutchinson or hangings of Quakers on Boston Common, defined a path that brooked little dissent. Like all orthodoxy, the Puritan establishment marginalized those it considered heretics—in this case, the Spiritual Brethren—driving out notions of mystical piety, the psychology of the affections, anti-preparationism, and the privative concept of sin.

Given the complexities of the ages in which Edwards and James were born, rhetoric played a key role in recalibrating the focal symbols of a culture emergent from a religious wilderness. Poetic refashioning inhabited rational argument so as to embody the primary values of an elusive grace and human attempts to trace it in a wilderness of competing ideas and values set in a time of existential homelessness. Both men ministered to the collision of ideas with retrospective norms and values so as to reorient individual and communal confusion, filling facts with meaning in such a way as to advance the tracing of truth and the sacred. In doing so, their writing sometimes functions as a self-consuming artifact pointing both towards and away from the normative present. We find poetic plasticity in Edwards's sermons and in his immersion in the images and shadows of nature that complement the pragmatic discernment of the most telling of questions, the nature of truly holy affections. James's metaphors of overflow and immersion illustrate the sacred paradox of language. In tracing the holy, both men's use of metaphor functions to embody and deny the signified sacred so as to embrace a propulsive intensity reflective of an unfolding reality. But this sacred trace required, above all, a poetic pragmatism in which the religious affections fuel the selective attention to fact in the making that is tested in a material world that awaits fulfillment.

This shifting language reflects and re-creates the transformed situation in which Edwards and James found themselves as they approached scientific innovations and religious decline. For Edwards, biblical images suggest a mode of typological interpretation afloat in a history of redemption that inspired the application of sacred story to everyday life, and with his artistic sensibility and searching analysis, to the natural world. His dynamic interpretation of typology reflects a metaphorical frame of mind that strengthened the sense of a pervasive divine communication. Edwards's typological thinking suggests diverse relations between God, self, and world that shapes his dynamic philosophy of excellence. Similarly, James's assertion that language is but a crutch emphasizes the metaphoricity with which he was so gifted. Famous images of fluidity and of widening, of an overflowing world of experience, point to the limits of words even as those words are empowered. In Edwards's world, religious affections applied poetic refashioning to the world, suggesting an experiential realization of an amplifying beauty at one with the advance of virtue so as to affirm and advance God's glory. For James, the poetic forms the best view of experience, an aesthetic funding active in the world by deepening and transforming conceptual analysis. The world was patterned, a mosaic without borders to which human action contributed pieces that sought transition or discovered termination.

James was quite familiar with Edwards's work due both to his father's and to Emerson's thought. Edwards's presence in *The Varieties* suggests the importance of his pragmatic evaluation of religious affections for James's thought. In the first lecture of *The Varieties,* "Religion and Neurology," James draws a distinction between spiritual and existential judgment so as to address the value of both scientific and aesthetic conceptions of religion in developing his analysis of the psychological dynamics of the workings of the spirit. But James's analysis suggests a preference for the spiritual or aesthetic appreciation of what he will call in the second lecture, "first-hand religion." This focus on spiritual judgment serves to place in context the potentially reductive and intellectually vicious consequences of existential judgment.

Here James makes clear his estimation of Edwards's value for his own work. Referring to Matthew 7:15-20, James offers "our own empiricist criterion ... By their fruits ye shall know them, not by their roots. Jonathan Edwards's *A Treatise Concerning Religious Affections* is an elaborate working out of this thesis."[15] James parallels Edwards's careful scrutiny of religious experience throughout *The Varieties*, but in such a way as to approve of religion in terms of its evolutionary value as a spontaneous variation that serves as a corrective to the scientific determinism that plagued his early adulthood. Feelings and ideas were part of the facts that fulfilled what James saw as a raw empiricism bereft of the human element. Thus James suggested that religious experience energetically upended determinism with vague gleanings of a richer expression of human purpose.

In arguing for the affective grasp of beauty within religious experiences, both Edwards and James contested the intellectual tendency towards anesthetic conceptualism and structural norms that valued custom and tradition as forces of orthodox conformity.[16] James would have recognized Edwards's description of "mere cogitation" as a predecessor of his concept of "knowledge about." While aware of the necessary virtues of conceptual language—Edwards offers a particularly telling discussion of what reading would be like without concepts—the prejudices of substitution too easily alienated feeling from the self and delegitimized experience.[17] Edwards's embrace of the doctrine of original sin and James's discomfort with the self-satisfied system building of those who imagined a block universe testifies to the risks of "knowledge about." The rational assessment of God that intensified the sense of human power or the vision of life in a block universe suggested a type of security that did violence to the experience of trail-blazing that defined thinking in a wilderness.

The defense of religious experience marks the struggle with such violence, but in the work of Edwards and of James, it also recognizes that "knowledge by acquaintance" functioned meaningfully, if with vulnerability, in relation to "knowledge about." This epistemological unity of heart and head emanated from the sense of an intimate reality both challenging to experience and strenuous to realize. The characteristics of their thought, consonant with the Antinomian concerns of the Spiritual Brethren and their descendants, speak of an aesthetic sense that inclines reasoning to participate in a concrete, yet incomplete, universe. Shaping the unfinished world through a concern for beauty that patterns creative action, religious experience bears witness to the human purpose as the expansion of glory or the fullness of meaning in a vast universe otherwise cold and alienating.

Suicide and Salvation in Edwards's Northampton

In a sense, Edwards was forced to employ an incipient pragmatism by the distress and disappointment of his ministry. The spiritual fires smoldering and igniting in wave after wave of revivalism in the small frontier town of Northampton, Massachusetts, forced Edwards to focus and refocus upon the question of religious experience. His thinking on this painful and practical ministerial dilemma led him to write one of his greatest works, *A Treatise Concerning Religious Affections.* Here Edwards took the unpopular position of quelling revivalism for fear of the damage it did to true religion, while affirming the mystery of saving grace that stymied rationalist religion. He admits,

> I am sensible it is much more difficult to judge impartially of that which is the subject of this discourse, in the midst of the dust and smoke of such a state of controversy, as this land is now in . . . as it is more difficult to write impartially, so it is more difficult to read impartially. Many will probably be hurt in their spirits, to find so much that appertains to religious affection here condemned: and perhaps indignation and contempt will be excited in others, by finding so much here justified and approved.[18]

Edwards's attempts to trace the sacred in the practical life of his congregation illustrates Reinhold Niebuhr's main theme in *The Irony of American History*. Niebuhr writes,

> The Biblical interpretation of the human situation is ironic, rather than tragic or pathetic, because of its unique formulation of the problem of human freedom. According to this faith man's freedom does not require his heroic and tragic defiance of the forces of nature. He is not necessarily involved in tragedy in his effort to be truly human. But neither is he necessarily involved in evil because of his relation to the necessities and contingencies of the world of nature. His situation is, therefore, not comprehended as a pathetic imprisonment in the confusion of nature. The evil in human history is regarded as the consequence of man's wrong use of his unique capacities. The wrong use is always due to some failure to recognize the limits of his capacities of power, wisdom, and virtue. Man is an ironic creature because he forgets that he is not simply a creator but a creature.[19]

Edwards understood all too well from his ministerial experience the critical function that irony plays in the advancement of true religion. Embracing a felt, if illusory, salvation, false affections catch the believer in prideful identification with the divine rather than the humility essential to the reception of grace. The fall that accompanies pride is haunted by irony; and irony's doubling of the self's meaning offers the opportunity for transforming humiliation into knowledge. This is where Edwards stands, between the assumptions of power by enthusiasts and rationalists alike, a position that makes him adopt a pragmatic approach for the sake of the true religion sullied by the pride of both sides. For Edwards, religious faith, if alive, catches the believer in a moment of unexpected self-awareness of the limitations and hypocrisies of his belief. The believer whose faith is alive is relentlessly brought to his knees by the unexpected in moments of grace that reveal, if only in a glimmer, the endless possibilities for self-renewal and the renewal of God's Creation. Because such moments occasion an expanded vision, they also act as a lure to wonder. Such wonder is elusive, yet real and transformative in its power to drive the believer on to a widened consciousness and an expansive heart. Charity is the offspring of religious irony, as awareness of human pretensions to knowledge, certainty, or righteousness fuel the desire to find a more complex reading of reality that illustrates what Edwards calls the complex proportions of Being as relation.[20] The calibration of the self that attends the perception of irony is, for Edwards, a type of repentance that is active, creative of new relations expressive of charitable love within the community.

The play of irony describes Edwards's ministerial career. The town was ablaze with religious fervor in the spring of 1735 as young people who once had socialized openly on the evenings following the Sunday sermon and weekly public lectures were now absorbed in Bible study and spiritual reflection. Adults were soon caught up in the young people's intense desire for holiness, and began devotional study and religious conversation to the point where the whole town, even during business hours, placed spiritual affairs above all else. A visitor to Northampton might well have believed that the world had been turned upside down, as commerce and daily custom were left behind for the coming kingdom of God. Edwards believed that the sudden changes within Northampton and neighboring towns were due to "an extraordinary dispensation of providence ... many seem to have been suddenly taken from a loose way of living, and to be so changed as to become truly holy, spiritual, heavenly persons."[21]

Edwards was confident, despite rumors to the contrary, that God had wrought a truly gracious transformation of the people of Northampton. His conviction did not seem wrong, despite obvious incidents of false enthusiasm and the warnings and suspicions of outsiders. Edwards was simply fulfilling his grandfather Solomon Stoddard's legacy of spiritual leadership in Northampton, and reaping the benefits of ministering to a town that had frequently experienced the mysterious action of grace since its founding almost one hundred years before. In 1733, several years after he succeeded Stoddard, the beginnings of the revival were first stirring, and threatened to spread across western New England. These enthusiasms had matured into numerous conversions and an ardent seeking after God among the majority of citizens. The young pastor could now feel justified in taking on the mantle of his illustrious grandfather. Edwards was so emboldened by these amazing events as to trumpet them in Boston; he wrote up a short chronicle of the revival for the Reverend Dr. Benjamin Colman, pastor of the Brattle Street church in the colonial metropolis. Dated May 30, 1735, the letter joyfully details seizures of the spirit "beyond almost all that ever I heard or read of."[22]

The miraculous events of the revival were short-lived, however. Two days after reporting "the extraordinary dispensation of providence," Edwards added a shocking postscript:

> My Uncle Hawley, the last Sabbath-day morning, laid violent hands on himself, and put an end to his life, by cutting his own throat. He had been for a considerable time greatly concerned about the condition of his soul; till, by the ordering of a sovereign providence he was suffered to fall into deep melancholy, a distemper that the family are very prone to; he was much overpowered by it. . . . He was in a great measure past a capacity of receiving advice, or being reasoned with.[23]

This tragic postscript signaled the end of the first wave of revivalism under Edwards, and began the transformation of his thinking towards a more sophisticated assessment of the vagaries of the religious mind desirous of personal assurance of election. Forced to amend the epistle to add the grim news, Edwards was now compelled to examine the failures of his pastoral leadership and the chaos and conflict wrought by the oscillation of religious enthusiasm and despair.

Edwards's postscript shattered his narrative of the good news of the revival. For Edwards and the people of the Connecticut Valley, the tragic results of this first surge of the Great Awakening signified a demonic rupture of what seemed to be visible, felt salvation history in the making. In the postscript, he blames Satan for Hawley's suicide and numerous other problems, prescribes a day of fasting to clarify errant souls in the congregation through this act of humility, and ends with the faint hope that the revival would continue to develop, as witnessed by the Durham parish. Edwards's hope for the presence of grace thinly accompanies the overwhelming sorrow and painful contrition that colors the horrifying news.

The lost promise of salvation was particularly traumatic for Americans living under the pressured expectation of the New Jerusalem. What Delbanco has called "the Puritan ordeal" was intensified in Edwards's attempts to recall the original purposes and assumptions of the Puritan pilgrimage in the face of its growing rejection in both religious and social spheres.[24] As Edwards wrote in 1742 in "Some Thoughts Concerning the Revival," "'Tis not unlikely that this work of God's Spirit, that is so extraordinary and wonderful, is the dawning, or at least a prelude of that glorious work of God, so often foretold in Scripture, which in the progress and issue of it, shall renew the world of mankind."[25] Hawley's death, and the hysteria it brought in its wake, raised serious questions about the value of the religious project in America just as Edwards was hoping to reassert such a call by offering powerful evidence of God's saving action.

The postscript to Coleman displays the visceral power and the shock of immediacy that such an event brings to its witnesses. The preacher's family was torn asunder by the violent self-destruction of Uncle Hawley, laying the groundwork for family tensions that contributed to Edwards's dismissal from the Northampton pulpit in 1750.[26] In the communities swept up in the revival, hysteria, despair, and disappointment racked converted and seekers alike as a wave of suicidal impulse swept the Valley, casting the meaning of the many conversions into doubt, and making clear only the ambiguous meaning of such revivalism.

Hawley's suicide was but the most horrifying sign that these spiritual events were not evidences of the outpouring of the Holy Spirit. As Edwards would later reflect, even the most saintly suffered from hubris and self-righteousness that led to problems within the community. Enthusiasm brought forth conflict of a particularly charged nature, as neighbor accused neighbor of spiritual failure, and congregants attempted to reject pastors who were without visible signs of grace. Melancholy and despair characterized the darker, more painful dimensions of spiritual striving. What if one could discern no signs of God's grace, but only faced the reality of a corrupted heart? Hawley was not the first person to experience melancholy in the midst of the revival; his suicide serves as the most severe reminder of the interior wrestling noted by friend and enemy alike of the Puritan mind in the throes of religious transformation.[27] "After this," Edwards writes, "multitudes in this and other towns seemed to have it strongly suggested to 'Em, and pressed upon 'Em, to do as this person had done."[28]

The revival confirmed conflicting beliefs in Edwards, as he held firmly to the reality and graciousness of the Holy Spirit and its presence in regenerate humanity, while he also became convinced that human beings could never arrive at an unambiguous and certain knowledge of that divine reality. True holiness could not be sufficiently confirmed so as to winnow out ideas dyed in hubris or despair. The conflicted pain of the need for such knowledge and its impossibility drove Uncle Hawley's suicide; in tandem with the prideful certainty of enthusiastic converts, it also killed the Connecticut Valley revival.

The lust for certainty and its impossibility led to dissension within congregations, despair among the unelect, and the fear that Satan had been unleashed and was reveling in attacks upon the pious. "Satan seems to be in a great rage, at this extraordinary breaking forth of the work of God," Edwards offered as explanation of Hawley's suicide.[29] The tumultuous events of 1735 radically changed Edwards's life and work, and dramatically shaped the future paths of his ministry and his writing. His horror and dismay at both the advocates and opponents of revivalism during the succeeding waves of the Great Awakening in the 1730's and 1740's motivated the creation of an analysis of religious psychology that constitutes a series of works culminating in the 1746 publication of perhaps America's most precise work on religious psychology, *A Treatise Concerning Religious Affections*.

In May 1737, Edwards addressed the congregation concerning the collapse of the revival, and confessed, "I do not know but I have trusted too much in man, and put too much confidence in the goodness and piety of the town." C.C. Goen suggests that Edwards changed the first edition of "A Faithful Narrative" in order to address this shocking realization by eliding expressions of confidence in the certainty of the conversion of sixty new church members.[30] Whether changed by Edwards or other editors, his questioning of the nature of truly holy affections signals the development of an increasingly subtle analysis of religious psychology based upon the painful irony concomitant with false religious affections.

Edwards's sophistication grew with increasing concern for the question of personal assurance that plagued Uncle Hawley and others. Northampton experienced no further revivalism for nine years; as Edwards observed in a letter to the Rev. Thomas Prince of Boston, "After that great work nine years ago there has been a very lamentable decay of religious affections, and the engagedness of people's spirit in religion."[31] This "dead time" ended with the Great Revival in New England, led by the itinerant preacher George Whitefield. Along with Gilbert Tenant, Whitefield set New England on fire, drawing enormous crowds of enraptured enthusiasts. In the experience of one ecstatic participant, Whitefield completely transformed the population: "It's a most blessed time, it's a mere heaven on earth; the people from dull carelessness, now are like the horse-leech at the vein, crying give, give!"[32]

Whitefield visited Edwards and preached in his Northampton pulpit in 1740. Edwards, despite his profound hope for true religious revival, remained skeptical of Whitefield's methods. Edwards's thinking made his method of investigation into experiential religion significantly different from that of Stoddard, or contemporaries like Whitefield and Tenant. His thinking evolved such that his own position became more sharply attuned to the belief that enthusiasm was even more dangerous than Arminianism to the advancement of Christian faith.[33] Not only was the extraordinary evangelist Whitefield charismatically compelling, the Northampton congregants were largely drawn to such exuberant preaching for its value to entertain rather than to save. Consequently, Edwards concluded that the provocation of enthusiasm led to the further ossification of a community that he describes bitterly as hard-hearted, "immensely harder than the hearts of idolaters, harlots, whoremongers, murderers, and sodomites."[34] Clearly, this reflected his growing dismay with the American experiment.

Edwards found the fevered and enthusiastic followers of Whitefield as scandalously unreliable in their confessions, dangerous to the mental health of the community, and as contributors to the arguments of Arminian opponents against experiential religion. To make matters worse, ministers such as James Davenport ranted and raved with an enthusiasm bordering on madness, further fueling the attacks of the opposition. Davenport whipped congregations into hysterical frenzies, and attacked ministers in their own pulpits on the grounds that they were unconverted, and could not discern the activity of the Holy Spirit.

For Edwards, the demonic shaped the extravagant motions of believers during the revivals:

> I don't know but we shall be in danger by and by, after our eyes are fully opened to see our errors, to go to contrary extremes. The Devil has driven the pendulum far beyond its proper point of rest; and when he has carried it to the utmost length that he can, and it begins by its own weight to swing back, he probably will set in, and drive it with the utmost fury the other way; and so give us no rest; and if possible prevent our settling in a proper medium.[35]

This drive to contrary extremes resulted from a blind intensification of the patterns of Puritan religious experience. Well-documented is the Puritan penchant for intense introspective scrutiny to the personal experience of the Christian drama of fall and redemption. Caught between the reality of original sin and the hope of salvation, between existence as a natural man and as a saint, the believer "settling in a proper medium" lived under a process of intense and ongoing calibration of the self, with the widest possible range of feeling and the ever-present danger of self-deception. This suggests the pragmatic dimension of Edwards's thinking, and anticipates the meliorism James argued is an essential element of pragmatism. But the ferocity of revival made such spiritual struggle far more extravagant, with communal pressure for awakening, the public witness of the converted, and the persistent and impassioned urging of the clergy all driving the psychic engines of those not yet affected by grace, mistaken or real. This complex landscape of communal feeling gave rise to the zealous enthusiast and the suicidal unconverted despairing of election, with many swinging wildly between these two poles. Excess was a natural result of such fervor. Thus Edwards observed the elect censuring their unconverted neighbors for being millstones on the millennium, and saw the suicidal motivated to self-destruction by abject self-degradation and shame. This called for the impossible, an utterly certain and final assurance of their state before God through a violent ritual of personal purification. In the revival, the abstractions of epistemology held the most visceral and fateful power.

Despite Edwards's constant reminders to parishioners that felt moments of grace do not establish the true cause of such experiences, spiritual pride became the repeated and primary sin. Edwards observed an overweening pride that forgets,

> There is a mixture of that which is natural, and that which is corrupt, with that which is divine. . . . The experiences of true Christians are very frequently as it is with some sorts of fruits, that are enveloped in several coverings of thick shells or pods, that are thrown away by him who gathers the fruit, and but a very small part of the whole bulk is the pure kernel that is good to eat.[36]

In 1751 Edwards reflected upon his experiences of revivalism in Northampton in a letter to the Rev. Thomas Gillespie of Carnock, Scotland. While noting problems inherent to the religious culture of Northampton, Edwards also observed, "God has been pleased in times past to bestow many special and distinguishing favors upon them." But Edwards further remarked that the people were often at odds with each other, either through ecclesiastical controversy of such intensity that it once led to physical violence or through class distinctions based upon land ownership. Undoubtedly, the two were related.[37]

Edwards also complained, "The people had got so established in certain wrong notions and ways in religion, that I found them in and never could beat them out of."[38] Part of the problem arose from the spiritual pride of the citizenry that could not be corrected by the timidity of their inexperienced minister. Though he had trained under Stoddard, Edwards was only twenty-three when he arrived in Northampton, and twenty-five when Stoddard died. In retrospect, Edwards confessed,

> Instead of a child, there was want [i.e. need] of [a] giant in judgment and discretion among a people in such an extraordinary state of things. In some respects, doubtless my confidence in myself was a great wrong to me; but in other respects, my diffidence of myself injured me. It was such that I durst not act my own judgment, and had no strength to oppose received notions and established customs, and to testify boldly against some glaring false appearances and counterfeits of religion, till it was too late. And by this means as well as others, many things got footing, which have been a dreadful source of spiritual pride, and other things that are exceeding contrary to true Christianity.[39]

The young Edwards faced a population raised under Stoddard's dominating guidance to embrace "a dogmatical temper; the townsfolk were also notable for their spiritual pride . . . that grand inlet of the Devil into the hearts of men." No doubt Edwards writes from first-hand experience when he says, "If it ben't discerned and vigorously opposed in its beginning, it very often soon raises persons above their teachers, and supposed spiritual fathers, and sets 'em out of the reach of all rule and instruction."[40]

Such opposition and disregard for pastoral guidance contributed mightily to Edwards's dismissal from the Northampton pulpit in 1750. It further manifested itself in reliance upon the technology of conversion and a confused epistemology in which illusion, speculation, and desire cloud the mind's evaluation of the nature and presence of grace:

> Particularly it was too much their method to lay almost all the stress of their hopes on the part steps and method of their first work, i.e., the first work of the Spirit of God on their hearts in their convictions and conversion, and to look but little at the abiding sense and temper of their hearts, and the course of their exercises, and fruits of grace, for evidences of their good estate. Nor had they

learned, and many of them never could be made to learn, to distinguish between impressions on the imagination, and truly spiritual experiences. And when I came among them, I found it to be too much a custom among them without discretion, or distinction of occasions, places, or companies, to declare and publish their own experiences; and oftentimes to do it in a light manner, without any air of solemnity. This custom has not a little contributed to spiritual pride, and many other evils.[41]

The "particular steps" to which Edwards refers were formally called the *ordo salutis*, or way of salvation, which served as a formula that shaped the experiences of believers. The steps could serve to falsify indications of the believer's spiritual condition by defining the behavior requisite to a particular state of grace, thus enabling false conformity to such a condition. In *Religious Affections*, Edwards asserts that the testing of spiritual provenance of the affections is not intended as a means by which public judgments may be made, but is intended only for the individual's own contemplation and self-assessment:

I am far from undertaking to give such signs of gracious affections, as shall be sufficient to enable any certainly to distinguish true affections from false in others; or to determine positively which of their neighbors are true professors, and which are hypocrites. In so doing, I should be guilty of the arrogance which I have been condemning. . . . It was never God's design to give us any rules, by which we may certainly know, who of our fellow professors are his, and to make a full and clear separation between sheep and goats: but that on the contrary, it was God's design to reserve this to himself, as his prerogative.[42]

Edwards's own personal experience, as well as his observations of parishioners, led him to refute the ordered stages of salvation. The ready-made mechanisms of conversion called into question honest self-scrutiny in regards to the uncertain process of religious transformation, made divine grace subject to human conceptual coercion, and constructed within the seeker a false sense of spiritual insight. Edwards recognized that his youth made it difficult to wean his parishioners from the ordered process of election taught to them by grandfather Stoddard. But his own sermons and analysis of spiritual experience constitute a heroic effort to disabuse the congregation of the prideful illusions that threatened their very existence as Christians. The threat was both mortal and eternal, as seen in the case of Uncle Hawley. Suicide and salvation worked intimately together upon those susceptible to melancholy and despair. Edwards was determined in his ministerial duty to address the horrific problems embedded in both the system of preparation and the fevered enthusiasm that could spin wildly and tragically out of control. Drawing upon his own spiritual experience, aesthetic sense, and keen intellect, Edwards developed a philosophy of excellence that attempted to trace the sacred through the pressured mind of the believer. In so doing, Edwards noted the power of the affections clarified through the attentive will as an act of creativity that pragmatically affirmed and advanced the charity possible in a world in need of such care.

Suicide and System-Building: James and the Problem of Certainty

The April 26, 1895, edition of the *Harvard Crimson* reported, "Professor James delivered an address before a large audience at the open meeting of the Christian Association in Holden Chapel last evening on the question: 'Is Life Worth Living?'" Published in the collection of essays entitled *The Will to Believe* in 1896, James's essay argues for the right to belief that may serve as an antidote to despair. James's address concerns "the profounder bass-note of life," and his aim was to argue that the physical order is partial, and "we have a right to supplement it by an unseen spiritual order which we assume on trust."[43] James was not supporting claims to certainty or the manufacture of idolatrous heresies or orthodoxies, whether religious or scientific. His point focused on the penchant for idolatry in any guise: "In this very University . . . I have heard more than one teacher say that all the fundamental conceptions of truth have already been found by science."[44]

For James, trusting in an unseen spiritual order instills the person with guidelines for living that breed hope:

> It is a fact of human nature that men can live and die by the help of a sort of faith that goes without a single dogma or definition. The bare assurance that this natural order is not ultimate but a mere sign or vision, the external staging of a many-storied universe, in which spiritual forces have the last word and are eternal—this bare assurance is to such men enough to make life seem worth living in spite of every contrary presumption suggested by its circumstances on the natural plane. Destroy this inner assurance, vague as it is, and all the light and radiance of existence is extinguished for these persons at a stroke. Often enough the wild-eyed look at life—the suicidal mood—will then set in.[45]

Trust is not certainty for James, but an experiment in hope that may sustain the person through the more difficult moments in life, and enliven the ability to contribute individual, concrete reflection of ontological wonder to a world in flux. To trust one's religious inclinations means to engage experience in a way that enables creative effort to live forward in the attempt to honor the process of creation that is selfhood. And such trust defines a relationship based on tolerance for a plurality of views, any or all of which may provide beneficial methods and evidence of the value of religion. James encouraged his audience to accept a world of *maybes* and of vagueness—the creativity that weds feeling, concept, and practical experiment and evaluation—that opens the human heart to process and possibility.

Thus it is not surprising that some one hundred seventy years after Edwards reported Hawley's suicide, James announced a protestant reformation in philosophy with the lectures that came to be published as *Pragmatism*.[46] As Luther and Calvin led reformations that sought to reestablish the basic tenets of Christianity without disruptive accretions, so James's reformation sought a return to the fundamental values of philosophical reflection as a quest for wisdom that reflected a deeper commitment to the human purpose of creating a more fulfilling and practical world. Such a return was not intended to worship the past, but was intended to reinvigorate philosophical reflection in relation to the future. James believed that philosophy is something all persons engage in, and something that can aid the discovery of truth and goodness in the practical affairs of daily life. Philosophy is also profoundly informed by human temperament, as James argues early on in the first lecture, "The Present Dilemma in Philosophy." Citing a passage from Chesterton's *Heretics*, James writes, "There are some people—and I am one of them—who think that the most practical and important thing about a man is still his view of the universe. . . . We think the question is not whether the theory of the cosmos affects matters, but whether, in the long run, anything else affects them."[47]

James attempts to reform philosophy so that it can serve the human community as a guide to living: "The philosophy that is so important in each of us is not a technical matter; it is our more or less dumb sense of what life honestly and deeply means."[48] Meaning has a prospective pulse for James, and describes a direction and a destiny rather than a past history and origin, though the present is funded by the past. Thus James begins his philosophical reformation with the recognition that thought is married to our beliefs and our values, in short, to the affections that drive our ideas and opinions. He sees the assumption that philosophy is simply technical thinking as lending "a certain insincerity to our philosophical discussions" because "the potentest of all our premises is never mentioned."[49] Temperament informs philosophical thinking, and is clearly shaped by it, particularly as it takes on the rhetorical guise of an impersonal science. Ways of seeing and the content of knowledge work hand in hand with temperament and feeling to establish the habit of being. Such boundaries of vision define a picture of normative reality and the assumed facts that underlie it. James, in *Pragmatism* as elsewhere, suggests that the human problem is the premature tendency to secure certainties and still the desire for shaping primordial experience into meaningful patterns.

Pragmatism, then, begins by embracing the notion that philosophy has the power to influence our practical lives in a profound manner, as theory bears both the imprint of temperament and yet also asserts itself to be a factual statement of reality. James writes in order to salvage philosophy from both the absolute idealism and the scientism of his age so as to enable its practical value to emerge. This is not to deny truth, but to place it in relation to the limitations and shortcomings of knowledge understood as a product of the human personality in all its complexity. For James, rationality is expansive and elastic, as it emanates from human feeling that is one with teleological impulse. As James argues in "The Sentiment of Rationality," "A strong feeling of peace, ease, rest . . . The transition from a state of puzzle and perplexity is full of lively relief and pleasure."[50] Philosophy is more meaningful when thinking involves feeling and the dispositions of temperament. Philosophical authority consequently requires some value or method that questions historical and cultural facts and assumptions as well as its own products, as an activity simultaneously aesthetic, conceptual, and practical. This is the methodological role that James has in mind for pragmatism.

This is well illustrated in Lecture 1 of *Pragmatism*. James cites the case of John Corcoran, a victim of suicide, as an example of the ways in which religious philosophy can optimistically rationalize the problem of suffering. For his friend and colleague, Josiah Royce, as well as for other philosophers, such a loss was simply to be understood as part of a larger whole in which evil and suffering worked to aid the creation of a larger good: "He (the idealist) means that these slain men make the universe richer, and that is philosophy."[51] In criticism of Leibnitz, Royce, and Bradley, among others, James makes a stand for the despairing and the suicidal, for philosophy to be responsible enough to accept reality as wide-ranging in experience, open-ended, and in need of new thoughts offering ideas for the meaningful construction of human life in an unfinished universe.

The relation of suicide to the system-building of philosophy made a similarly stark statement for James: human beings are blind to the wide possibilities of life, and crave and cling to even the most pernicious certainties and securities, experience notwithstanding. For many persons, life has no options other than those expressed by a determinism that precludes human action. Optimistic idealism similarly negates the person, as it brushes the reality of loss and tragedy under the carpet of neatly woven systems of thought. To James, the human predilection is to accept such dead-ends as healthy and supportive of life. Contemporaneous philosophy failed to address the needs of the suicidal or the lost soul, as certainties and explanations make pretense to settle unanswerable questions. For James this meant the loss of a valid option, and consequently a loss of experience, of diversity of ideas, and of possibility. Certainty and explanation reveal the ironic predicament of human beings, and deny the melioristic character of the pragmatic approach to the verification of ideas and beliefs. Belief, when made an idol, carries a virulent irony, while trust, when relational, returns the person to the ongoing stream of experience.

James's concern for human despair and the question of suicide was both personal and intellectual, and arose from his own and other family member's struggles with such painful questions. In a sense James's work reflected a commitment to a type of therapeutic philosophy. The opening chapter of *Pragmatism* served as a continuation of James's lifelong attempt to address the question of melancholy and suicide as philosophical issues, and as such, questions that force the renovation of concepts and methods of thought. James's analysis of philosophy's dilemma puts forth the argument that the attempt to build systems too often results in dogmatic opinion about the one true vision. The use of temperament to describe an individual's quality of mind serves two important purposes: it sees arguments and assumptions arising from personal disposition as well as intellection; and it expands the concept of reason far beyond the constricted boundaries established by much nineteenth-century science and philosophy. In these cases, normative assumptions, dogmatic arguments, and the given facticity they express are made out to be questions, beliefs, and opinions. James writes,

> Metaphysics has always followed a very primitive kind of quest. . . . The universe has always appeared to the natural mind as a kind of enigma, of which the key must be sought in the shape of some illuminating or power-bringing word or name. That word names the universe's principle, and to possess it is, after a fashion, to possess the universe itself. But if you follow the pragmatic method, you cannot look on any such word as closing your quest. You must bring out of each word its practical cash-value, set it at work within the stream of your experience. It appears less as a solution, then, than as a program for more work, and more particularly as an indication of the ways in which existing realities may be changed.[52]

This position is made abundantly clear by an examination of James's life. Restless creativity and burdensome despair characterize the general pattern of his inner life. James adopted a variety of identities throughout his life. His first great love was art, and his talent justified his desire to become a painter. Discouraged in this endeavor by his father, James first turned to science; a medical degree was the only degree he ever earned. But James never cared for medicine, and turned to psychology, from which he moved to philosophy as a career. His adult life saw him work as teacher, scholar, and public lecturer, but his hunger for experience and change also meant he traveled widely in Europe and the United States. James's life can perhaps best be described as an attempt to immerse himself in the overflowing richness and energy of reality such that the life of the self was in a continual process of change. He craved an intellectual life of risk and adventure in which limits and boundaries were shunned for the transitions and motions of emerging vision.

The discovery of creative freedom distinguishes the birth of James's philosophical career, a calling no less powerful than that of Edwards's. James experienced a particularly devastating bout of melancholy while in his twenties and early thirties that derived in large part from a strong sense of alienation and meaninglessness in what he perceived to be a mechanical universe. James would suffer depression throughout his life, but its power was particularly overwhelming for him as a young man when he could find no context in which to understand his suffering. James's experiences of despair and meaninglessness arose as he wrestled with the need for a professional vocation as opposed to his desire for creative expression and thought. His spiritual crisis involved vocational confusion, obsessive philosophical questioning, and a self-perceived lack of moral courage that whirled together to make his life a state of "philosophical pessimism and general depression of spirits about my prospects." These spiritual and mental disturbances were accompanied by insomnia, back pain, eye trouble, and gastro-intestinal distress. He later remarked, with apparent understatement, "I was entirely broken down before I was thirty."[53]

The analysis of James's youthful melancholy has become almost a cottage industry, and the scholarly attention paid to his twenties almost overlooks the significance of his lifelong struggle with depression and its relation to his creative advances in philosophy. Perhaps the most significant aspect of his illness was the total affect on his being: his physical, mental, moral, and spiritual vitality were intimately related in his depression. The young James had a strong sense of moral responsibility that, when combined with a healthy appreciation of his own estimable talents, added a deep and abiding frustration and self-loathing to his years of dread and melancholic incapacity. James keenly felt the need for an intellectual arena in which to find meaningful work, and he obsessively questioned the need for the active power of free will and the sense that he lived in a universe receptive to his creativity. As a well-read young medical student brought up in a household filled with conversation about the intellectual currents of the day, James was quite aware of the ascension of scientific materialism as a normative worldview. This was a great cause of his despair, as he felt "swamped in an empirical philosophy. I feel that we are nature through and through, that we are wholly conditioned, that not a wiggle of our will happens save as the result of physical laws."[54] He would later conceptualize this feeling in the essay whose title grimly recalled his earlier struggles, "Is Life Worth Living?":

> We of the nineteenth century, with our evolutionary theories and our mechanical philosophies, already know nature too impartially and too well to worship unreservedly any God of whose character she can be an adequate expression . . . visible nature is all plasticity and indifference—a moral multiverse as one might call it, and not a moral universe. To such a harlot we owe no allegiance; with her as a whole we can establish no moral communion.[55]

James found no comfort in his father's theological musings, either. While Henry James, Sr., had found solutions to his own youthful melancholy through an idiosyncratic interpretation of Swedenborgian theology, such a system was too far in the monistic camp for his son. For William, such monism led to the inevitable defense of evil as necessary to the order of life. Rationalism and the speculative theological and philosophical systems that it constructed offered no balm to his obsessive philosophical questioning, offered "no explanation of our concrete universe, it is another thing altogether, a substitute for it, a remedy, a way of escape." Such philosophy "lets the world wag in its own way, feeling that its issues are in better hands than ours and are none of your business."[56]

James's diary of late 1869 clearly notes the affect that the idea of a world with no moral or spiritual component played upon his sense of creative power. The problem appeared to be how to function in a world bereft of meaning or freedom; he could not simply act by ignoring the evil realities or the moral needs of the world, yet he felt this was what modern life demanded of him. His inability to find a philosophy to live by created a fear and paralysis that made for a painful conflict between his sense of duty, and ideas and feelings that made action meaningless. James hit bottom when he was twenty-seven and harbored a fear of insanity that led him to thoughts of suicide. He typified the divided self of *The Varieties*, as he was convinced of determinism and yet committed to his intuitive sense that he had free will and was a responsible actor within the world.

The concept of the divided self points to the ironic dilemma of the person caught between two senses of meaning who had not yet found a way to resolve them. For James, as for Edwards, embrace of the fallibility of belief erased the power of the ironic to cast one into pained and rueful reflection. The divided self was healed by the propulsive intensity witnessed within religious experience, an intensity that imperfectly unfurled in poetic language that reconstituted reality, a poetics necessarily pragmatic so as to bind the self to the authenticity of its experience as it entered a world in need of repair.

Chapter 2
A New Reach of Freedom

Edwards and James give high estimation to the quality of experiential religion due to its intensification of the creativity necessary to address a world in need of repair. However, the apparent persuasiveness of determinism, whether couched as theological predestination or scientific determinism, stymied each man's early thinking on the relationship between religious experience and the creative imagination.[1] Belief in creative freedom in the face of fixed boundaries of thought challenged each man personally and intellectually. In their thinking, both Edwards and James attest that religious experience teaches that a world bound and sorted constricts the mind, limiting vision to the retrospective confines of custom and tradition. Relationship with a spiritual dimension of life by its very nature breaks down barriers. Experiential religion liberates the imagination to activity in a spiritual wilderness beckoning creative experimentation.

For Edwards, creative freedom comes with the arrival of what he calls "the new sense" that brings to life awareness of human participation in the divine theater. James affirms in *The Varieties* that religious experience brings a "new reach" of freedom that liberates the individual for strenuous and creative effort. These ideas emerge from the spiritual wilderness of Edwards's experiences in what he calls the pastures of God, and that James sees in the vague yet deeper reaches of a wider environment or "more." These are visions of the creative freedom central to the American experiment. Whether in terms of the personal freedoms or political liberty of the people, Allen C. Guelzo observes,

> Free will has possessed American imaginations . . . free will is a question which links theology and metaphysics with ethics, with psychology, and with epistemology, all of which are easily recognizable as major American intellectual industries . . . it is our national gargoyle, our favorite device for keeping conscience in the rocking chair.[2]

Edwards makes very clear the semantic confusion that accompanies much interpretation of the term "free will," and James puts forth the idea of "free will determinism" as a typically puckish spin upon the problem from a pragmatic perspective. James's advocacy of a pragmatic theory of free will rests upon the functional value of the term rather than anything approaching the Arminian sense of human power that Edwards attacked. James understood the common sense upshot of determinism in his notion that life must be lived in relation to suffering and a lack of optimism: "life has real losses and real losers."[3]

But James's interest in experiential religion sees the widening of self and community as an activity that moves dynamically between center and margin of the field of consciousness to reacquire freedom from the achievement of conceptual analysis and the ease of rational fluency. The truth "salted-down" may orient the mind, but it lacks the freshness and vitality of prospects uncovered in what James calls "consciousness existing beyond the field."[4] Such a program, rather than exalt individualism, as scholars routinely interpret James's thought, seeks to jet the individual into the experiential matrix, both to contribute to and to partake of the wealth of opportunities expressed in the dynamism of the novel occasions present as transitional junctures. This is a social model of self and universe that is a highly dynamic model of exchange between the most profuse varieties of relations and disjunctions.

This suggests one of the most basic differences between James's experiential metaphysics and Edwards's relational ontology. James shuns systematic theology's construction of God as absolute knower that holds all things and beings in existence for its failure to assist human work in the world. Instead, James prefers a God in the making that functions without coercion or the support of absolute certainty. He knows that human beings do not see traditional doctrines describing God's qualities, such as those of aseity or of predestination, as commensurate with human reality, and that such ideas are subject to misuse according to human self-interest and authoritarian tendencies. For James, radical sovereignty limits rather than liberates human potential. The idea that human beings exist within an interactive and experiential environment filled with risk and uncertainty does not allow for work stoppages or moral holidays because of the demand that human activity be held to the bar of responsible participation in such an environment.

Edwards and James share a concern for malleability and process, but Edwards embraces the theological absolutism that James rejects. Edwards's bedrock faith is given tremendous depth and nuance by his concept of God as Being in General, which reflects a dynamic metaphysics of relations. Human freedom of choice exists within an Augustinian system in which responsibility to Being in General becomes both spiritual demand based upon necessity and delight found in freedom of responsible choice. The will is not free, but dyed in the history of the human species, and hence in the necessity forced upon Adam and the liberty redeemed by Jesus Christ. Further, the individual will is dispositionally colored by the history of its own actions and tendencies, painted with the subtle complexities of affectional pointillism to create a self-portrait that may change in relation to its attraction to light or shadow. As Boller observes, "Predestination, as Edwards saw it, was an energizing doctrine which gave zest and sting to life."[5]

James's resistance to an absolute knower in his theory of radical empiricism belies the presence of a widening more that suggests a finite God somehow aiding human beings in their spiritual experimentation. James's radical empiricism makes possible a pluralistic panpsychism that returns the sacred to the world of experience as a living possibility of a power that makes incursion into the human world. The relationship of mutual possession that James sees in religious experience frees the person from gods and absolutes that do not allow creative work to be done because given to systematic reductionism.

Creative freedom exists as a mediating and constructive power operative between deterministic laws and principles and unseen potentiality. The model that James constructs of pure experience suggests a continuous reality beyond the distinctions of self and world, subject and object, such that the human penchant for systematic and retrospective conceptualization is an illusion when taken as lending comfort and certainty to a world that is chaotic and uncontrollable. The dangerous tendency of human nature is to become habituated to retrospective or conceptual ideas, values, and beliefs such that there is a sense of rational fluency when, for James, full rationality paradoxically necessitates incoherence and the vague in attempting self-definition. Pure experience for James calls into question the fragmentation of experience such that knowledge is limited to logical systems that lead to human alienation from authentic existence in a world in which continuity flows chaotically and in seemingly infinite relations, transitions, conjunctions, and disjunctions. James's philosophy of radical empiricism is an attempt to describe the nature of creative freedom in the construction of the human community, and it suggests both an avenue for change and an indictment of custom and tradition. The role that experiential religion plays in James's radical empiricism is crucial for his comprehensive vision, for experiential religion demonstrates the shifting creative center, the wider self through which novel experiences and ideas emerge to enter into and reshape the seemingly deterministic block universe into an open-ended and pluralistic universe.

Like Edwards, James needed to discover a universe where human agency played a part, and creativity was a possibility. As young men, both experienced the powerlessness wrought by the assumption of a mechanistic universe, whether conceived through a concept of God as cruelly deterministic or of a universe, including human feeling and experience, modeled only on the principles of natural science. James, too, desired a creative participation in reality: "My old trouble and the root of antinomianism in general seems to be a dissatisfaction with anything less than grace. . . . The aesthetic sense or imagination . . . merely craves, and what it craves is to maintain itself in play free from laws."[6]

Chapter 2

Personal Liberty and Radical Sovereignty in Edwards's *Personal Narrative*

One of the most famous of New England conversion narratives, Edwards's *Personal Narrative* appears to have been written in the late 1730's in order to address the problems of preparationism and of spiritual pride and hypocrisy within the Northampton congregation.[7] Unlike the straightforward and somewhat simplistic confessions of seventeenth-century converts, as a minister's spiritual autobiography, the *Personal Narrative* was artfully crafted to take full effect of its author's stature as the spiritual leader of the community.

Edwards seeks to instruct the reader on the discernment of truly holy affections through the captivating story of his own painful search for grace, thus providing to the town an example of the spiritual trials of their minister. But the *Narrative* is even more subtly layered with the complex relations between the quest for self-knowledge and the psychological and theological ideas that Edwards seeks to develop and to impart to the reader. Within the *Narrative* Edwards implants many of the ideas central to his spiritual and intellectual life. These threads unravel to reveal the intimate relationship between his religious experiences and his thought. Thus the *Narrative* weaves intellectual and affective dimensions of human experience in a complex fabric that suggests Edwards's disapproval of enthusiasm and the uncritical religious confession and reflection that come in its wake.

Perhaps nowhere else in his writing does Edwards reveal his response to the fluctuating moods of the Connecticut Valley in the 1730's more intimately than in the *Personal Narrative*. Though Edwards claimed that the *Narrative* was written for personal reasons, its elision of certain aspects of his earlier, less carefully crafted *Diary,* its repetition of experiences recounted in other of his revival writings, and its careful rhetorical construction of authentic as opposed to false religious affections mark it as a public document aimed at his local audience.[8] Above all, the *Narrative* addresses the problem of false affections by illustrating the personal experience of true religious vision arising from the influx of grace.

Edwards's *Personal Narrative* is atypical for the genre, lacking the careful construction of the ordo salutis commonly seen in the preparationism dominant in the communities of the Connecticut River Valley. Edwards's individuality marks his resistance to the mechanics of conversion, and this shapes the *Narrative* as revelatory of the author's rather original conception of experiential piety and his attempt to sort out, for himself and for his audience, hypocrisy from authenticity of spiritual apprehension. After Uncle Hawley's suicide and the chaos of the little revival, the critical question of Edwards's ministry had become that of the nature of true religion. As the son of a minister he witnessed various "seasons of awakenings," and had long contemplated the question of truly holy affections: "it is a subject on which my mind has been particularly intent, ever since I first entered on the study of divinity."[9] The *Narrative* embodies this question in autobiographical form, and not without homiletic intent. Edwards demands followers and opponents alike reflect upon the nature of true religion. To question the mystery of grace and its apprehension is to express loyalty to that very same mystery. Thus would the hypocrite be thwarted.

What led the young Edwards to pursue such a question with the tortured intensity that the reader finds in his earliest autobiographical writings? This was the crucial religious question for the seriously devout, and was certainly a constant topic for discussion of his father, Timothy Edwards, and his grandfather Stoddard. But as both the *Narrative* and the *Diary*, which was written some twenty years beforehand, illustrate, young Edwards, for all his brilliance, was bewildered by both the nature of his relationship with the divine and by the means for receiving grace. His study at Yale of the new psychology and physics no doubt contributed to his difficulties, leading him eventually to create new and startlingly modern theories about the nature of mind. But striking to the reader is the sense of despair and anxiety that marks his early diary entries and their later refinement in the *Narrative*. Generally concurrent with the *Diary* is a series of "Resolutions," one of which typifies Edwards's state of mind:

> Resolved, to act, in all respects, both speaking and doing, as if nobody had been so vile as I, and as if I had committed the same sins, or had the same infirmities and failings as others; and that I will let the knowledge of their failings promote nothing but shame in myself, and prove only an occasion of my confessing my own sins and misery to God.[10]

The following "Resolution" resulted from an entry of July 30, 1723, and further amplifies the intensity of Edwards's concerns over his state before God: "Have concluded to endeavour to work myself into duties by searching and tracing back all the real reasons why I do them not, and narrowly searching out also the subtle subterfuges of my thoughts."[11] A similar pattern of oscillation between despair and hope, self-condemnation and praise of God that defines Edwards's life, runs throughout his autobiographical writings. Such an unsteady motion through the boundaries and fringes of consciousness was both a proven and tested method for the Christian pilgrim and a painful and confusing disorientation of identity. The result for Edwards and his followers was an ongoing interrogation of the nature and limits of self-identity that, ideally, fueled both the becoming of the aspiring saint and the becoming of God and the Creation. As we have seen from the case of Uncle Hawley, it also could lead to suicidal despair.

The *Personal Narrative* is an exercise in "narrowly searching out all the subtle subterfuges of my thought" in the form of spiritual autobiography. It lacks the precision and rigor of *Religious Affections*, but demonstrates a literary artistry that was undoubtedly intended to appeal to his parishioners and offer hope to those caught in the slough of despond over their state before God. To hear of their minister's travails and to conceive of the possibility of knowing divine love even while in the midst of a psychic maelstrom enabled the seeker to carry on with hope, and not put an end to himself from self-degradation or despair. And in seeking to ferret out the self-deceptions and illusions of the mind's darkest corners, Edwards was able to take the hypocritical enthusiast to task. By showing the eternal motion of the pendulum of grace and despair as it affected the very leader of the congregation, Edwards pointed out the absurdity of the hypocrite's oft-expressed and arrogant humility.

The *Narrative*'s compression of historical time suggests the quasi-fictive quality of autobiography and the superior estimation of salvific history or mythic time held by Edwards and his audience. The *Narrative* moves through various episodes of Edwards's life to portray the spiritual ruminations of a pilgrim, and to suggest the transcendence of historical events through moments of grace that break through nature to bring about a change in the individual and the Creation. The construction of spatial and temporal liminality takes place in the *Narrative* with greater subtlety and much less force than in another of Edwards's literary masterpieces, "Sinners in the Hands of an Angry God." There the floorboards creak with the threat of a fall into hell, and time is given the most intense feeling of contingency, as death waits momentarily for someone, anyone, in the congregation to be transported to an eternity of nothingness.

In the *Narrative*, and normative for the seeker after holy affections in all of Edwards's work, liminality is a desirable state. Existence is authentic in the circular self-reflection of the individual enmeshed in the contest between nature and grace, fall and redemption. The central character of the *Narrative* is always on the threshold between self-sacrifice and the elision of the 'I' and self-expansion in the widened fields of a new sense of God that reinscribes the reborn self. Our hero appears, disappears, and reappears as a person refreshed by grace. This leaves the reader with a concept of the self that is chaotic and dynamic, a skein of past, present, and future continually unraveling and being rewound. This is too optimistic a picture, however. The self is often lost in a welter of conflicting values and confused ideas that magnify the anxiety or deepen the melancholy of the sufferer lost in perplexity.

Even at an early age, Edwards felt the sting of losing his emotional interest in the divine, and confronted the pain and regret of the guilt-ridden person aware of self-deceit but unable to fight it or the return to sin. The *Narrative* begins with repeated episodes of backsliding by the young Edwards. Troughs of regret concerning self-deception and remorse over what has been lost or proven to be illusory follow waves of enthusiasm. A childhood prayer booth and an illness "in which he brought me nigh to the grave and shook me over the pit of hell" were not enough to establish grace in the aspiring young Edwards. Instead, the inevitable conclusion to these episodes was that "I entirely lost all those affections and delights and left off secret prayer . . . and returned like a dog to his vomit, and went on in the ways of sin."[12]

Perhaps the most powerful structural element within the *Narrative* is the conception of divine sovereignty, for with Edwards's spiritual transformation, a changing understanding of God as sovereign occurs, and his conception of reality is revolutionized. Sang Hyun Lee has remarked, "Supremely important for him was the principle of God's absolute sovereignty in all aspects of reality, both the material and the spiritual."[13]

Edwards writes of divine sovereignty and the problem of predestination with clear awareness that this is the most troubling of questions for his parishioners. It is also the most important idea within his theology:

> From my childhood up, my mind had been full of objections against the doctrine of God's sovereignty, in choosing whom he would to eternal life, and rejecting whom he pleased; leaving them eternally to perish, and be everlastingly tormented in hell. It used to appear like a horrible doctrine to me. But I remember the time very well, when I seemed to be convinced, and fully satisfied, as to the sovereignty of God, and his justice in thus eternally disposing of men, according to his sovereign pleasure. But never could give an account, how, or by what means, I was thus convinced, not in the least imagining at the time, nor a long time after, that there was any extraordinary influence of God's Spirit in it; but only that now I saw further, and my reason apprehended the justice and reasonableness of it.[14]

The influx of the Holy Spirit transforms Edwards's vision, creating the first indication of the new psychology that he was to develop in relation to the most powerful and bewildering attribute of God, that of the foreknowledge that allows for the predestination of the creature. The question of one's state before God generated a fevered compulsiveness during revivals such that the melancholic, like Hawley, suffered an intensified despair leading to suicide. But Edwards now sees that the doctrine of predestination was not to be interpreted deterministically. Predestination, long held to be a horrifying doctrine intended to drive the believer to intensified self-scrutiny and the tangible proof of salvation through hard work and material gain, Edwards now beholds as "a delightful conviction." His former reading of the sovereignty of God was as much an illusion as the sources of the enthusiast's hubris in believing that false affections were the sign of election.

What was the source of such illusion, and how was divine sovereignty in truth "delightful"? The key to understanding Edwards's experience and love of the doctrine of God's sovereignty rests in the notion of delight that symbolizes Edwards's view of reality in both aesthetic and relational terms. The shift in vision that Edwards experiences with the influx of the Holy Spirit points to a primary functional change in Edwards's concept of the affectional dynamic of mind. Because of original sin, the seeker after God is incapable of the spiritual vision or sense that enables delighting or glorying in the Creation. Therefore, the idea of God's sovereignty would appear as a terrifying doctrine capable of instilling suicidal despair in the seeker afflicted by obsessive imaginings. The turbulent energy of a community in the midst of a revival intensified such fear.

The idea of predestination was never to be thought of as the extension of a deterministic model of reality, however. Predestination was misunderstood from Calvin onward. In *John Calvin: A Sixteenth Century Portrait*, William J. Bouwsma discusses the elements of the doctrine that made for its repeated misinterpretation:

> For Calvin, predestination is both biblical and a necessary corollary of God's power. . . . But here, as so often with Calvin, there is another side to his thought: he hardly dared "simply" to affirm predestination. "God's secret election" was an impenetrable mystery to him, and he was intensely opposed to speculation on the subject, which had already made the doctrine "a sea of scandals." . . . He thought it "terrible" that, as Scripture compelled him to believe, "only a small number, out of an incalculable multitude, should obtain salvation."[15]

Bouwsma adds that Calvin changed his mind as to the placement of the doctrine of predestination in the *Institutes of the Christian Religion*, moving it in the final edition from consideration as part of the doctrine of providence to that of salvation. This is due to his reconception of predestination in terms of the life of faith, in which the doctrine "promotes zeal and industry to live purely," and enables appreciation of divine sovereignty and humanity's absolute dependence such that "we shall always be safe." Thus the doctrine "evokes gratitude and inspires confidence" in the believer; it could even be used to explain social or familial hierarchy so as to "give comfort in a changing world."[16]

But the doctrine of predestination served more to invoke horror or spread apathy than to provide comfort and assurance. Instead of being read as a spur to the acceptance of Christ and an earnest seeking after God, it had the opposite and perverse effect of stopping people in their tracks with a fearful fatalism. Edwards echoes many of his predecessors in arguing against such a view:

> They say, To what purpose are praying and striving and attending if all was irreversibly determined by God before? But to say that all was determined before those prayers and strivings is a very wrong way of speaking and begets ideas in the mind which correspond with no real thought with respect to God. Decrees of our everlasting state were not before our prayers and striving, for these are as much present with God from all eternity as the moment they are present with us.[17]

Edwards is not merely saying that whatever we do God already knows from eternity. Rather, his concept of God establishes God's eternal life as incommensurate with the world with its temporal and spatial realities. The Creation functions along divinely ordained laws and principles that allow both for the ongoing dynamic of nature and the capacity of sentient beings to realize particular experiences and things given the cohesion of sufficient causes. This defines Edwards's notion of causal necessity and personal liberty or contextual freedom of choice. Thus, the potential for being saved or being damned both exist given the sufficient causes. That Christ is freely offered to all is clearly the crucial point of many of Edwards's sermons, most notably "The Excellency of Christ" and even "Sinners in the Hands of an Angry God." Encouragement of the seeker to accept the love of Christ that is freely offered is paramount in Edwards's ministry.

To return to the *Narrative*, the idea of delight in God's sovereignty reveals the dramatic changes within Edwards's state that led to the birth of the new sense, or the sense of the heart. God, understood as Being in General, beauty, or excellence, offered to Edwards a vision of the vast potentialities available to those who had experienced "a wonderful alteration" of mind. Such an alteration was not simply the capacity to see as a spectator, but as a participant in reality; the capacity for relation was born as an ability to work with the potential goodness established by divine creation to create a real good, beauty, or excellence that transformed and fulfilled reality. Thus the revolution of Edwards's idea of God's sovereignty not only meant the erasure of a feared determinism but also, more profoundly, established the seer as a co-creator of the good or beauty dormant within the Creation as actual, realizable potential. The individual had the personal liberty to build out the community of God through right action just as those who rejected the creative possibilities God offered for the augmentation of being and the promotion of the good fell away from being into nothingness. Edwards was able to arrive at his sense of delight in this vision of divine sovereignty by witnessing it as the rule of love and goodness.

Such creative freedom comes alive in the *Narrative* in a series of experiences following upon the transformation of Edwards's appreciation of the doctrine of God's sovereignty. The capacity to delight in this idea underscores the experiential or relational dimension in the birth of a new habit of vision or alteration of mind. This is also described as "another kind of sense," as "a new sense," and as a "a new sort of affection." Edwards's religious psychology slowly emerges from the *Narrative* in harmony with the transformation of the self and a movement through God's two books, Scripture and Nature. A scripture passage proclaiming the sovereignty of God becomes the occasion for the emergence of the new sense:

> As I read the words, there came into my soul, and was as it were diffused through it, a sense of the glory of the Divine Being; a new sense, quite different from anything I ever experienced before. Never any words of Scripture seemed to me as these words did. I thought

> with myself, how excellent a being that was, and how happy I should
> be, if I might enjoy that God, and be rapt up to him in heaven, and be
> as it were swallowed up in him for ever! I kept saying, and as it were
> singing over these words of scripture to myself; and went to pray to
> God that I might enjoy him, and prayed in a manner quite different
> from what I used to do; with a new sort of affection. But it never
> came into my thought, that there was any thing spiritual, or of a
> saving nature in this.[18]

Edwards perceived God in a new light, enabling spiritual reading of the Bible. His experience of reading is startling, for language comes alive in a way quite different from that of normal experience. This section of the *Narrative* is the experiential counterpart to the extraordinary discussion in *Miscellany #782*, "The Sense of the Heart." Here Edwards builds his argument on the distinction between signs and actual ideas in the mind's interaction with its experiential environment. By an actual idea Edwards means the real affectional excitement of a thing or a concept within the dynamic system of relations that he defines as consciousness. The term 'sign' simply refers to such an idea without any affectional sense being stirred. Knowledge is either speculative, a "mere cogitation," which Edwards defines as "a kind of mental reading wherein we don't look on the things themselves but only on those signs of them that are before our eyes"; or it is experiential, a form of apprehension in which "the mind has a direct ideal view or contemplation of the thing thought of," which is an "inward feeling or sense."

In *Miscellany #782* Edwards challenges the reader to take one page and read it with the full experiential power of actuality as opposed to the bare signification that defines the vast majority of our linguistic exchanges:

> Now [if] we use signs instead of the actual ideas themselves, we can
> sufficiently understand what is contained in that page in a minute of
> time, and can express the same thoughts to another in as little time by
> our voices, and can think ten times as swiftly as we can read or speak.
> But if, in order to an understanding of what was contained in that
> page, we must have an actual idea of everything signified by every
> word in that page, it would take us up many hours to go through with
> it. For taking in all the ideas that are either directly signified, or
> involved in relations that are signified by them, it would take us up a
> considerable time before we could be said to understand one word.[19]

Edwards structures *Miscellany #782* around his interpretation of Locke's psychology, in which Locke distinguishes between actual ideas and signs. Signs are mental abstractions, and are employed without attention to the experience designated or the origination of the word in that particular experience to which it refers. Actual ideas are apprehensions of the experience itself; signs may stand as a designation of such experience, but they cannot communicate the actual idea itself. Edwards's Platonism comes through in this distinction, for Edwards held that objects were created as actual ideas in the mind of God and were imaged or shadowed forth by their natural or corporeal counterpart that is an actual idea different from that in the mind of God not in kind, but by degree of actuality. Signs are necessary for social survival and development, for they allow for discourse to function representationally. The concept of sign, whether used as a technical linguistic term or as a metaphor for instance or occasion, was unstable on account of the fallen nature of humanity: the human interpretation of signs is always fallible. Only in deep and prolonged contemplation of a word could the reader experience the actual idea being shadowed by linguistic signs, and reap the complexity of relations which revealed both the beauty of such an idea and the poverty of both its linguistic representation and of human understanding. As Edwards notes, apprehension,

> wherein the mind has a direct ideal view, or contemplation of the thing thought of . . . is vulgarly called having a sense. . . . Persons cannot have actual ideas of mental things without having those very things in the mind; and seeing all this latter sort of mental things, that belong to the faculty of the will or the heart, do, in great part at least, consist in a sensation of agreeableness or disagreeableness, or a sense or feeling of the heart.[20]

This leads us to a further distinction between signs and actual ideas. For Edwards, to apprehend true knowledge of a thing, idea, pleasure, or pain, and not simply dwell inauthentically in an abstract reference to these things, "we must have that very idea in our minds." The actual idea was the very reality for Edwards. He beautifully illustrates the difference between the mere cogitation of signs, which is the activity of the understanding or head, and apprehension, or consent to, the actual idea, which is the province of the heart, with two striking images. Edwards tells us that the difference between mere cogitation and the ecstatic embrace of actuality is akin to the difference between being told what honey tastes like, and really tasting honey. Or even more powerfully, Edwards asks us to imagine the difference between being told what it is like to be in love and actually being in love. This distinguishes a sign from an actual idea, which is the act of experiencing a particular thing or idea in itself.

We can also see in Edwards's two notions of the sovereignty of God in his *Personal Narrative* another example of the difference between mere cogitation about an idea and actual experience of an idea. The change in Edwards's conception of the symbol, the sovereignty of God, is not simply a change in his own sense of the need to subject himself to such an idea. Rather, it is a fundamental change within his own religious consciousness, as is indicated by the attention lent to reading and the interpretation of language. Language has come alive in a different way for Edwards through the influx of grace that conveys the means by which he is able to appreciate the actual idea of God's sovereignty, not as direct experience, but as mediated through the mind's powers of symbolization. Language as sign alone conveys little or no religious meaning, is but cogitation. Language spiritualized, however, carries the power of relation and recollection of actuality, of authentic divinity. The recognition of divine glory and Edwards's relationship to it enables a resymbolization of the sovereignty of God such that God is understood not as external rule, but as a dynamic, communicating being. Such is in keeping with what Perry Miller calls Edwards's rhetoric of sensation, an employment of language that enables the auditor to actualize an experience of divine terror or beauty in a way that resonates with experiential reality.[21]

Signs are necessary and useful tools for individual and social communication and progress. But signs may also alienate the person from experience; the traffic in signs habitually removes the reader from the experience of things and ideas, and this is particularly dangerous given the ultimate importance of humanity's spiritual struggles. Young Edwards misread the doctrine of God's sovereignty by taking it as a sign of a horrible determinism, as he had no experience of the actual idea of divine sovereignty. Yet with the influx of grace and the gift of the new sense, he reads all of the Creation in a revised way such that he experiences its actuality, is able to enter into relation with its ontological reality in a way that augments his own consciousness. Beyond the experience of an actual idea is the new, yet continuous, mind born with every new relation. For in the energetic apprehension of an actual idea, the whole person changes as the relational pattern that defines consciousness shifts and grows.

This is what the *Personal Narrative* conveys. The experience of the holy spirit not only transforms the entire mental process, but it draws Edwards into a relation in which the ego is suspended and the self engaged in a relationship far greater than itself, suggesting a Christ-like kenosis. He is "rapt up to him in heaven . . . swallowed up in him." His transformation is such that he sees reality in a completely new way, enabling him to gain a new "apprehension" of Christ and his redemptive work. Singing, prayer, abstraction from the world, and an inability to express his experience accompany this feeling of "inward sweetness." All such mental activity implies the transformation of discursive modes of thinking within the context of the awakened sense of the heart. As Miller notes, Edwards reveals his rhetoric of sensation in the *Narrative* by using a sensory vocabulary to describe spiritual experience. But beyond this affecting and keen interpretation of spiritual perception is the sense of a process of relation with the divine and its manifestations in the Bible and the Creation that moves from a moment of unity to its aftermath, the reconfigured soul moving through a spiritually alive creation.

The sense of union with the divine suggests a more complex notion of unity as relationality when Edwards begins to contemplate nature. As he "walked abroad alone, in a solitary place in my father's pasture, for contemplation," Edwards began to view the glory of God in all things, and to understand God's attributes of majesty and grace as "a sweet conjunction: majesty and meekness joined together . . . a sweet, and gentle, and holy majesty; and also a majestic meekness; an awful sweetness; a high, and great, and holy gentleness."[22] Such conjunction points to the ways in which God brings opposites together so as to communicate the meaning and extent of the complex patterning of relation that defines God's being. Theologically, God as "Being in General" consists of an infinitely complex and dynamic relationality which, breaking in on the believer through the influx of the Spirit, shatters habitual patterns of conception. The more Edwards looked at the divine nature, the more fully did he experience an ongoing ecstasy in which the self was continually drawn towards new horizons of vision. This is in keeping with Edwards's notion of beauty as an expanding system of relations, with God, as Being in General, the most beautiful or excellent of all. All of the elements of nature that Edwards takes in are beautiful in and of their own existence as divine creations, but it is in their mutual relationship that a complex beauty or excellence is manifested, overwhelming the senses and yet denoting an inspired pattern of relations. Such a pattern reverberates in the mind as a series of complex ideas drawing out into new proportions of being the very dynamic relationality that now defines the method and content of awakened consciousness.

Rhetorically, Edwards was able to point to the dramatic energy and variation within the nature of God by using the conjunction of opposites, such that the reader's own conceptions were propelled into confusion, introspection, and clarification. But above all, to conceive of God as majestic and meek, holy and gentle, awful yet sweet, signals the mind's new power to symbolize relations between weakness and strength, earth and heaven, as a means to fulfillment of the bare and fallen world. The gulf separating the human from the divine is bridged through the new sense, which enables apprehension of divine ideas manifest in God's two books, Scripture and Nature. Such a capacity of symbolization enables the reconciliation or conjoining of opposites that is at the heart of Edwards's conception of the excellence of Christ. The new sense is a type of Christ-mindedness; as Edwards notes, it is a type of "personating" of Christ.[23] In such a new life comes a realization of possibilities and potentialities dormant within the believer's creative imagination. Language becomes action when understood and employed symbolically, for now it has the power of communicating divine ideas to those able to recognize its depth and actuality.

The capacity to conjoin opposites underlies Edwards's awareness of the new sense as a mediating or esemplastic power that ends the self's alienation from reality. This power enables the actualization of an infinite variety of possible relations, whether simple or complex. In "A Divine and Supernatural Light," Edwards argues that such a power can only arise from supernatural grace that is above nature, and qualitatively different from anything corrupted by the Fall:

> In the renewing and sanctifying work of the Holy Ghost, those things are wrought in the soul that are above nature, and of which there is

nothing of the like kind in the soul by nature; and they are caused to exist in the soul habitually, and according to such a stated constitution or law that lays such a foundation or law for exercises in a continued course, as is called a principle of nature. Not only are remaining principles assisted to do their work more freely and fully, but those principles are restored that were utterly destroyed by the fall; and the mind thenceforward habitually exerts those acts that the dominion of sin had made it as wholly destitute of, as a dead body is of vital acts.[24]

Not only does sanctification bring a new principle to the soul, it revitalizes and reorients the other elements of consciousness, establishing Edwards's organic concept of mind. Mind is married to a Christ-like consciousness that works for the redemption of the Creation:

This knowledge will wean from the world, and raise the inclination to heavenly things. It will turn the heart to God as the fountain of good, and to choose him for the only portion. This light, and this only, will bring the soul to a saving close with Christ. It conforms the heart to the gospel, mortifies its enmity and opposition against the scheme of salvation therein revealed: It causes the heart to embrace the joyful tidings, and entirely to adhere to, and acquiesce in the revelation of Christ as our Saviour: It causes the whole soul to accord and symphonize with it, admitting it with entire credit and respect, cleaving to it with full inclination and affection; and it effectually disposes the soul to give up itself entirely to Christ.[25]

The sense of the heart is, then, a "symphonizer" with Christ, a model of consciousness that seeks to harmonize those elements discordant to the vision of God as the expanding and dynamic ground of Being. Edwards's experience of nature suggests that just such a transformation has taken place. He has a vision "of being alone in the mountains or some solitary wilderness" much like Jesus in the desert, and he returns from such contemplation to "a solitary place in my father's pasture," suggesting an Edenic return. There he experiences a paradise: "God's excellency, his wisdom, his purity and love, seemed to appear in everything; in the sun, moon, and stars; in the clouds and blue sky; in the grass, flowers, trees, in the water, and all nature; which used to greatly fix my mind."[26] Thunder and lightning were now not frightening, but sweet in their communication of God, serving to remind the reader of the change in Edwards's attitude towards divine sovereignty. This new experience of thunder and lightning suggests Edwards's changed thinking on the concept of predestination and the illogic of arguments for freedom of the will. Delight now consists in the opportunity to witness, and play a part in, the divine drama of the cosmos. The theatre of the Creation gives the person an active role in the expression and expansion of glory through creative effort and moral action available through personal liberty. Conversion establishes a relationship that one has the choice to work at and develop, or take for granted or abuse.

Edwards's capacity to see the divine presence within the creation signifies an awakening to grace, but such gracious affection was entangled with the fallen nature of man, requiring the believer to undergo a process of continuous spiritual revolution. When "A Divine and Supernatural Light" was first delivered in Northampton in 1734, Edwards was still somewhat naive regarding the complexity of religious transformation. As he noted in his writings on the awakening following Hawley's suicide and the unbridled and prideful enthusiasm of many in the town, grace is inevitably at play in territory that, if not largely held by the devil, is at least in direct confrontation with natural inclinations existing within a fallen reality. The hyperbole of "A Divine and Supernatural Light" met the harsh reality of human pride and egotism in the events of 1735, with the result being that Edwards, if not the town, became both sadder and wiser.

Nature offers further aid to the believer, if he attains a way of reading the Creation for divine purpose or meaning. Nature assists the believer, but once again in a way that reinforces the dialectical nature of faith and the processive quality of an existence that is an ongoing internal pilgrimage. For Edwards, then, nature joins the Bible as a source of divine communication to be plumbed by the reader for kernels of wisdom that are propulsive, which unfurl so as to expand the relation between self-knowledge and knowledge of God. Edwards's vision is of a cosmos permeated with symbols of divine presence and activity. The intensity of the Puritan mind ecstatically devoted to God's sovereignty, and thus energized with an ardent self-scrutiny, further motivated the struggle to discover the workings of divine glory. To Edwards, language has the capacity to render spiritual knowledge imperfectly, as it carries a mystical possibility correspondent to the mysticism of nature and spirit that are subject both to misinterpretation and to clarification of vision.

Edwards uses the term "image" for the concept of symbol. He sees the clear separation of image and idea as emblematic of the alienation of the human from the divine, of the seeker from the end. If we see through shadows, we see through darkness. The irony is that the complexification lent to the reader by symbolization reveals yet further work to carry out in the propulsive intensity of language that constantly unfurls, seeking ever more complex relation. Religious experience as a process of symbolization, or spiritual sight, drives the seeker on to further dimensions of meaning and fuller powers of moral action. The demand of Edwards's concept of a dynamic selfhood is the ongoing expansion of vision through an experimental piety that is continually being reconfigured by pragmatic testing of experience.

Despite recounting numerous occasions of holy beauty, Edwards shapes the *Narrative* as an ongoing and pained oscillation between God's grace and his own depravity. He writes, "I know not how to express better what my sins appear to me to be, than by heaping infinite upon infinite, and multiplying infinite by infinite."[27] There is a certain pride to such claims of sinfulness, but it gives to the *Narrative* structure the feeling of the Puritan dynamic, making the author, his audience, the world, and language all subject to revelation's power both to conceal and disclose the nature of reality. Such a pattern of experience also prodded the enthusiastic hypocrite to seek more deeply; if the minister longed for "humility, brokenness of heart and poverty of spirit," how could his followers deny their own fallenness? The clear reward for such self-emptying was mystical union that brought forth the experience of divine love: "My heart panted after this, to lie low before God, as in the dust; that I might be nothing, and that God might be ALL, that I might become as a little child."[28] This immersion in the divine creates spontaneity expressive of a will restored to harmony with Being in General.

In structure and content, the *Personal Narrative* invokes the repetition of a pattern of pride and blindness, an oscillation of fall and humiliation that leads to kenosis and divine union. The pride of the believer swirls up again despite the experience of supernatural grace, reminding those who assume their election of the vast incompleteness of their struggle. The brokenness that drives self-emptying and the reinstantiation of the cycle of temporal fall and redemption is ongoing in history, as Edwards's repeated statements of his clearer vision of his own sinfulness following upon his increased awareness of God, remind the reader. The believer seeks fulfillment by comparing his expanding awareness of the holy with the incongruity of his own desires and actions, and comes up shorter and shorter of the goal.

The cycle of fall and redemption is repeated within the *Narrative* a number of times and in a variety of forms, and is intermixed with reflections on "the greatest delight in the holy scriptures," "the advancement of Christ's kingdom in the world," "the glory of the third person in the Trinity," and "the bottomless, infinite depths of wickedness, pride, hypocrisy, and deceit, left in my heart."

Edwards takes such dogma and makes it come alive; the taste of Christ's excellence is as vibrant as the taste of honey, the generosity of free grace as miraculous as actually being in love. This is a mark of the utter brilliance of the *Narrative*, for Edwards is able to give experiential feeling to ideas that many of his parishioners took as confusing or dull lessons at best. The way in which the gift of grace arrives is not detailed theoretically or formulaically, but is made into a story that is passionate, even thrilling. And the life of the self is made a life of adventure and risk in which the human dilemma of being both creature and creator is developed not as a tragic tale, but an ironic one in which the two polarities form a conjunction that reflects a warming and clarifying light. The liberty available in the freedom of choice realized through conversation with a communicating and sovereign God, in the response to daily life as an expression of God's will, resolves such irony.

Edwards's conception of the sovereignty of God before and after the experience of grace illustrates the awakening to a sense of a knowable reality in which he could participate. Without entering into a sense of a reality that is open to participation, no one can function in any but the most alienated of ways. The discovery of a living and communicating cosmos to read gives birth to the master trope of a life: the ongoing turning to new circles of meaning as the power of symbolization unfurls ideas and relations that destine consciousness to creative action. Edwards's *Personal Narrative* is a lesson in the power of the religious mind that, through literary artistry, seeks to provoke such vision in the reader.

The *Personal Narrative* offers insight into Edwards's ideas on freedom and the nature of the will also. The will for Edwards is not merely a faculty in which choice takes place, but is energy shaped by disposition or affection. As Perry Miller observes, "The will lies inside the tissue of nature, and is caused by 'something' outside itself.... Man transmits stimulus into effect ... He is in the chain of events, and he cannot interrupt it; his motion is not, and nor ever be set in opposition to it."[29] Being as relation means that freedom comes not in rebellion from engagement with such excellence based upon an assumption of individualism and the sovereignty of reason, as in Arminian claims to the freedom of the will. Personal liberty, on the contrary, exists as creative engagement with the beauty of being itself. As Edwards writes, the experience into which we are born funds our agency:

> All events whatsoever are necessarily connected with something foregoing, either positive or negative, which is the ground of their existence; it follows, therefore, that the whole series of events is thus connected with something in the state of things, either positive or negative, which is original in the series: i.e., something which is connected with nothing preceding that, but God's own immediate conduct, either his acting or forbearing to act.[30]

Such relationship, from one perspective, limits the freedom of the individual in making choices independent of the funded commonwealth of ideas and experiences that Edwards traces in origin to the divine mind, but which James sees as a given of the world of experience. Both thinkers recognize that deterministic forces tend to imprison the human person unless he is liberated by spiritual intuition. From the perspective of the affectional or engaged will, the overwhelming richness of reality offers infinite potentiality for experimentation.

Edwards's engagement with the divine occurs through the erasure of spectatorship, individualism, and the freedom of the will understood as a type of self-divination in which any and every human choice is possible. Edwards experiences saving grace through the paradoxical apprehension of responsible freedom in the sanctification of the heart that he calls the new sense. Thus Edwards is gifted with the capacity to envision beauty, to consent to, or feel with, the patterned relationality of the Creation. Melancholy and despair are overcome by such an event because the sense of a deterministic and cruel predestination is erased. Moral purposiveness becomes possible because there is a community of being with which to engage, and a pattern of potentiality welcoming to such engagement's efforts to amplify being through consenting acts of charity. The experiential engagement that comes alive with the new sense makes the person an artist or poet, and the ethical life a pragmatic poetics calibrated to the remaking of self and world. That this is the case is clearly illustrated in Edwards's artistry within the *Personal Narrative*. For here Edwards, through the story of his own growth in grace and entry into a world of attraction and plenitude, makes the ego's triumphal confidence an absurdity of meaninglessness that transforms the affectional energies and center of attention of the self to the beautiful totality in which it is enveloped. As Elisa New observes of Edwards's transformation of vision,

> The eye undergoes the experience of seeing, an experience that abrogates the priority of either subject or object. . . . Beauty is the representational countenance of forces subsuming, rather than subsumed by, desire. It is the dermal outer membrane of a Being so densely prodigious and enveloping that consciousness flatters itself indeed to think mere acuteness of will could compass such abundance.[31]

James's Melancholy and "Everlasting Possession"

James struggled with similar problems of determinism, but in the late nineteenth-century terms of science and positivism. Like Edwards, James forges a means of creative engagement with reality that is honest to the world of new ideas and to his own intuitive sense of moral purpose and spiritual meaning. The breakdown of subject and object and the employment of a twofold theory of knowledge enable James to create a means of moving through the world as a self in transition, ever sculling ahead towards wider channels in the stream.

James, like Edwards, was also looking for an avenue by which to enable the best elements of philosophical reflection to serve human need rather than scholarly self-indulgence traveling under the guise of system building or logic chopping. James firmly believed that philosophy should address all human concerns and problems as honestly as possible, which accounts in part for his call for a confession of temperament and motives on the part of the philosopher. He counted religious thinking and belief as the most valuable force within a humane philosophical worldview. His high estimation of the value of religion existed despite the presence of religious dogma, which he viewed as a malignant ossification of religious experience, a tomb of retrospection. He wished to harness religion's valuable contributions to human insight and meaning so as to inspire and motivate creativity and moral action. James's vision was removed from the exigencies and pains of communal religious life, and existed in the academy; and yet the urgent need for a vital religious perspective was, in its own cultural framework, as necessary for him as it was for Edwards.

The transformation of James's consciousness developed slowly, as he sought solutions to his despair in European excursions, and study and contemplation at home. In some sense, James needed to gather the strength to follow his inclinations that the creative life of the imagination should carry the weight of public, moral insight. This was despite the repudiation of human creative freedom offered by materialist philosophers and Darwinists concerned with both science and social structure, ideas he found compelling yet painful, and against the grain of common sense and human feeling. Returning home in 1869, James was able to develop his philosophical commitments to a sense of freedom and creativity in conjunction with exposure to a group of young philosophers who named their group the "Metaphysical Club." The unpublished fruit of this conversation was James's reply to Chauncey Wright's materialism, "Against Nihilism." Here James attacks Wright's view that all is a "nulliverse":

> The assertion that we must admit no kind of existence but plenary existence, and that therefore things only exist once . . . contradicts the vague but deep notion of common sense that in each thing, beside its happening to exist as a matter of fact now, there is another kind of meaning which we may call ideal . . . the thing has a meaning, serves a purpose, is a cause, or an end. . . . I suppose more is meant than this - something, namely, like an other and a primordial thing on a plane behind that of the phenomena, and numerically additional to them.[32]

James's argument against Wright forces him to reveal his own feeling that meaning exists as a revelation of an ideal, and that such meaning is purposive. His appeal to common sense implies the acceptance of the assumption that human beings have the freedom to interact with reality both as subject to its laws, but also as a creative force within the extension of meaning that defines reality. James's arguments reveal the division within his own mind. Trained as a medical doctor, son of a theologian and philosopher who encouraged his study of the scientific theories of the day, a lover of art and once a budding painter in his own right, James turned to philosophy as a means to mediate all of these competing interests. This is clear in his dual conception of the temperamental motivations behind the project of philosophy, as seen in this reflection, probably written in 1868:

> Philosophies owe their being to two impulses in the mind: (1) that after absolute intellectual unity or consistency; (2) that after an object we guarantee for our interests. The first breeds critical and sceptical systems, idealisms, etc., the second religions. For by leaving out our feelings from the present act of philosophizing, and simply looking at them as states, one may reach more or less easily a consistent total conception. But when the feelings are in energy, their peculiarity of

> positing objects for themselves forces us, or bribes us, as some would say, to define the rest of the universe in a different way from that perfectly intelligible one in which it appeared to us when considered abstractedly. Do we succeed, is the only question. If we do, we are better philosophers, for our synthesis has included an order of facts disregarded by the other set of men - namely, the desire of the heart to be a match for the whole universe and not shrivel to an infinitesimal accident within it. The way is open to us - we walk it at our own risk.[33]

James's "desire of the heart to be a match for the whole universe" reveals his strong calling to work at philosophy to defend the creative, emotion-laden aspects of human nature not accounted for by overly systematic thought. Surely he had felt himself to be "an infinitesimal accident" in response to the materialist universe, but now he declares himself as courageously devoted to the energy of feelings in their creative function as part of a more expansive concept of reason. His description of the systematic interpretation of the universe as appearing to us "when considered abstractedly" is interesting; his use of the adverb rather than the adjective paints a wry picture of the rationalist philosopher removed from all experience. The young James was concerned for both the fully human and the fully practical in philosophy, for by the inclusion of all of the elements of experience—by not being abstracted from experience itself—"we are better philosophers." This also makes the human a creator, as the stasis of a correspondence theory of truth is replaced by a view of truth and reality that is malleable, capable of growth, and dynamic.

The "desire of the heart" is not unlike Edwards's sense of the heart in its concern to bring the person into relationship with reality through an experiential testing of ideas and actions, and thus avoid the alienation that follows upon the traffic in signs that James sees in relation to a correspondence theory of truth. How can one engage reality if he is alienated from it by engaging it through copies of it that deny acquaintance? Much later in life, James will continue to ponder the feelings and values behind philosophizing, perhaps most fully in *Pragmatism*. James's notion of the event of truth, its verification and validation, points to a concept of agreement that has provocative resonance with Edwards's notion of the sense of the heart and excellence's dynamic quality. James defines the truth-event or verification as follows:

> Our ideas 'agree' with reality. They lead us, namely, through the acts and other ideas which they instigate, into or up to, or towards, other parts of experience with which we feel all the while - such feeling being among our potentialities - that the original ideas remain in agreement. The connexions and transitions come to us from point to point as being progressive, harmonious, satisfactory. This function of agreeable leading is what we mean by an idea's verification.[34]

Perry observes, "It is abundantly evident that for James the urgency of philosophical problems arose from the conflict between science and religion; and it is equally evident that, so far as he himself was concerned, the solution must lie in a reconciliation and not a conquest."[35] James's melancholy was in part determined by the fact that he found materialistic philosophies persuasive, but not humanly meaningful or compelling. The empirical attitude could not be discarded, however, but could be turned around as a methodological aid to the investigations of the heart:

> The nihilistic objection that the substance adds nothing to the phenomenon, having no other connotation other than that of being substance to this phenomenon, does not exactly hit the mark; for the essence of the substantial judgment added by us to our apprehension of the phenomenon is, 'It is meant so! This being meant is that which separates 'real' phenomena from figments and fancies. . . . The theoretic insight into the necessity of things is not vouchsafed us, and the empiricists so far are right. But this practical stability constitutes the most important part of the philosophic quest.[36]

As James early knew, speculation without verification was a dead end, and held no meaning for the actualization of life in its fullest. The construction of the good necessitated the practical assessment of human experiments in the development of an ethical community. Without such "practical stability" the way of the heart could be confused, the value of religious meaning lost in a fog of enthusiasm and self-interest. Though James did not witness the chaos of a revival run amok, as Edwards did, he did know that there was tremendous energy exhausted on the construction of philosophical systems and religious beliefs that had no relation to reality, and that belief in such worldviews could and did hurt both the individual and the community. For James, the affirmation of the desire of the heart meant not only that feeling profoundly informed philosophy, and was not an escape from the insight of materialist systems, but was a responsible attempt to reconcile opposite points of view, each with credible claims to make. Such an affirmation also meant that James had liberated himself through his recognition of the value and power of his imagination and of his ineluctable search for life's meaning.

Such a concern for practical outlooks suggests an early development of Jamesian pragmatism, which also emphasizes the importance of experiential testing and the wastefulness of abstract speculation or stubborn adherence to ideas not capable of being verified by fulfillment in a meaningful terminus. A diary entry written by James in 1868 illustrates the early origins of this perspective: "Every good experience ought to be interpreted in practice. Perhaps actually we can not always trace the effect, but we won't lose if we try to drop all in which this [is] not possible."[37]

While James was convinced of the validity of empirical philosophies, he did not feel that empiricism went far enough. Philosophy needed to take seriously the human heart and its desires for ideas and beliefs not theoretically provable. Thus all experiences needed to be understood in terms of their wider relations; those which had none could be ruled as strictly subjective, and consequently of no cash-value in the stream of experience where the construction of the good took place. Such a position was a risk and a pilgrimage, a direction leading to intellectual adventure of the sort that James would become famous for, but it was motivated by what he would later call a "mystic sense of inner meaning."[38] James was led early on in his philosophical musings to consider that the imagination could best embrace the thicket of reality through a radical empiricism that sought to take account of both scientific and affectional facts.

This is further illustrated by the continuation of James's thinking on the nihilism of Wright. In 1873 he commented on the relation between the positivist and the transcendentalist in his reading notes on Masson's *Recent British Philosophy*:

> That a thing should merely be or happen is the all in all of it for the positivist. What more, he says, can one ask, than concrete actuality? But the transcendentalist asks some guarantee of that being, some assurance that it is 'intended' by the universe. . . . He postulates thus a sort of duplication of all existences: (1) their positive actuality; (2) the hold their idea has upon the rest of nature. . . . in addition to its actuality it has a potentiality when it is not, and that such potentiality means that whatever is now calls for that phenomenon in its time and place. In other words, it is not an accident, but continuous with all the rest of things - it is meant. To be able to say of each phenomenon, this is meant by all that is, would be to achieve the philosophic task and bind all that is into unity. It would, moreover, achieve the moral and religious task. For each phenomenon that confronts us is an occasion for our reaction. We know it by meeting it actively - in the *kennen* sense. If, moreover, in the *wissen* sense we know that it is meant here and now to meet us, we know it all round.[39]

This is an intriguing piece of reflection, for not only does James elaborate upon his distaste for positivism, but he clearly invokes the affectional and moral value of religion, recognizing it as a valid enterprise alongside systematic philosophical programs. The weight of human history's long interest in, and attention to, religion does not justify its constructions, "but as a whole their (religious worldviews) massive effect is too great to be overpowered."[40] Furthermore, the end of philosophy is also the end of morality and religion, and suggests continuity as a type of communion in which the fact of existence is an expression of meaning. The binding into unity—and bear in mind the etymological roots of 'religion' as re-ligare, the binding of all things in community, a vision of ongoing relationship—demands a reaction, an active encounter, an experiential knowledge that witnesses the affirmation and augmentation of potential realities.

This dynamic relationality is what James signifies by the phrase "it is meant"; meaning signifies a destiny, a direction, a call for further work. James here anticipates the coherence theory of truth-processes of *Pragmatism*. Such intentionality motivates an activity and expansion of relation that drives towards unity, completion, or an end that is yet dynamic in its richness. And that end calls forth a perfection of knowledge in both acquaintance or relation, and understanding or explanation; the knowledge of the latter is recognition of the laws regulating the actions and requirements of natural events. Thus, knowledge is "round": perfected in both the relational knowledge of all in all through the phenomenon of acquaintance and understood empirically in relation to its natural existence. Meeting and meaning are coterminous in the actualization of potential realities, and understanding offers an explanation of physical laws that enables such actualization to be grounded in "practical stability," a precursor to pragmatic verification. The "roundness" of the completed transit of knowing by acquaintance and knowing about points to the ways in which James's two-fold theory of knowledge comprehends the Coleridgean theory of imagination, and particularly how Emerson interprets it in his essay "Circles."

James's emergence as a philosopher in the 1860's and 1870's provides him with a number of ideas and interests that he will contemplate throughout his life. Two of the most important of these have to do with the propulsive nature of his thought and the sense of a penumbral 'more' that lures human beings towards the creative exploration of what James calls "the ontologic sphere." These are closely linked in James's thought:

> Our notion of a future time with its material content forms a sort of matrix ante rem into which in its time the res fits. . . . Desires, again, and judgments that things would be better thus than so, involve the feeling that apart from their actuality things have a certain coercive hold on being. . . . From all these different sources there grows up round about the actually present in consciousness an atmosphere of reference to something more which haunts it. This 'more' may be the margin of otherness in time and space; it may be the truer determination of the instant, whether as the real which is to correct instant expectation, the rectification which is to correct instant perception, the desirable end which coerces instant feeling, the mere doubt which corrects instant dogmatism, or the reflection 'this is subjective' which corrects instant ontology. The present cannot move unaccompanied by this escort, this ontologic sphere in which it lies embedded, and which prevents us from accepting it schlechthin as absolutely given. . . . The here and now, in addition to being the seat of actual feelings, becomes a sort of locus of intersection of the network of ideal relations arising from association, anticipation, reflection, desire, etc.[41]

This feeling of "something more" establishes an engagement with experience in its ability to serve as a margin or limit principle that offers correction to human pretensions. As such it is both an instigator of the ironic and a lure to creativity in the satisfaction inherent in the aesthetic free play that leads to agreement. The idea that the mind merely exists to copy a static reality cannot exist within such a philosophical belief, nor can the human spirit:

> I for one must confess that if by an effort of abstraction I am able for a moment to conceive of the world in Humean terms—of representation sprouting upon representation by absolute happening, of everything being only once, of evolution with nothing involved, of our mental life, for example, as having come to be with no ideal preexisting determinant of it—I feel as if the breath was leaving my body.[42]

James's confession seals his spiritual commitment, if it does not define it. His Humean fantasy leaves him bereft of experience, and hence of life. James suggests an empiricist version of chaos, and envisions, again, the mechanistic reality that so crippled him only a few years before. As he sees clearly now, such a life of material existence alone lacks the feeling of "being meant." The breath leaving his body suggests the spirit's absence from such a world, and implies the creative force that returned life to him. The breath or spirit of life was for James discovered with philosophical courage and the conviction of his belief that grace could instill a disinterested aesthetic sense that promoted meaningful advance into, and expansion of, the world of experience, the desire of the heart that propelled one into the free play of relationality. Such creativity required science to anchor it in the real so that the construction of the good could develop free of the chaos and confusion inevitable, ironically, to the life of an abstracted mind. Thus James suggests that aesthetics and ethics are synonymous in the connection that he draws between aesthetic creativity as the advance of coherence that necessarily requires verification with the dynamic process of the experiential stream that describes his philosophy of radical empiricism.

James scholars have made much of the melancholic years of the 1860's and 1870's; many especially note the influence of the French philosopher Charles Renouvier in drawing James out of his despair. In reading Renouvier and accepting his notion of free will, "the sustaining of a thought because I choose to when I might have other thoughts," James formulated an answer to his own despair that compressed his many feelings and ideas into a workable approach to living. He writes of this experience,

> My first act of free will shall be to believe in free will. . . . Not in maxims, not in Anschauungen, but in accumulated acts of thought lies salvation. Hitherto, when I have felt like taking a free initiative, like daring to act originally, without carefully waiting for

> contemplation of the external world to determine all for me, suicide seemed the most manly form to put my daring into; now, I will go a step further with my will, not only act with it, but believe as well, believe in my individual reality and creative power. My belief, to be sure, can't be optimistic - but I will posit life (the real, the good) in the self-governing resistance of the ego to the world. Life shall be built in doing, suffering, and creating.[43]

Renouvier's ideas enabled James to coalesce and symbolize his thinking so as to break out of his divided state, and make an affirmation of a personal philosophy dyed in a spiritually haunted orientation to life. What Renouvier enabled James to do at this point in his life was articulate in clear terms the many ideas and conflicts that had long been brewing within him. Upon examination of James's diaries, notebooks, and letters, it is clear that James was wrestling with the question of creative freedom and the nature of philosophy before reading Renouvier. What is intriguing about this notebook entry is the encapsulation of James's personal philosophy as "doing, suffering, and creating," involving the pressure of the ego in resistance to the world. This echoes James's musings on meeting life actively, resisting its "pastness" in order to construct the real, which promises the good, in a creative way. James's transformation reveals a belief in both the value of a future orientation in thinking and the sense of "something more" that offers the opportunity of an acquaintance with new possibilities and the intersection of more complex relations. The interplay between action and correction defines human experience, and enables a creative synthesis that constructs novel relations expressive of the good that is yet still subject to the same process of revision. The suffering referred to in this interaction suggests the play of irony that divides and yet propels the self to a new depth of mind.

That James's transformation is sincere is proven by the biographical facts of a life understood and embraced as processive. "Doing, suffering, and creating" is a phrase that symbolizes the propulsive experience of the search for meaning as a spiritual quest to construct the good. Action in the world begets the correction of idea and vision; ironic self-perception drives the act of creativity, forging a reconfiguration of the self as engaged with a reality that is understood as a fabric of relations. James's belief in free will bespeaks a transformation of vision.

"Doing, suffering, and creating" is also a phrase that expresses James's dynamic view of life, and the elements that will emerge as his philosophy of radical empiricism exist in these early years of his philosophical career. James understands the limitations of thought existent within the empirical guidelines of what is given in experience, and yet he resists the reductionism of "paltry empiricism."[44] This enables him to thicken his empiricism with the affectional facts, values, and ideas that the individual may discover in engaging with the world, and that may offer novel patterns of meaning as they enter into the free play of a world of overflowing experiential richness. In some sense, James had to invent radical empiricism as a way to survive as a moral agent inspired by a pragmatist imagination long before he works out, in a more elaborate way, his philosophy of radical empiricism.

Through his melancholy and the reflection that it forced upon him, James experienced a spiritual, philosophical, and psychological rebirth that enabled him to participate in the creative activity of life. Human action enters into the matrix of relations that defines reality; suffering is inevitable, and takes place through the correction of ideas, opinions, and beliefs that persons bring to reality. Here the world of bare materialism is the enemy to be overcome by the impression of thought upon thing, original action that is creative of another self and another world in a way that draws upon Romantic theories of the imagination. James's former desire to reject determinism through suicide reveals not only the heroism he sees in original thinking, but also a dissent from the deadliness of mechanistic philosophy by a final pyrrhic victory. His ability to go beyond suicide to a belief in creativity and responsible freedom signals the advent of a new worldview, a new blueprint for action in which life defined as the reality of goodness demands the remaking of the crude world of materialism by the struggle of the philosopher. The consequent avoidance of pathos and the transcendence of tragedy signal the advent of faith, as hope enables the birth of possibility and the awareness of irony that drives vision and revision. Such irony takes on diverse facets within James's thinking: his two-fold theory of knowledge corresponds to the dialectical relationship between vision and revision in the drive for full meaning. This becomes critically important to the pragmatist imagination that believes that things are "in the making."

Religion was perhaps the driving, if vague, energy motivating James's reflections and his emergence as a philosopher. In 1873 he wrote,

> Religion in its most abstract expression may be defined as the affirmation that all is not vanity. The empiricist can easily sneer at such a formula as being empty through its universality, & ask you to cash it by its concrete filling, - which you may not be able to do, for nothing can well be harder. Yet as a practical fact its meaning is so distinct that when used as a premise in a life, a whole character may be imparted to the life by it. It like so many other universal concepts is a truth of orientation, serving not to define an end, but to determine a direction.[45]

James had found his own direction through the vague affirmation of the common sense valuation of faith and of the affections that demand and fund such a faith. This provided a tremendous source of freedom for James, enabling his desire of the heart, the construction of the good through disinterested exploration of, and creative engagement with, reality, to establish its relevance with courage and conviction. James would later confirm this belief in *The Varieties*:

> If religion is to mean anything definite for us, it seems to me that we ought to take it as meaning this added dimension of emotion, this enthusiastic temper of espousal, in regions where morality strictly so called can at best but bow its head and acquiesce. It ought to mean nothing short of this new reach of freedom for us, with the struggle over, the keynote of the universe sounding in our ears, and everlasting possession spread before our eyes.[46]

Thirty-five years after James's youthful assertion of belief in his own creative power, the difficulty of forging ahead against a world constructed of sensation, determinism, and retrospective and systematic ideas continued to hamper his philosophical endeavors:

> Pent in, as the pragmatist more than anyone else sees himself to be, between the whole body of funded truths squeezed from the past and the coercions of the world of sense about him, who so well as he feels the immense pressure of objective control under which our minds perform their operations?[47]

The desire for freedom, the creative demand suggested by the intuitive feeling that human life holds a propulsively expansive meaning, the belief in strenuous effort to build a moral universe, all of the doubts and values that plagued James's personal crisis and emergence as a philosopher continued to accompany James, defining his mature life and the trajectory of his career. The reduction of human life to a mechanistic model by deterministic philosophies underscores a belief that Edwards shared due to the painful lessons of Northampton revivalism. The world-picture envisioned by a particular epistemology may hold a compelling and hypnotic power that can tragically fate human ends to illusory limitations and a deathly blindness.

The achievement of creative freedom tempers the trance-like effect of false imaginings and limited systems of thinking. For Edwards, this was found in a divine sovereignty that was infinitely glorious. God for Edwards was of such utter beauty that the human person should be wholly and joyfully grateful for the opportunity to participate in the divine drama; any other notion of freedom was a type of alienation from human destiny. For James, the uncertainty and risk of life not guaranteed by a transcendent absolute meant that the person had the opportunity to act despite the forces compressing the will. While Edwards embraced relationship with God's sovereignty as the best, and only, opportunity for meaningful creative action, James witnessed the opportunity to press through the scientific and philosophical determinisms of his day to perhaps—perhaps— discover a relationship with a vague spiritual reality that was both liberating and morally instructive in a way flexible enough to enable a wide variety of experiments. The susceptibility that describes Edwards's notion of the sense of the heart and James's mystic sense of inner meaning, his spark of the heart, defines a new focal point of willed attention, a shift in the center of energy, such that religious experience becomes creative of novel approaches to ontology and epistemology. The rise of the religious imagination and of a reality poetically advanced as an enriched empiricism arises from the despair of life witnessed as an unresponsive and alienating reality.

Chapter 3
Heart Religion and the Pragmatist Imagination

In the Book of Ezekiel, the wheel of the spirit is a symbol of inspiration that has served as a source for modern conceptions of the imagination. Ezekiel writes, "Whithersoever the Spirit was to go, the wheels went, and thither was their spirit to go; . . . for the spirit of the living creature was in the wheels also."[1] Moving through and over the world of experience, uniting human energies in its transfiguring power, evoking solidarity between the living and the dead, the wheel of the spirit embodies and refigures human knowledge. The biblical image of Ezekiel's wheel aptly configures the pathos and triumph of the mind's fate as it shapes itself, its communicative transactions with the divine economy, and the world of being and things in either expansive or contractive ways. Such imaginative reconfiguration traces the sacred, an evanescent light across the cosmos and under the invisible particles of the Creation, in seeking the full richness of life.

S.T. Coleridge employs the image of Ezekiel's wheel to describe God's providential role in the birth of the creative imagination and its symbolic activity. In *The Statesman's Manual*, Coleridge writes, the imagination is

> That reconciling and mediatory power, which incorporating the Reason in Images of the Sense, and organizing (as it were) the flux of the Senses by the permanence and self-circling energies of the Reason, gives birth to a system of symbols, harmonious in themselves, and consubstantial with the truths, of which they are the *conductors* These are the Wheels which Ezekiel beheld, when the hand of the Lord was upon him, and he beheld visions of God as he sate among the captives by the river of Chabar. . . . The truths and the symbols that represent them move in conjunction and form the living chariot that bears up (for *us)* the throne of the divine humanity.[2]

Symbolization invokes the hope of divine communication and the claim for providential historical transformation through a type of "circum-inscription," or "writing around" that evokes the two-fold system of knowledge that Edwards understands as heart (affections) and head ("mere cogitation"), and James sees as "knowledge by acquaintance" and "knowledge about." Edwards and James find the spatial form of the circle in motion suggestive of the dynamic character of experiential religion as it emerges from the tension between deterministic systems of thought and the intuitive sense of creative freedom available to every person. The models of knowledge that they offer convey such circling energy, and thus resonate with Samuel Taylor Coleridge's theory of the imagination.

Ezekiel's wheel inspires a sense of hope and purpose for a world that perpetually appears mechanistic and fixed by law, as it suggests that the human heart in particular operates analogically to providential circling as a creative power enabling engagement with reality. Edwards interprets Ezekiel's wheel as an image that illustrates divine providence in the revolutionary dynamic of natural, moral, and spiritual life:

> All is the motion of wheels. . . . They go round and come to the same again; and the whole series of divine providence, from the beginning to the end, is nothing else but the revolution of certain wheels, greater and lesser, the lesser being contained within the greater. What comes to pass in the natural world is, in this respect, typical of what comes to pass in the moral and intelligent world.[3]

The circle, like the heart, is a metonym for human experience, both symbol and cipher of the world. It indicates the possibility of a marriage of spirit and matter that "circum-inscribes," and thus advances, reality as a social universe of overlapping circles of activity.

Such an activity of circumscription and processive advance describes the pragmatist imagination as it carries out James's assertion that the world of persons and things is "in the making." He writes,

> What *really exists* is not things made but things in the making. Once made, they are dead, and an infinite number of alternative conceptual decompositions can be used in defining them. But put yourself in the making by a stroke of intuitive sympathy with the thing and, the whole range of possible decompositions coming at once into your possession, you are no longer troubled with the question which of them is the more absolutely true. Reality *falls* in passing into conceptual analysis; it *mounts* in living its own undivided life—it buds and bourgeons, changes and creates. Once adopt the movement of this life in any given instance and you know what Bergson calls the *devenir reel* by which the thing evolves and grows. Philosophy should seek this kind of living understanding of the movement of reality, not follow science in vainly patching together fragments of its dead results.[4]

This is the image of the turning-place where life itself is affirmed and augmented. Here creative freedom works to make a real addition to the world through experimentation and risk. James's model evolves in part from the morphology of conversion developed by the deeply imaginative Puritan Protestant tradition in England and America. The pragmatist imagination functions to widen and thicken realities and experiences such that we become aware of the gaps, blind spots, fatigue, and disjunctions within our assumptions about reality. James takes this lack of awareness as a major contributor to the preserved conceptual decomposition and discursiveness in thought. The radical empiricism that James favors sees "more imagination of realities" such that we are exposed to both the thickness and the tragedy of human life.[5] In the work of Edwards and James, the heart, as synecdoche for the fullness of human cognition as it incorporates the widest possible range of feeling, fuels the pragmatist imagination.

In joining heart religion with the pragmatist imagination, the relationship of Edwards and James to the romantic theory of the imagination as envisioned by Coleridge and Emerson arises. The blindness of human beings in binding human assumptions and knowledge to retrospection and the archaeological rather than to the propulsive prospectivism advanced through imaginative activity marks the dilemma that Edwards and James address in their high estimation of religious experience. Here also is found the marriage of idealism and materialism that defines the enriched empiricisms of both Edwards and James. Critically important and intriguing here is the presence of beauty as a vital factor in this propulsive expansion of vision, and not as retrospective aestheticism that reflects narcissism. Beauty's synonymy with Edwards's idea of true virtue and James's concept of truth as a species of the good empowers the imagination. Religious experience drives the synonymy of aesthetics and ethics that remakes community by necessitating public consensus, thus refashioning the space of public life and democracy according to a model of strenuous or agonistic effort requisite to such power.

Dewey draws from Coleridge's theory of the imagination to offer a pragmatist imagination suggestive of Edwards's and James's own concepts. Dewey writes in *Art as Experience*,

> [Imagination] designates a quality that animates and pervades all processes of making and observation. It is a way of seeing and feeling things as they compose an integral whole. It is the large and generous blending of interests at the point where the mind comes in contact with the world. When old and familiar things are made new in experience there is imagination. When the new is created, the far and strange become the most natural inevitable things in the world. There is always some measure of adventure in the meeting of mind and universe, and this adventure is, in its measure, imagination.[6]

The response to the despairing consequences of determinism involves the approval of human affection as a mode of cognition that fuels engagement with a world unfinished and in process. Engagement with a reality that is malleable and receptive to human involvement offers a sense of possibility that neither Edwards nor James previously grasped. The image of Ezekiel's wheel suggests the position of the person between the presence of mystery and mechanical law in which feeling or the heart operates to radiate the individual's sacred trace outward into the world of dynamic ideas, persons, and things. Thus Edwards sees the process of divine emanation and human remanation as a circling activity definable as glorying or delighting in being. For James, the world of experience "means an abandonment of theoretical constructions that may have become habitual, and even incorporated in accepted modes of speech, like the terms *mind* and *body*."[7] For James, the phenomena "person" designates a holistic reality that serves as a center of creative activity: "everything circles round it, and is felt from its point of view."[8]

The ontological wonder that both Edwards and James experience and recommend exists as a clarifying moment of engagement or delight that motivates the struggle to affirm Being in General or realize the penumbral self within the forms of natural existence. This moment of participation occurs most clearly within the experience of holiness or the sacred, and results from spiritual feeling that conceptual analysis cannot contain. In realizing ontological wonder, Edwards and James bracket Romantic thinkers like Coleridge, who develops a theory of the creative imagination akin to Edwards's concept of the sense of the heart or the mystical sense of inner meaning that James endorses.

Like Edwards, James sees in vaguer terms that there is something wrong at the heart of human nature that is adequately addressed only within the realm of "'*something there*,' more deep and more general than any of the special and particular "senses" by which the current psychology supposes original existents to be revealed."[9] The experience of something more thickens the self's awareness by feathering a spiritual power within reality that expands the meaning of a life. These strands of mutual possession create the freedom to engage the overwhelming world of experience as intensely vibrant and beautiful. From these lightest strands of being the heart radiates concentrically, spinning out the transitions and relations that augment being itself in the particular forms of life with which the person engages. Such radiality or circulation of the heart affirms others, glorifying for Edwards the creation and the Creator, while for James building-out the unfinished universe in a way that reflects the possibility of a cooperative salvation.

Edwards and the Pragmatist Heart

Edwards inherits the Puritan concept of the heart as a metaphor for the organic nature of the person as a feeling, willing, thinking being. The synecdoche of the heart rests upon biblical anthropology, the renewal of spirituality within Reformed traditions, and the revived interest in humoral psychology in the late sixteenth and seventeenth centuries witnessed in numerous works akin to Burton's *Anatomy of Melancholy*. Puritan devotionalism emphasized a living relation with God that, when intensified, resulted in new modes and methods of spiritual practice that marked a shifting concept of the person.

The image of Ezekiel's wheel suggests motion between the ideal and the material that inhabits the human mind as the spiritual energy of creation that Edwards and James express in building metaphysical visions in which the claim for reality as constituted by experienceable relations upholds both an orientation to the future and a belief in creative freedom as a viable expression of responsible agency. While James readily admits to a "vague vision" that tries to avoid the theocentric claims of absolute idealism, he does suggest a "More" beyond human consciousness that aids in the furtherance of human values and goals, and that is apprehended in the widening of vision accomplished through experiential religion. The vagueness of James's vision results from his desire to emphasize the future orientation of agency within the world of experience, and to shun claims about God or ultimate reality that serve no functional purpose and in fact encourage a work stoppage, in moral and religious terms. When James states, "I myself believe that the evidence for God lies primarily in inner personal experiences," he asserts his belief in the affectional facts discovered by the "spark of the heart" that are both ideal and real, haunting personal experience with the vague but genuine demand to bring such spiritual perception into the real world of struggle. He writes, "The truth of 'God' has to run the gauntlet of all our other truths. It is on trial by them and they on trial by it."[10]

The heart is the master trope for human experience, as illustrated by the Puritan model of sanctification. Surprisingly to modern persons, until the late seventeenth century, medical observers also considered the heart the center of identity and intellect, as well as the center of feeling. Barbara Lewalski writes,

> The heart (is) synecdoche for the Christian himself, the stage for the whole of spiritual experience. The basis for taking the heart as John Weemse succinctly states is a synecdoche: 'In natural generation the *heart* is first framed; and in supernaturall regeneration, it is first reformed. . . . The life of Grace begins in the *heart* first, and is last left there." . . . Other biblical metaphors for the Christian life are often couched in terms of actions upon or actions of the heart.[11]

Lewalski finds the heart synecdoche present in descriptions of the Christian life as a battle between light and darkness; in the interior agon of Christian warfare; in the pilgrimage from sin to grace; in spiritual union or marriage; in images of cleansing, purgation, weeding, rooting out, pruning; and in the figure of the temple as ark or altar in which the heart is located. She notes the origin of these images and metaphors in biblical texts, citing Jeremiah 31:33 and Ezekiel 36:26 as central to the interpretation of divine regeneration of the human through the activity of the spirit.[12]

The precision with which Protestant poets and divines analyzed the inner workings of the religious mind is continued in the exquisite care with which Edwards parses the many variations of experimental piety so as to discern truly holy affections in *Religious Affections*. The heart synecdoche is a commonplace even today, and for thinkers like Edwards and James, the heart becomes a metaphor by which the central role of feeling in experiential religion may be described fully and suggestively. Immediately comprehensible to all, yet expressive of complex relations between experiential and conceptual knowledge as they inform human agency, the heart metaphor encapsulates the circuit of the wheeled spirit, the connection between the graciousness witnessed in experimental religion and the human vessel that enables spiritual action within material reality. The diastole and systole of the heart's circulatory power finds an analogue in the relationship between revelation and reason, the ideal and the real, self and other, and individual and community that powerfully conveys Edwards's spiritual philosophy. For James, the use of traditional religious metaphors within his more modern analysis of religious experience has the effect of thickening the poetic vagueness that he frequently employs simultaneously to evoke both spiritual presence and absence.

The rhythmic pulse of being originates in the heart, as Emerson so eloquently observes, an organ of boundary-breaking power that defines selfhood as normatively liminal.[13] As the heart beats, so life progresses or degrades, but there is no escape from the onward pulsation even as the human builds walled fortifications against the heart's outward drive. The heart metaphor informs the enriched empiricisms that Edwards and James develop as alternative paths of being or forms of theological philosophy that offer a mode of thinking and acting sympathetic to the visionary mode of being that holds freedom and the openness of the future as paramount values. The metaphor of the heart communicates the primacy of purposiveness.

Conceiving the heart in these diverse dimensions of human experience makes clear the organic model of reality with which both Edwards and James wrestle in their conception, analysis, and critical approval of religion within the context of the metaphysical implications of an experiential worldview. As the organic metaphor for the rhythmic pulse of vitality and growth, the heart serves a central function in the tentative solutions to the problems posed by the demand for freedom in a world in which religious and scientific doctrines are determinative. The heart metaphor suggests energy and limitation, growth and vitality checked by the end of a life given the opportunity to participate in a sphere of being wider than itself. The historical dimension of human existence frames the experience of the heart and the momentary freedom of creativity within a transient present. Retrospective and prospective vision shape the act of experiencing or testing of the self in such a way as to limit and define human knowledge through the making and breaking of focal centers of attention. The human struggle is repeatedly to find creative freedom through "advantageous connexion" that, while marking the event of truth and its aesthetic dynamic, does not reify such truth as fixed or final.[14] Nor does it leave the aesthetic apart from ethical and communal implications, for the action of success or failure as a truth-event transforms the pattern of social life and well-being.

The self is thus a society of relations embedded within a reality that is also intensively social. Engagement of the self with reality defines a social dynamic in which liminality is a normative state. This supports James's claim that consciousness does not exist as an entity, but functionally, to enable free participation in the organic system of a pluralistic universe. In a similar vein, Edwards describes consciousness as a kind of "feeling within itself,"[15] suggesting a resonating cognitive pulsation.

Edwards's interpretation of Ezekiel's wheel informs his concept of the sense of the heart and its relationship to consciousness in terms of a communicative circulation of the divine presence in all beings and things. "The providence of God is like a wheel," Edwards writes, as is the creation shaped ex nihilo by divine delight, where revolution defines the process of the seasons reflective of the invisible, spiritual realities that natural processes and things in their beauty suggest.[16] The saint operates as a vessel of divine care for the Creation in the resonating power of the sense of the heart capable of conjoining relations that affirmatively augment Being in General through charitable action constructive of community. Reality for Edwards may be described as concentrically complex to an infinite degree. Such a model further suggests that the Creation is concentrically social, and this is in accord with Edwards's notion of a Trinitarian God creative of a holy family through an inherent delight. God is envisioned as a creative, communicative being, and this quality defines radical sovereignty because it marks the uniqueness of divine communication as the creative power of being itself.

Edwards describes divine sovereignty with the unusual view that it is delightful, and this is because God is radically sovereign as a communicating or interactive being. Edwards's description of God as Being in General is extremely helpful in providing a clear transposition from traditional attributes of God to a sense of James's "something more." The communicative circuit of the divine mind, the circling recombination that Ezekiel's wheel inspires, ultimately revolves in mystery even as the human portion of experiential religion drives the radial figuration of self and world. Instead of the traditional notion of the incommensurability of God with any human conception, James uses his notion of pure experience and of the More as pragmatically meaningful limit principles able to avoid absolutistic and systematic habits of the philosophical mind. Similarly, Edwards's notion of Being in General suggests a dynamic and unfolding process to which humans attend, but which may never be fully grasped.

These philosophical positions define a model of the human actor agreeable to the intuitive sense that determinism does not tell the full story. Edwards's enriched empiricism and James's radical empiricism are rooted in early experiences of personal conflict, develop over time as fully fleshed out worldviews, and situate themselves as programs that redefine their respective concepts of religion. These models of experiential reality bear witness to visions of reality as rich and generous, but requiring the hard human struggle to interact with, and build-out the implications of, spiritual experience in the real world. Edwards sees the development of the Christian community as reliant upon such metaphysical implications. Similarly, James's view of cooperative salvation depends upon the principles inherent in radical empiricism.

For Edwards, the heart functions as an image of organic dynamism that finds analogues in both the nature of reality and in the function of language. In a fragment included in *Images of Divine Things*, Edwards writes,

> In the conception of an animal and formation of the embrio (sic), the first thing appearing is the punctum saliens or the heart, which beats as soon as it exists. And from thence the other parts gradually appear, as though they all gradually proceeded and branched forth from that beating point. This is a lively image of the manner of the formation of the new creature. The first thing is a new heart, a new sense and inclination that is a principle of new life, a principle that, however small, is active and has vigour and power, and as it more beats and struggles, thirsts after holiness, aims at and tends to every thing that belongs to the new creature, and has within it the foundation and source of the whole. It aims at perfection, and from thence are the issues of life. From thence the various things that belong to the new creature all proceed and branch forth and gradually appear, and that more and more. And this principle, from its first existence, never ceases to exert itself, until the new creature be compleat and comes to its proper perfection.[17]

Edwards's concept of being as relation profoundly informs his notion of the sense of the heart. The organic quality of Edwards's thought and the exceedingly careful employment of language that marks his work compel a careful scrutiny of the term "sense of the heart," despite the easy associations of the term to ideas of spiritual feeling and insight. That these associations do in fact inform the complexity of the concept illustrates Edwards's genius in the employment of direct and accessible metaphors that yet carry significant precision and depth.

Edwards begins *Miscellany #782* with the distinction between sign and actual idea, and arrives at two basic points: that the use of signs, though a cause of error, is necessary for social life and development; and that to truly apprehend knowledge of a thing, idea, pleasure, or pain "we must have that very idea in our mind." This leads Edwards to distinguish two activities of mind, distinctions made only for the sake of discussion: cogitation, which is of the understanding or "head"; and apprehension, which appertains to the will or "heart." The heart concerns inclination or disposition as it responds to pleasure or pain; it signifies the energetic self-relation of the unified self as it participates in "a direct ideal view or contemplation of the thing thought of." Such an ideal view or beholding of an actual idea "is what is vulgarly called having a sense."[18]

The sense of the heart is an energy of perception and creation that draws ideas within the context of relationality that is the self (a kind of feeling within itself). Immediately conjoining the idea within its present (though passing away) context so as to generate a new system of relations constitutes the self as both proportionally dynamic configuration and act responsive to the wider community of being. The sense of the heart is an energy unifying the self relationally/aesthetically and consensually/ethically with the context of its own being and with Being in General. Edwards notes that all objects of knowledge concern "the wills or hearts of spiritual beings," and that such spiritual knowledge is indeed our only real concern."[19] The actual ideas excited by experience strike the mind like a stone thrown into a pond that generates resonating waves formative of concentric patterns of relation. The excitement of concentricity, of dynamic relationality, is the exercise of the sense of the heart. Such exponentializing excitement is a beholding that is also a generative organizing of experience capable of enacting consent to being enlarging of self and Creation. Experiential immersion is the drawing of a circle from the overlapping yet retrospective accretions that fund consciousness. As such it requires both breaking known boundaries and reinscribing a new circumference and a transformed center of attention. The phenomenon of inscription, or, more accurately, circumscription, conveys the power and limitation of language as it seeks to represent such boundary-breaking and boundary-making. These activities inform the two-fold theory of knowledge Edwards adopts in the terms "heart" and "head," and in James by the terms "knowledge by acquaintance" and "knowledge about."

The gap between human and divine understanding is so great, "that a due sense of those (spiritual) things is never attained without immediate divine assistance."[20] The gift of illumination that enables a sense of the excellence of divine things transforms the self in its inclination or interestedness:

> In the renewing and sanctifying work of the Holy Ghost, those things are wrought in the soul that are above nature, and of which there is nothing of the like kind in the soul by nature; and they are caused to exist in the soul habitually, and according to such a stated constitution or law that lays such a foundation for exercises in a continued course, as is called a principle of nature. Not only are remaining principles assisted to do their work more freely and fully, but those principles are restored that were utterly destroyed by the fall; and the mind thenceforward habitually exerts those acts that the dominion of sin had made it as wholly destitute of, as a dead body is of vital acts.[21]

The illuminated self has a new foundation as the basis of its activity; this new habit, energy, or disposition is a law or principle of nature. God restores the human to active participation in the Creation, returns the human to life, by returning to the person the law or principle that enables the new sense to operate as an element of God's own creative self-enjoyment. Such illumination is "so much of God, of his nature, so much a participation of the deity: It is a kind of emanation of God's beauty, and is related to God as the light is to the sun."[22]

The sense of the heart, then, is the energy, habit, or law that restores or fulfills human being to its rightful capacity to participate freely in the Creation. It is a unifying sense, what the Cambridge Platonists called a "plastic nature" that beholds, relates, and contextualizes the self in relation to the actual ideas of the Creation that are images *and* shadows of the perfected actual ideas in the mind of God. It is a sense as it perceives of experience by grasping the actual idea; and it is of the heart because, as Edwards notes,

> However small (the heart) is active and has vigour and power, and as it more beats and struggles, thirsts after holiness, aims at and tends to everything that belongs to the new creature, and has within it the foundation and source of the whole. It aims at perfection, and from thence are the issues of life. From thence the various things that belong to the new creature all proceed and branch forth and gradually appear, and that more and more. And this principle, from its first existence, never ceases to exert itself, until the new creature be compleat and come to its proper perfection.[23]

The sense of the heart's drive for "more and more" speaks to both the continuous calibration of the self in relation to being and to its participation in the fulfillment of the Kingdom that is ongoing in time. The energy of love or consent that affirms being is not private or limited, but engages the community even as it has engaged the community of Being in General. The will to be is the will to holiness, and requires a mental energy capable of beholding and responding to actual ideas in complex relation. The excellence of Christ is here the best teacher; for the hypotactical and pluralistic oppositionalism that Christ artfully displays speaks of and to a mind capable of conjoining, through the activity of the heart, seemingly contradictory realities in an appreciation of unity in relation, expansively generous in its consent to being. The sense of the heart propels the self to ongoing transformation through the chiastic play in which actuality and its verbalization work together and fall asunder in historical time, creating a growth in the capacity to love that is a "symphonization" with Christ. This is the true end of the Creation, the capacity of human love to augment Being in General by its radiation or remanation of love or consent to God. Human love or consent thus can cause God to grow and become happy: "this light, and this only, has its fruit in an universal holiness of life." [24]

But this spiritual sense reanimated by divine light operates in a fallen reality in which darkness makes its daily appearance, and all of human existence is fraught with the potential of "evil imaginings," self-interested acts, and a valorization of cogitation over affection. The economy created by cogitation serves a system of signs that substitute for experience, making social life more facile, but also creating alienation from the world of experience, and hence from the teleological impulse so central to divine communication and purpose. One might well argue that the famous sermon "Sinners in the Hands of an Angry God" is itself a meditation on the dangers of cogitation. The use of what Miller has called "the rhetoric of sensation" functions to return the Enfield congregant to life by reminding him of contingency in an intensely visceral fashion. By separating the person from the fullness of experience, the view of sin or privation of the good in the practical realities of poverty, suffering, and injustice, are invisible in their pained actuality. This finds a parallel in James's notion that we need to work cooperatively towards the possibility of salvation. Life has real losses, according to James, and human contributions to rejection of members of the species and refusal to work actively towards a richer environment diminish the potentiality of the world of experience. James states in *Pragmatism* a belief repeated throughout his works: life is dangerous, and demands strenuous effort.[25]

The heart and the head ideally function in such a way as to strengthen the full power of thinking, as it is informed by both affections and cogitation. Edwards reiterates that rationality gains depth of power by the new principle of the sense of the heart as it transforms consciousness, and the deepening of the understanding further strengthens the hinge or fulcrum upon which the affections rely for their power of discernment. The habituation to cogitation, however, limits the ability of the self to unravel the skeins of its own imprisoned will. What James in *The Principles of Psychology* describes as the "substantive moments" or "resting-places" habituate and enmesh the will in its own dispositional tendencies, and constitute an arena of agonistic struggle for the person. Liberation from cogitation may only occur through the awakening of the sense of the heart by sanctification, and the benevolent consent to one's fellow community members that pragmatically affirms and advances the vitality of both the individual and the community.

This complicated theater of human mental life is the stage on which the Great Awakening played out its scenes, and it illustrates the perplexing problems of discernment of true religion that Edwards faced. Recall that in the postscript of his letter to Rev. Colman, Edwards followed the tragic news of Uncle Hawley's suicide that triggered mass hysteria and accusations of Satanism amongst neighbors with the hopeful report of new exercises of the Holy Spirit in a nearby village. His *Personal Narrative* follows suit: it expresses the dilemma of spectatorship and the horrifying mystery of predestination; the chaos and confusion of discernment of truly religious affections; and the sanctifying work of the Holy Spirit in laying a new epistemological foundation that transforms the person by enlivening the soul. Conversion signals a process of becoming that reconfigures, though with incomplete assurance, Edwards's concepts of self, language, and sainthood, but the powerful lure of hope and promise drives such becoming.

The Plural Centers of James's Vision

Though present in various texts, the image of the heart does not serve as the central metaphor in James's thought. One is hard-pressed to think of any one metaphor that sticks to James, for he exemplifies an extreme intellectual restlessness. James's lack of comfort with any one metaphor for human feeling and his frustration with the limitations of language ironically shape him as a sophisticated stylist ever searching for the phrase that might capture the ungraspable dynamism of the thickness of reality. His intense demand is that we keep language as dynamic as possible to be true to the experiential richness we encounter. Many writers have tried to define James's center of vision; the ink spilt in such a quest would undoubtedly amuse James. In reality the center of James's vision is the fact there can be no center, but only a processive circling out into the world of experience. Jill M. Kress writes,

> The discourse of consciousness in the Jamesian text produces an equivocal version of the self—sacred, central, inward core, *and* wandering, tenuous flow of experience. In the Jamesian account of consciousness, words keep us suspended, questions are left unanswered, theories remain open-ended. . . . He is continually gesturing toward what exists outside of his narrative. . . . James creates a series of metaphors out of which consciousness materializes, yet he systematically deconstructs his own creation throughout the course of his career. Metaphor, however, seems to regenerate itself. Liquid metaphors, nuclear metaphors, ethereal metaphors, corporeal metaphors – consciousness measures inwardness with figures such as these. What we inherit from James are both the tools to construct the self and the subsequent claim to continually remake it.[26]

Some of the terms James uses include feeling, affection, disposition, acquaintance, passion, will, and habit to denote the radiation of feeling as a cognitive power. His preference generally is to construct metaphors that express process over form, as in his metaphor of the stream of consciousness. His notion of the "melting mood" carries the meaning of the warm or tender heart through the application of an adjective typical to the psychology of the humors and the image of heat as a transformative power. But we might also read the melting mood as a metaphor for the cognitive experience of metaphoricity itself. Kress is right in seeing James as constructing his rhetorical strategy through the idea of the vague; this, in some sense, is why Edwards's sense of the circulating heart-mind and Emerson's notion of circling perhaps anticipate Jamesian vagueness best, for both work from models similar to the twofold theory of "knowledge about" and "knowledge by acquaintance" that seek knowledge "fully round" and yet historically relative and destined for ongoing transformation. Another image applicable to James's restless vagueness is of the self as disperser of rays to other selves. This image is present in both Edwards's writings about the saint's personation of Christ and in James's concept of the self as spiraling wheel. But as John Wild notes, James is committed simply to arguing for the value and power of "knowledge by acquaintance":

> Would the notion of being (existence) have any meaning for us, if it excluded what we feel and perceive by direct acquaintance? . . . The aim of radical empiricism is to avoid both these extremes (abstract interpretation and original concreteness) by the use of concepts in cooperation with feeling and perception in such a way as to clarify the original meaning without destroying it. This requires a patient and painstaking process of elucidation in which what was at first inarticulate, floating, and untranslatable gradually becomes articulate, fixed, and communicable, without too great a loss of its original concreteness and certainty.[27]

The cognitive value of feeling shapes one of James's best-known phrases, "the will to believe." John Smith observes with irritation the misreading of James's concept in his book *The Spirit of American Philosophy*:

> There is no idea in James, or in any other American philosopher for that matter, which is more widely known and more universally misinterpreted than the will to believe. James does not argue that you not only can, but that you should, believe anything you care to believe and that, with regard to anything you desire to be true, you can force yourself to believe it to be true against all evidence if only your will is strong enough.[28]

Those misreading James's will to believe doctrine make him into a kind of philosophical Teddy Roosevelt, a thinking man's rough rider running over rational assessment of belief. But James narrows the avenues by which the will to believe may travel with his concept of live and dead options, and his major concern in the essay is to define the will in the terms of disposition or affection. The essay is not an argument about logical bases for believing, it is a psychological statement concerning the nature of human being as affectional being.

Interpreted in this way, "The Will to Believe" is an essay that expands upon James's assertion of "the spark of the heart" as an intuitive sense that there is more to life than the deterministic model of reality offers to the thinking, feeling person. Thus James enters into a universe of experiential engagement akin to Edwards's engagement with the divine through the new sense. Through the cognitive power of feeling, and the trust in temperament that James claims as ineluctably human, he brings to birth a creative freedom based upon the impress of mind and heart upon the universe. This is his original notion of the spark of the heart as an existential energy by which the person may courageously, if not optimistically, protest against a reality understood as fixed. D.M. Yeager asks suggestively whether the misreading of James's essay is not a sign of the need to embrace certainty and retrospection within the confines of systematic analysis: "Might readers *need* to believe that James said something other than he did? Do contemporary presuppositions and preoccupations bias us toward misconstrual?"[29] Yeager's question raises the possibility that the very taxidermy of thought that James sought to address with essays such as "The Will to Believe" has obscured the meaning value of James's thought by misinterpretation.

The will as described by James in the essay is, in fact, very similar to the spark of the heart, and suggests that will is not an exercise of choice, but a habit or disposition that propels action in the world of experience to be tried by engagement with reality. The Jamesian will is like Edwards's "feeling within itself," a welter of responses overlapping one another, knowing one another, and temperamentally inclining one into the world. Whether one's ideas find meaningful transitions and fruitful terminations is the adventure—and the risk—that is at work as the free play of ideas that the pragmatist imagination claims as the human purpose.

James's creative engagement with totality during his period of spiritual awakening in the 1860's and 1870's provides the first written reflections upon the idea of the will as a dispositional energy manifesting prior affectional facts, Like Edwards's theory of the affections, it operates like a spring that moves the person into the world as a type of interactive circling out driven by focal attention and emphasis upon a particular set of relations. Thus James sees the heart as the circulating center of the human being. This affirms the cognitive value of feeling and defines the self as liminally dynamic:

> The deepest thing in our nature is this *Binnleben*, this dumb region of the heart in which we dwell alone with our willingnesses and our unwillingnesses, our faiths and fears. As through the cracks and crannies of caverns those waters exude from the earth's bosom which then form the fountainheads of springs, so in these crepuscular depths of personality the sources of all our outer deeds and decisions take their rise. Here is our deepest organ of communication with the nature of things.[30]

This passage conveys James's validation of feeling as the *sine qua non* of religious insight. As mute, it is pre-reflective and pre-linguistic. The Jamesian heart is synonymous with the affections and the will. The crepuscular state is one in which the twilight experience of transformation takes place, verifying the liminality of selfhood. James's image of the heart returns us to Emerson's "whole fact," which begins the draft lecture of *The Varieties*, and appears in the final text in James's concluding remarks:

> A conscious field *plus* its object as felt or thought of *plus* an attitude towards the object *plus* the sense of a self to whom the attitude belongs—such a concrete bit of personal experience may be a small bit, but it is a solid bit as long as it lasts; not hollow, not a mere abstract bit of experience, such as the 'object' is when taken all alone. It is a *full* fact, even though it be an insignificant fact; it is of the *kind* to which all realities whatsoever must belong; the motorcurrents of the world run through the like of it; it is on the line connecting real events with real events. That unshareable feeling which each one of us has of the pinch of his individual destiny as he privately feels it rolling out on fortune's wheel may be disparaged for its egotism, may be sneered at as unscientific, but it is the one thing that fills up the measure of our concrete actuality, and any would-be existent that should lack such a feeling, or its analogue, would be a piece of reality only half made up.[31]

The additive nature of the whole fact, at least in James's analysis, suggests the widest diversity of ideas and values haunting us as wider circles of relationality in which the self is embedded. But unlike the verticality of Edwards and Emerson, James makes the wheel not that of divine providence or the transparent eyeball in which the divine absorbs the human in transcendent union, but the wheel of fortune rolling out one's life through the connection of real events that constitutes concrete actuality. James sees in such a concrete reality a wider self at work to aid human effort.

James employs various images to suggest the liminality inherent in the circling energies of the spirit, an idea that arises from the influence of Emerson. The essay "Circles" in particular informs James's method of circumscription in *The Varieties*. James's mature thinking on panpsychism further reflects the influence of the process of circumscription as a model of the complex interaction of persons and things as they concatenate or overlap within a radically empiricist and pluralistic universe.[32]

The idea of the heart driving for "more and more" illuminates James's first utterance of his concept of "an atmosphere of reference to something more which haunts it."[33] It, too, occurs in relation to the activity of the heart, more accurately, the network of feelings and ideas in which the self is temporally embedded, past flowing through the present and into the future. The concept of the More carries out a variety of tasks for James that marks this initial discussion as a precursor to his philosophy of radical empiricism. It serves as a critical principle that erases the subjectivism of "instant ontology" and other ungrounded assumptions; as the margin of otherness in time and space; and it surrounds and energizes what James will later call the "storm-centre."[34] Critically important is that the More symbolizes a propulsive dynamism that partakes of the archaeological while transforming it into the present moment in a way that gives continuity priority as the defining characteristic of reality. Thus, like Edwards's sense of the heart, James's valuation of feeling suggests not a reduction of experience into subjectivism, but a transactional dynamic in which feeling or affection serves to engage and traverse the thicket of reality. In this way, the creative freedom of the person engaged with reality finds life more complex and elusive. But life also promises greater richness of relation (beauty), more profound human meaning (the truth-event), and possibility of cooperative and communal advance into unknown regions of thought and experience (salvation).

But, as James notes, "the trail of the human serpent is over everything."[35] The problem of retrospective custom and the self's habituation to inherited forms of conceptual substitution remains a stumbling block, almost a pathology, for the way in which James wishes to conceive of creativity. Experience, while funded by the past, sculls forward, dipping into the stream and creating an ebb and flow.

James is very careful not to adopt a notion of a spiritual sense, as Edwards does in his sense of the heart, for even the idea of sensation used metaphorically reduces the vague openness of the world of experience. Instead, he uses the word 'feeling,' reinstating vagueness into it to suggest both "knowledge by acquaintance" and "knowledge about." James refers to "the mystic sense of hidden meaning" in "A Certain Blindness in Human Beings," but the qualifier "mystic" upends the idea of sensation alone as insufficient as an approach to empirical reality, which reveals what James suggests are deeper layers of meaning. In *The Varieties* he uses the phrase "sense of reality,"[36] but this also embodies an intuitive element. James also wishes to reinstate the vague in order to place all assumptions into question, and thus to drive the mind forward into the world of experience. Experiences labeled religious may arrive "in the form of quasi-sensible realities directly apprehended."[37] James maintains the tension of the vague to foster human responsibility for building-out the affections and "the reality of the unknown" within the matrix of experience. Without this testing of our beliefs and intuitions, James argues, we do a disservice to the truth of god(s) and humanity (and all other potential truths) by neither testing them in, nor contributing them to, the human community. Religious experience is about trying and being tried in an integrated and complex transaction between self and world. Risk and struggle characterize these attempts to advance the community and the self. "Quasi-sensibility" is a term offering much insight into James's thinking, for it verifies his philosophical "in-betweenness" in which he necessarily situates himself amongst idealism and empiricism, arche and telos, substantive and transitive. This is also the ideal community, the ethical republic, and takes its cue from the model of oneness and manyness seen in the American project of *e pluribus unum*.

As we have seen, James applies the two-fold theory of "knowledge by acquaintance" and "knowledge about" to the conception of religion, and he appears to give priority to acquaintance, at least in the gathering of affectional facts. This appearance of priority in part defines James's rhetorical agenda in *The Varieties*, as it supports his stated purpose of defending religion from academic philosophers and of advancing experiential religion as of utmost functional value to the compassionate widening and ethical truth-gathering of the human community.

As with Edwards's criterion of fruitfulness, James's assessment of the value of religious experience ultimately rests upon its public, communal value. This means that "knowledge about" is equally integrated into the process of human cognitive experience as the shaper of acquaintance that propels further circling-out into the phenomenal world.[38] Both thinkers recognize that it is seductively easy to interpret the primacy of the affections in an imbalanced way by forgetting the complex and integrated relationship between heart and head, "knowledge by acquaintance" and "knowledge about." This balance is critically important on a number of levels, for it defines the process of creative freedom as necessarily about the tensile relationship between oneness and manyness. Such tension leads to the liminality that is so central to the self as creative contributor to the cooperative process of salvation because it defines the interchange necessitated by active engagement with a relational reality. The American wilderness may serve as a reservoir of religious insight and charitable action, but it is truly existent as a light to others, and not as a state of self-aggrandizement, but one of humble affirmation of all varieties of human being and community. To privilege one form of knowledge over another is to imbalance the entire schema of concentric sociality that defines the strenuous advance of a moral universe.

That being said, James approaches his topic for the Gifford Lectures of 1900-1901 with a commitment to prospectivism and an emphasis on the courage and strenuousness of the heart or will that does privilege knowledge by acquaintance for rhetorical purposes. His initial criteria for the judgment of religious phenomena are spiritual or metaphysical, followed by serviceability in relation to the communal verification of the truth process: what is the meaning or value to the world of experience of a particular claim or assertion of religious experience? He writes,

> Their (religious claims) value can only be ascertained by spiritual judgments directly passed upon them, judgments based on our own immediate feeling primarily; and secondarily on what we can ascertain of their experiential relations to our moral needs and to the rest of what we hold as true. *Immediate luminousness*, in short, *philosophical reasonableness*, and *moral helpfulness* are the only available criteria.[39]

James has been criticized for privileging "roots" over "fruits" in comparison to Edwards's *Religious Affections*, but such evaluations take James's powerful rhetorical posture in *The Varieties* as a sign of disequilibrium in his assessment that may not be in fact the case. James's rhetorical posture addresses not his own inner need to claim theological sources for religious experience so much as a desire to broaden the focus of vision when it comes to the evaluation of religion. James is not making a confession so much as seeking to avoid the dismissal of evidence helpful to understanding the value of religious experience for the moral life of the human community and for the correction of systematic and reductive intellectual ossification, whether scientific, philosophical, or theological.[40]

James carefully introduces a contrast between the retrospective habits of cultural inheritance and the prospective search for meaning. This contrast parallels the temporal dimension of Edwards's distinction between heart and head, which Emerson also describes at the beginning of *Nature* as prospective and retrospective vision. Like Emerson, James rejects "this circular wave of circumstance": "I propose to ignore the institutional branch entirely, to say nothing of the ecclesiastical organization, to consider as little as possible the systematic theology and the ideas about the gods themselves, and to confine myself as far as I can to personal religion pure and simple."[41] By shunning institutionalism, James works to return his readers to the world of experience, and will use the testimonies of extraordinary individuals to point to the powerful yet indefinable quality of religious experience. His first step in carrying out this mission is to break out of the circle of retrospection and drive towards a definition of living religion. For Edwards, the problems of the church institution in relation to rational religion and enthusiasm are not yet sufficient to command an anti-institutional perspective. The seeds of such anti-institutionalism are present, however, in the conflicts and controversies over ministerial authority, claims to spiritual experience, and the habituation to spiritual delusion that shadow the revivals.

In moving from second-hand borrowings of religious experience to first-hand accounts, James establishes a dichotomy between retrospective vision, which understands life through the forms of the past, and prospective vision, which lends the mind a propulsive character. These types of vision invoke the two-fold system of "knowledge about" and "knowledge by acquaintance" that in turn constitute ways of knowing made distinct for the purposes of analysis, but that work intimately in cognition. In Lecture 2, "The Circumscription of the Topic," James moves from circumscription understood as a reduction of experience through abstract conceptualization, to the vague sense of religious feeling that originates with the expansion of power that he constructs as a relationship to a "More" or "wider self." Thus Lecture 2 and Lecture 3, "The Reality of the Unseen," anticipate lectures on healthy-mindedness, the divided self, the sick soul, and conversion. Prospectivism as it informs experiential acquaintance through the mind's tendency to live forward shapes the structure and argument of *The Varieties,* and much of James's work, in a powerful way because of its necessary relation to questions of freedom. While Edwards's providential notion of history is necessarily teleological, James envisions a propulsive purposiveness uncertainly navigating a pluralistic universe.

For James, circumscription, understood as the construction of concepts, reveals the tendency to value laws and dogmas above the wilderness of ideas and values. Thus it is not surprising that he offers a vague definition of religion as "the feelings, acts, and experiences of individual men in their solitude, so far as they apprehend themselves to stand in relation to whatever they may consider divine." An ever-increasing presence of the vague informs the polarity of subject and object by which James attempts to define religion. His circumscription of religion works to consume itself, as individual conceptions of religion are compared and contrasted with the notion of the divine in such a way that subject and object eventually become secondary constructions in an open-ended and processive vision of a spiritual freedom that establishes creative engagement with a reality understood as relational. Edwards carries out a similar task in "The Excellence of Christ"; the conjunction of opposites, when piled up, breaks from the sense of a unity of being that may be salted-down. Instead there is a renewed sense of the beautiful complexity or excellence of the experiential matrix as it eternally unfolds in the transactional relationship between the human and the divine.

James seeks to immerse his audience in experiential religion, to bathe them in religious feeling, and through such baptism accomplish a thick, and thus truer, description that inspires a revival of interest in religious experience. He breaks the reductive power of conceptual thinking by infusing his discussion with the idea of the vague, which represents richness, plurality, and prospectivism for James, all of the dimensions and dynamics reduced by conceptual thinking and definition.[42] Thus the audience's assumptions about religion are subverted by

James's attempt to point them towards the first-hand acquaintance of religious experience itself. Eugene Fontinell writes of the expansiveness of James's concept of the vague,

> James's desire to reinstate the "vague and inarticulate" is . . . not a defense of obfuscation or romantic cloudiness. Paradoxically, it is an effort to describe our experience as rigorously as possible and to avoid any procrustean cutting of experience so as to fit neatly into what can be named or conceptualized. . . . This in no way denies the legitimacy and even necessity of extrapolating from or speculating upon our personal experiences. It does, however, caution against explaining away that which is present in our immediate experience.[43]

The reinstatement of the vague to the circumscription of the topic is James's major strategy in the second lecture, and thus informs the style and substance of the entire work. His definition of religion as the solemn and serious relation of the individual to an enveloping and primal reality is further undercut by his admission that "we are dealing with a field of experience where there is not a single conception that can be sharply drawn . . . the boundaries are always misty, and it is everywhere a question of amount and degree."[44] The vague and the misty occasion James's appeal to pragmatic criteria in the assessment of religious experience's value. He emphasizes the meaning and value of such experiences in order to avoid both conflicting claims for religious authority and the dissolution of the self into an Emersonian transparency that produces an optimism capable of overlooking the problems of suffering and of evil.

James employs the strategy of the vague to compare the stoic moralist with the passionate happiness of Christian saints. Note that he draws yet another set of analogues to the prospective and the retrospective. He writes, "The difference is as great as that between passivity and activity. . . . You feel that two continuous psychological universes confront you, and that in passing from one to the other a 'critical point' has been overcome."[45] These states are akin to "an arctic climate and the tropics"; James employs the oppositions of hot and cold drawn from humoral psychology's descriptions of vitality and stasis. Such heat or passion is particularly important, as it "should be regarded as the practically important *differentia* of religion for our purpose."[46] For James, the stoic moralist with his admirable "athletic attitude" inevitably breaks down under the weight of the human condition:

> We are all such helpless failures in the last resort. The sanest and best of us are of one clay with lunatics and prison inmates, and death finally runs the robustest of us down . . . all our morality appears but as a plaster hiding a sore it can never cure, and all our well-doing as the hollowest substitute for that well-*being* that our lives ought to be grounded in, but, alas, are not![47]

The dualism of subject and object and the coldness of retrospection and circumscription collapse due to the wide range of existential dilemmas that leave the person bereft of conceptual explanation and the protective illusion of certainty that accompanies it. This is precisely why religious melancholy is one of the factors preparatory to religious transformation: the horror of our moral death becomes the occasion for our spiritual birthday. The living death of despair and breakdown is converted to the life of a wider selfhood: "Religious feeling is thus an absolute addition to the Subject's range of life. It gives him a new sphere of power."[48]

Within the second lecture, James moves from the conceptual reduction of experience towards a vague sense of feeling or acquaintance that originates with the leveling of assumptions concerning the self and its power. In *The Varieties*, James will further define this dimension of emotion as a shift in the boundaries of the self such that relation to a "More" or "wider self" is created through which real saving experiences come.[49] This is pointed to by the notion of an "everlasting possession spread before our eyes" that is "a new reach of freedom."[50] Possession is not constructed in relation to a subject possessing an object, of one possessing another in an imbalanced power relation, but as a dynamic state of mutual empowerment that reconciles oppositional dualisms, propelling a rich growth of relationship. This lack of subject-object diremption underscores the presence of a radically empiricist worldview at play in *The Varieties*.

The "stoic resignation to necessity" is overcome by a "passionate happiness" in which the range of possible relations is spread out before *our* eyes. The self undergoing religious transformation does not arrive at a solitary ascension, as with Emerson's transparent eyeball, but a vision of the possibility of salvation achieved cooperatively, and within the real dust and dirt of daily human struggles with tragedy and evil.[51] Reality is a relational environment analogous to a community in which the amelioration of suffering comes about through creative action that attempts to discover fulfilling relations expansive of both vitality and possibility.

Thus James sees creative action and charitable service constitutive of "the workshop of being."[52] The intimacy that forms community expresses itself in acts of consent and dissent that enrich the potentialities present within such a view of reality. Thus the pragmatic notion of salvation is a cooperative process that mimes the truth-event as a concatenation of affirmative connections. Truth is thus communally verified as the transition of a process of complex interactions that correlate to Edwards's concept of excellence.

This conception of religious experience also points to James's theory of radical empiricism, as it sees subject-object diremption as a conception secondary to an experiential acquaintance that is aware of the intimate interdependence and activity of disjunctive and conjunctive relations teeming with transitional tendencies and possibilities for growth. On the level of conscious human beings, the real possibility of salvation exists in the discovery of a wider selfhood; freedom finds a new reach in the capacity to engage creatively with the community of being receptive to actions that help "build-out" an unfinished universe. James's metaphors of the "More" and of the "finite god" are vivifying in that they rely upon the strenuous will of the person transformed by religious experience to expand and enhance the possibility of a salvation that is communal through action, a divine vagueness serving as a lure to creativity. The person and the invisible vitally inform one another in a way in which individual identity is maintained through a "harmonious adjustment to the unseen order."[53] This adjustment achieves a construction of the good through a pragmatic circling towards the true direction that in its tracing of the sacred joins with the directions offered by others.

In *The Principles of Psychology* James describes consciousness as a stream in which both continuity and process result from the activity of selection that subsumes experience into a conceptual framework linked by transitions. Focal attention centers the self in the world of experience, stabilizing the self while it experiences a context of past and future transitions or relations that redetermines the feelings, concepts, tendencies, and directions of consciousness. In *The Varieties* James moves to the circle and the field as his metaphors of consciousness. The self centers itself by circumscription, and discovers new fields by affectionally "circling out." Throughout his description of the field of consciousness, James speaks of the shifting center of energy that drives the self in its relations both to the fringe or penumbra that surrounds it as an indeterminate margin and to the interactive world of experience. Religious experience transforms the center of energy so that its focus becomes that of the sacred trace that, through fleeting incursions, has formed a relation with the person that transforms the focus and range of vision towards horizonal possibilities in this "new reach of freedom."

The self as a circling activity, a centrifugal force, exists as what James calls "the center of reference and activity" analogous to the heart's systole and diastole that, given reality's pluralism, functions in relation to "centres (which) disperse each other's rays."[54] This is an image that, upon inspection, bears remarkable resemblance to Edwards's vision of the proportional excellence of the benevolent community. Thus both the activity of "knowledge by acquaintance" and "knowledge about" always operate within a wider field of indeterminate margins while also constructing a center of interest or excitement around which the self interacts with the activities of other centers of reference and activity. The person grows through a centrifugal activity that is responsive to the wider fields of experience and yet maintains its integrity through a center that is both continuous and processive as past and present slip with it towards the future. The ongoing expansion of the self's relational context is open to a concentric widening or expansion similar to the continuous circulative growth of Edwards's sense of the heart or of the circling activity of Emerson's boundary-breaking heart. Recall that in his first draft of Lecture 1 of *The Varieties*, James writes of this concentric widening as a centrifugal power beyond linguistic description.[55] This paradoxical "living moment" suggests the active holding in being of every moment in a way that conflates mystical insight and concrete experience. James's suppressed desire for the ideal breaks free momentarily as he waxes poetic about the living moment having "something of absolute." Such an experience describes "this higher vision of an inner significance . . . this mystic sense of hidden meaning," as a dynamic state oscillating between the ideal and the concrete that inspires the strenuous mood.[56]

As with Edwards, man as self-evolving circle is expansive in relation to the apprehension of wider spiritual realities. Edwards would see this as the resonating circulation of the inspirited saint that he calls delight, remanation, or glorying, the affirmative augmentation of otherness that charitably enriches the Christian community, expanding spiritual and moral beauty, and making God happy. James finds that, in the living moment of experience, the self is a spiraling wheel streaming radially from a vortex of past existence and growing into a novel reality. The living moment of the centrifugal widening of selfhood defines the experience of activity that both centers the self and circles out to new regions of experience that are remade by the dispositionality of the self.

James uses language in as dynamic a way as possible, though he realizes that at best "concepts are stepping stones, and words are canes and staves. They give some help, of a disjointed kind . . . it is an imperative human function to go on verbalizing and formulating *as if* the end might so be reached."[57] By necessity he returns to the act of circumscription as a type of linguistic circling which, though crippled, struggles on inspired by the possibilities and relations offered by the living moments of experience. Verbal formulation stands in here for "knowledge about," and reasserts the Jamesian demand for the full circling of the self as experiential and rational. When linguistically constructed as circumscription, the writing-around or chronicling of the self's activity makes the historicist dimension of James's thought apparent.

James seeks to make immersion in experience the goal of human thought and activity, not as subjectivism, but as interactive responsibility. He wants to balance conceptualization with acquaintance so as to garner the fullest possible insight from the interaction of self and world, and to build the capacity for the recognition of patterned relations in the form of analogy, similarity, and dissimilarity of the dynamic activities of experiential transactions. This defines the activity of circling as propulsive. James's thinking becomes ever more vehicular in carrying mind forward, to the point where consciousness exists only secondarily to pure experience, and language is driven past any concept of metaphoricity or symbolization that may become reified, to the transitory and verbal that always point ahead and away from themselves.

But at the same time, the building-out of the universe requires reconceptualization as part of the process of circling. James's streaming becomes a real fugation, a fleeing to experience and away from the vicious intellectualism and moral claustrophobia that lead to paralysis and despair. And yet part of the attack upon such reductionism comes through the necessary remolding of reason in its discursive function. James anchors the heart knowledge gained through experiential acquaintance with the demand that a practical connection be made that addresses human need. As he writes in "Reflex Action and Theism," the "speculative voyage (must be) washed ashore on the *terra firma* of concrete life again."[58] Religious experience best enables such intensity of creative engagement with the plural fields that define reality, for religious experience breaks the bonds of necessity and circumscription for James. Through a vivifying vagueness, the heart expands concentrically to apprehend and act upon the "glimpses of relation which we divine rather than see, for they shoot beyond the field into still remoter regions of objectivity, regions which we seem rather to be about to perceive than to perceive actually."[59]

These glimpses of relation provide the most treasured insights into the human condition for James, for they present the genius, the visionary, and the prophet with the novel revelations with which to bring savor and zest to the world of retrospective custom so as to challenge the deterministic mechanism that appears to drive material reality. Once again, this illustrates the high estimation given to the embrace of liminality as a way of life dependent upon the ongoing circling out into experience that expands the vista within, renewing relation to something more, a wider self. Even as James values the making of new conceptions that serve as building blocks of reality, he realizes that, like language, such blocks are simply stepping-stones in the pilgrimage of homeless humanity towards a cooperatively constructed yet piecemeal salvation.

Chapter 4
The Art of Expansiveness

Edwards and James each struggles to unearth a vision of the human as a widening self that experiences life as a storm-centre expressive of the flux of moods and motives that batters the habitations of custom. The famous description of Edwards on horseback returning home with a coat pinned with scribbled fragments of vision, James's view of life as a developing landscape witnessed by the train passenger glancing backwards while speeding forwards illustrate the immersive mood that describes the enriched empiricisms each thinker attempts to invoke.

The immersive mood suggests that bare empiricism is not empirical enough, as the ideal and the potential are left out. These men bear witness to an inclusive reality, Edwards moving vertically and James horizontally, towards a more intimate universe. Religious experience supplies an expansive view of the material world, and attempts to amplify reality through actualization of the potentialities present in the thicket of life. Ugliness is anathema to right living; all that is beautiful is practical, in this case because of the actualization of virtual potential into beauty as a form of being. Religion is humanity's most important business because it melds the beautiful and the practical, furnishing a pre-reflective depth of feeling that transforms the thin world of custom and conceptual system into a tangle of complexity that demands pragmatic interpretation. The environment requires an integration of the aesthetic and the practical that changes insight to knowledge, history to promise, and immediacy to hope. Religious affections motivate the thickening activity of Edwards's notion of being's consent to being and James's concept of everlasting and mutual possession, illustrating the process by which deep feeling within consciousness gives rise to practical demands that transform the chaos of reality and received convention into creative action. Such action realizes a richer agreement or harmony that establishes more human truth and dignity.

Rather than "paltry empiricism,"[1] Edwards and James embrace forms of enriched empiricism that direct motion forward because inclusive of potentials felt but not seen. And religious experience provides the most powerful sense and motive for such inclusion. What James calls the thrilling mystery of fact aptly evokes the radically rich environment prompted by experiential knowledge attuned to a harmony inclusive of dissonance. Mystical sensibility enables a form of acquaintance that seeks a more comprehensive or holistic view of reality in the act of being's consent to being. Empiricism is too exclusive in its admission of experience, and both Edwards and James seek a view of reality far more inclusive. The idea of an enriched empiricism is described alternatively in images of potential fulfillment, for Edwards in the glory of God, for James in the full fact of a pluralistic universe. In each case, beauty becomes a central metaphor and method to describe and advance the richness emergent from religious experience.

Enriched empiricism describes forms of the American dream that make various claims for the exceptionalism of something beyond a nation-state, a vision embraced by the tradition of the Spiritual Brethren from which the experimental piety of Edwards and of James evolves. The counterbalance of idealism and empiricism that suggests the metaphor of enrichment, of Edwards's sovereign God and James's finite god(s), reveals historical transitions in American religious thinking that beckon idealism in different directions that suggest related but distinct perspectives. While Edwards's thought reveals a "shadow empiricism" fraught with both the dangers of illusion and the promise of a supernatural illumination of the I/eye, James's view of things invokes a "shadow idealism," a penumbral fringe that acts as an intuitive lure to creativity.

In each case, the notion of enriched empiricism embraces a cultural vista defined by promise of a history that is redemptive, a fulfilling of fact that makes real that which is envisioned. And because this relies upon affection or acquaintance, intimacy describes engagement with an ever more complex patterning of relationship. Paltry empiricism alienates through the thin description of reality that suggests that estrangement is the normative state of human persons. In fact, such bare facticity reveals the falling away from being that Edwards notes as privation and James as alienation.

This embrace of promise and its fulfillment makes these versions of empiricism dependent upon reading the words "sense" and "feeling" as vague and ambiguous metaphors employed to bridge physical and metaphysical worlds. Invoking partiality, uncertainty, and a vivifying vagueness to suggest language's limitations and a shadow world of penumbral affect and fringe relations, the sense of the heart and the mystic sense are terms that operate to persuade the reader to trace the sacred. Feeling is cognitive, and directs interest, a focal attention that enables an intuitive and poetic perception that sees into the world by integrating other forms of knowing. Such poetic vision subsumes retrospective vision through an archaeology of concept, and imagines prospectively as coruscating lines of consent or engagement lead to a deepened intimacy tested for its fruitfulness or paltry worth. It relies upon conceptual knowledge in order to imaginatively see into the world ever more deeply. This enables the advance of conceptual knowledge through the affirmation of fertile tendencies and potentials or through the termination of avenues of experience that find no transit. Such imaginative vision also enables one to see with the other sympathetically. What one wills to bring forth with the imagination bears moral responsibility that serves to adjudicate conflict, and deepens moral beauty through a disinterested consent that affirms and advances the life of the community.

The vehicularity of the religious imagination makes the search for capable words particularly demanding. For Edwards the transformation of biblical typology into a system of symbols provided a rich approach to the poetic fashioning of the world altered by religious affections. Despite his eloquent and witty use of language, James saw words as dangerously seductive. His view that language could not possibly capture the overflowing stream of experience meant that he employed a variety of metaphors and images that attempted to grasp the overwhelming richness he aimed to describe. The shadowy and the penumbral inscribe capable language as virtual potential that is real and expectant, best grasped by an aesthetic sense that reshapes self and world in its drive for agreement, order, and symmetry. For James, the shadowy and the penumbral spark delight, clarity, and fluency when illuminated as practical dimensions that fit the world of lived experience.

The crafting of common terms such as sense or feeling utter complex invocations of an amplifying vagueness. This marks the propulsiveness so central to each man's thought as the circling energies that unearth the crush of determinism so as to awaken an intimate reality of everlasting possession whose transitions and termini are pragmatically self-evident. The dispositional and focal nature of the human person instructed by the cognitive immediacy of feeling is the formative power potentially additive to the ideal of the full fact. And because fullness functions as an end, all forms of knowing enter into the visionary project. Perceiving the world, divining the world, and consenting with the world imaginatively circle in unison to refashion one another so as to inquire of the world and drive its advance. This entails seeing as simultaneously aesthetic and ethical, envisioning a complex pattern of relationality that is beautiful along natural, moral, and spiritual planes formative of a holistic environment. For Edwards and for James, beauty and the life of practical action are synonymous. Sense, affection, and feeling are terms of disposition and fulfillment within the currents of retrospective and prospective experience. Believing is not conceptually thin but experientially thick as an expression of that which one loves, of the affections that color and drive the will's focal attention and action.

The metaphysical visions arising from various claims made in consequence of religious affections underlie the quarrel between rational system building and theology and philosophy understood as forms of art. Both Edwards and James are philosophically and theologically poetic in temperament and method. Edwards argues, "Mere existence be accounted a beauty,"[2] and asserts that the misery of life is endured because persons "cannot bear to lose sight of such a beautiful and lovely world."[3] His typological vision entails the sense of the heart that is grasped by, and expansive of, an intimate relation to reality through the creative imagination. Biblical, natural, and historical types map divine activity, enabling the interpreter of religious affections to trace the sacred as an ongoing process of the becoming of self, world, and God.

Similarly, James witnesses in the mosaic philosophy descriptive of the pluralistic universe "new reaches of life succeeding on our most despairing moments."[4] In another view, James sees that "philosophies paint pictures," making the thinker akin to the lover in being "the organ of a higher need than the bare practical."[5] James's metaphysics of religious experience describes a thickening potential within the nature of reality best apprehended and energized through a mystic sense of hidden meaning grounded in complex beauty. Poetry and art reflect religious experience. In *The Varieties* James writes,

> The sense of deeper significance is not confined to rational propositions. Single words, and conjunctions of words, effects of light on land and sea, odors and musical sounds, all bring it when the mind is tuned aright. Most of us can remember the strangely moving power of certain passages in certain poems read when we were young, irrational doorways as they were through which the mystery of fact, the wildness and the pang of life, stole into our hearts and thrilled them. The words have now perhaps become more polished surfaces for us; but the lyric poetry and music are alive and significant only in proportion as they fetch these vague vistas of a life continuous with our own, beckoning and inviting, yet ever eluding our pursuit. We are alive or dead to the eternal inner message of the arts according as we have kept or lost this mystical susceptibility.[6]

Central to this restoration of the living world of dynamic activity is the poet able to charge language with the power to break the world constructed by rational proposition. The depth of meaning attributed to religious experience and its pragmatic value rests in an amplifying resonance that demands capable words expressive of new vistas. For Edwards, typological language enabled interpretation of history and being both, the one through biblical interpretation, the other through spiritual reading of the Book of Nature. Taken together, God's two books describe the ways in which the potential for glorification of God could transform a world of shadow into one of dazzling light.

James did not inhabit a biblical landscape. His validation of religious experience through testimony, poetry, and the experimental piety supported by the right to believe came together with his psychological and philosophical explorations to create a vibrant and rich writing style. James's controlled desire for the ideal breaks free momentarily as he waxes poetic about the living moment having "something of absolute." Such an experience describes the mystical germ, a dynamic state oscillating between the ideal and the concrete that inspires the strenuous mood. And yet he maintained that language is a crutch.

According to Edwards and James, radial gestures emerge from religious affections to provide the deepest clues to life's meaning, and so enact this poetic function of human agency. As Frank Bidart suggests, "Pattern, form . . . whose infinite repeatability within matter defies matter" gives rise to the boundlessness achieved by the religious imagination as it envisions something more and hidden.[7] The poetic function "brings unconscious inward knowing together with conscious, outward knowing."[8] Beauty as pattern and form finds inscape, defying matter yet demanding verification. Thus the poetic function conveys a synonymy of the aesthetic and the ethical that pragmatically seeks good ground. Enriched empiricism assumes a pragmatic poetics.

Because arising from religious moods, the action of the imagination is necessarily asymmetrical aesthetically and ethically. As action, it is on the way forward, and thus embodies both beauty and irony. Asymmetry is its dynamic force, wilderness its environment. Modes of knowing experientially and knowing conceptually, modes of heart and head, describe a relationally rich environment that necessitates the wildness of a future orientation that yet invokes the ironic situation of human limitation.

Within this unmapped territory, the revolving moment of conversion is the central turning-place that James describes as the workshop of being. Working at the wheeling of being, the religious imagination actively shapes existence even as it necessarily foretells its form, its future containment. As James writes in "Philosophical Conceptions and Practical Results," "The poets and the philosophers themselves know as no one else knows that what their formulas express leaves unexpressed almost everything that they organically divine and feel."[9] Feeling and divining descend into language that is necessarily limited by its conceptual shape.

In emphasizing mood and feeling, Edwards and James invoke the drive of the heart for something more that is described respectively as Being in General or ontological wonder. For Edwards, God or Being in General delights in its Creation, while for James human being wonders, and in so wondering seeks a home impossible to find. Edwards attests that God is a communicating being from whom the person may receive inspiration, a word that he begins to transcribe into the modern language of imagination, suggesting a move away from a human reality defined by illusion and a consequent falling away from being towards nothingness.

But for James "all homes are in the finite"[10] because beginning is always elsewhere. Whereas Edwards's vision of home may best be described by H.R. Niebuhr's eloquent confession that "we are all immigrants unto the empire of God,"[11] James understands life as embodied yet homeless. Edwards sees the self in the sun that lights the horizon, the sun to which the human responsibility is to remanate light, an event achieved through the personation of Christ. James has an eye on a horizon that disappears into the next as a wider spiritual environment lures forward towards harmony and clarity as inclusivity of relations. The tensile complexity of transition and terminus, of mutual possession and real loss, breaks down limits and thus breaks open claims to a block universe, rending paltry empiricism asunder.

Edwards's concept of excellence and James's radical empiricism assume an experimental piety that tests the consequences of religious affections within the shadow world of material reality. Such experimentation invests thinking with the consent to being that illuminates and advances material reality. James's desire is to paint of experience a philosophy in which the human concern is to build out an unfinished but growing pluralistic universe that offers the possibility, but not the guarantee, of a cooperatively made salvation. For both men, thinking imbricates revelation and creation in a way suggestive of Edwards's philosophy of excellence and James's mosaic philosophy of radical empiricism. The teleological purpose of the human being bends the ideal to the empirical in attempts at a comprehensiveness that acts as a self-consuming artifact.

The "dis-positioning" spontaneous to religious experience realizes an immersive mood that is antecedent to subject-object diremption. It destabilizes focal attention so as to give rise to a new center of interest. The religious imagination awakens an enlivened disposition or attention that transforms the seer and the seen, bringing forth the rhythmic repetition of discovery and abandonment. The enriched empiricisms of Edwards and of James embrace the mystery of fact by bringing religion and science together in a holistic vision of an experiential world angled by shadows and fringed with the potential intimacy of mutual expansiveness. Perception, vision, and value result in a synonymy of beauty and the good such that intimacy with an expanding reality is unbound. Poetry and science implicate one another in practice by echoing heart and head, knowledge by acquaintance and knowledge about. The mystic sense of the heart provides ways of engaging a world of rich complexity in which immersion calls out to analysis and pragmatic advance. The aesthetic, it must be remembered, operates within each of these modes of being, and is alive or dead dependent on prospective affection and disinterest or retrospective custom and self-interest. The delight or beauty of experiential immersion shifts vision in a way James describes as knowledge by acquaintance, and impels forward prospectively. The aesthetic further describes the shaping of conceptual knowledge as a result of analysis and systematic thinking. Pragmatic advance enacts these modes of knowing as the consequential fact in the making that propels forward and sees backwards simultaneously as relation or termination becomes salted down as true within the streaming of experience.

Edwards and James each craft a metaphysics of experience that displays signal elements of their religious thinking. These elements describe a perspective that includes the organic relationship of a growing reality within which the purpose of the human person seeks to affirmatively augment such reality through an aesthetic refashioning pragmatically tested. Inclusive within this philosophical frame is a view of reality as incomplete, and growing through spiritually funded imaginative acts that reshape factual experience in such a way as to repair a reality fallen or alienating. Such imaginative acts trace the sacred that haunts the human person, and seek to inscribe it in the world through pragmatic poetics, an infinite repeatability that makes matter meaningful by wedding inner and outer experience. Pragmatic interpretation does not define a metaphysical worldview of visionary experience, but supports its advance.

Enriched Empiricism and the Expansion of Excellence

Edwards's philosophy of excellence presents an image of divine creation so intensely vibrant that the ideas of the divine mind take on a phenomenological cast of compelling reality. The divine ideas, as Edwards sees them, have such power as to be creative of actual substance, leading to the suggestion that Edwards envisions an enriched empiricism emerging, through aesthetic perception, from a world of shadows. Such aesthetic perception, Edwards's sense of the heart, reveals a fusion of biblical and natural types or symbols that move in vertical and horizontal directions to energize a process of becoming. Such a process unveils the ontological fulfillment of God or Being in General and the communal realization of the redemption of history through the fulfillment of divine glory within the created world. Invoking the sense of the heart, Edwards's version of enriched empiricism seeks out excellence through consent to or "feeling with" reality that is poetic refashioning pragmatically tested.

In his *Personal Narrative*, Edwards, overwhelmed with the beauty of nature and its correspondence with scripture, loses the power of speech, illustrating James's notion that the poet and philosopher divine more than they can express. The divine mind overwhelms conception, suggesting the ongoing process of the self's response to the shadow empiricism of the material world as a consent to being that affirmatively advances Being in General. Thus we see Edwards portraying the life of faith as a practice of humility and kenosis in which the communicating God is ever more fully actualized in the world. Religious affection is a spring to action that fulfills the potential inherent in the creative self-delight of God. And the languages of the Bible and of nature reveal divine power and presence that compels the work to realize glory in the world by the saint. Such work is carried out through the crafting of capable words that resonate within the world through poetic action pragmatically interpreted. Recall Bidart's suggestion that "Pattern, form/ whose infinite repeatability within matter defies matter." The poetic function weds inner and outer, divine and human, glimmer and substance so as to transform the world into a fullness suggestive of the enriched empiricism both Edwards and James invoke as authentic ways of seeing and being. Infinite repeatability tells how such fullness rhythmically becomes, as the patterning and forming of beauty finds inscape through instress, deepening matter's meaning, which to be authentic demands verification. The wheeling of Ezekiel is a revolution in which the poetic function of circling between inner and outer conveys a synonymy of the aesthetic and the ethical that pragmatically seeks good ground. Infinite repeatability characterizes the human potential for inscribing the invisible and the interior in the world of bare facts. Wonderment and feeling, willing and testing—all dynamics of the pragmatic interpretation of religious experience—direct the saint to the communicative nature of being that tells and is retold.

Edwards's marriage of idealism and empiricism seeks to be true to a reality in which God communicates being in a fashion that makes religious determinism and the controlling power claimed by rational religion into second-hand faith. For Edwards, the world is a dynamic and continuous locus for human agency understood as a form of conversing with the divine, but as his ministerial experiences painfully told him, such conversation could be deceitful chatter rather than words capable of tracing the sacred. The enrichment of human experience required a pragmatic grounding.

The need to overcome the falsity of a dualistic and alienated reality with the vision of an intimate creation forges his enriched empiricism, which employs metaphors of light and gravity, and the language of typology understood in both metaphysical and historical ways through the intertextuality of the Bible and the Book of Nature, to shape creative action. Experience in the world traces the beauty of Being in General manifest as the divine mind. While revealing the presence of God, such a world is susceptible to the widespread illusion that Edwards sees as the poverty of the human mind bereft of divine light, and thus at risk of a dizzying falling away from being towards nothingness. The tension between fallenness and salvation symbolizes the mixed nature of the saint and the haphazard history of redemption in the attentive tracing of the sacred in the world.

Edwards's powerful sense of mystical piety suggests that it is through created things that one may perceive the divine when in fact it is the divine mind communicating itself in the form of the images and shadows made available to the perceiving heart. The unregenerate ego, blind to the divine substance of images and shadows, adopts a sense of autonomy and control that mocks the concept of freedom as defined within the relationality of being. Edwards's new sense reveals an idealism qualified by empiricism, creating a shadow reality in which objects have a real existence that is yet unfulfilled due to human blindness and self-interest. George Rupp writes, "Edwards's tendencies also evidence the countervailing emphases entailed in Edwards' empiricist orientation."[12] Edwards's philosophy of excellence incorporates the ideal and the empirical in part due to his faithful attention to the Creation; as Janice Knight observes, "Edwards's idealism was always balanced by a sense of the importance of nature as a vehicle for God's progressive communications."[13] This suggests that the actual ideas discovered through the sense of the heart's focal attention configure the glory of God in the world. This enriched empiricism arises from the sense of the heart and its commitment to concretion that addresses, but does not heal, the fallen human situation and the painful irony it reflects.

The fall from grace that embodies privation is the lens through which Edwards views the human dilemma and the possibility of expansiveness. As Perry Miller observes, Edwards's notion of the sense of the heart seeks to address the paucity and possibility of enlarging the presence of God. He writes in his Introduction to *Miscellany #782*, "Edwards's sense of the heart . . . is rather a sensuous apprehension of the total situation important for man, as the idea taken alone can never be." Suggesting Edwards's notion of mere cogitation and its potential for becoming a form of what James calls "vicious intellectualism" ("the treating of a name as excluding from the fact named what the name's definition fails positively to include"), Miller adds that the problem of good and evil, in the spiritual wilderness of America, asserts that meaning matters and matter means. "The word then becomes one with the thing," Miller adds.[14]

In "The Mind #1" Edwards begins the exploration of his philosophy of excellence in a statement that anticipates by several years the "Author's Preface" to *Religious Affections*:

> There has nothing been more without a definition than excellency, although it be what we are more concerned with than anything else whatsoever; yea, we are concerned with nothing else. But what is this excellency? Wherein is one thing excellent and another evil; one beautiful and another deformed?[15]

True religion, then, is one with excellence, and with the pragmatic imperative of the "Twelfth Sign" with which Edwards concluded *Religious Affections*. This pragmatic inflection is evident in his earlier entries in his notes on *The Mind*, as excellence depends upon transitions and connections that augment God as Being in General.

Edwards describes excellence in terms of relations, which is a topic central to his early essay "Of Being." Edwards, having seen a remarkable congruity between the biblical notion of glory and Newton's discussions of light and of gravity, argues that being relies upon the gravitational relation between infinite numbers of discrete atoms. Early on in the essay, Edwards makes clear that "to find out the reasons of things in natural philosophy is only to find out the proportion of God's acting."[16] For Edwards, the idea of gravity strikes a biblical resonance, for he interprets Newton's concept through a notion of the sovereignty of divine communication as weight or impress that shapes the laws and principles of the physical world. The extension of an object into space and its particular range and speed of motion is determined by its dynamic state in relation to other atoms. It is shaped and made tensile and energetic by the attraction of each to another, thus forming entity or being. Analogously, persons exist in being by relation, a relation held in tensile motion by God as Being in General expressing the gracious power of will so as to effect a dynamic creation that is by ontological necessity relational. Such relation exists through attraction; on the intelligential level, such attraction takes on various degrees of consent to Being in General.

Edwards moves towards describing reality as an enriched empiricism in asserting, "Space is God . . . all the space there is without the bounds of the creation, all the space there was before the creation, is God himself."[17] The two books of divine communication, Nature and Scripture, together guide the believer. The intimate intertextuality inhering within God's activity creates a conversation between the ideal and the real aimed at the creature's salvation. Salvation history is the process whereby the actual potential of the creation becomes fulfilled in the glorious delight or consent to its possible realization by the community of intelligential being. The God anterior to, and unbounded by, the creation when spiritually sensed through genuine religious experience provides the possibility for the enrichment of reality. Thus God grows and becomes happy. Space becomes place as homeless humanity comes home through the communication of God into a fallen world. Edwards's concept of God as Being in General creates a picture of absolute dependence coursing throughout human experience, but it is a dependence of love, not power or authority. God's sovereignty rests in God's omni-communicative disposition so as to realize a world alive with divine energy or glory. Edwards's understanding of contemporary science and psychology adds to this picture by offering him new concepts that aid his attempts to find language for his novel insights into divine activity.

Edwards's language on the substantial reality of ideas is confusing, as he attempts to work through his studies of Locke and Newton in light of his powerful sense of a living, omni-communicative God. The traditional understanding of Edwards as an idealist is upended, and an enriched empiricism shadows forth through the transformative power of the regenerate heart. Edwards's description of the ideas cast by divine communication creates a shadow world due to the fall from grace that defined human existence. The difficulty for intelligential being arises from the rejection of the natural order manifest in the fall from grace that denies the authorship of divine creativity. Diverse and penultimate economies of faith propagate within human culture, and offer circumscribed homes enticing for their comfort, security, and seeming ultimacy. For Edwards, these failures to trace the sacred constitute a failure to inhabit reality, to enact the active tendencies and forces of personality within the community so as to contribute novel possibility. Spectatorship emerges as a result of the breakdown of human attendance to the divine theatre, and for the limitations of the natural man constitutes a structural habit established with the Fall that becomes extended by the elaboration of dispositions and tendencies drawing one away from Being in General.

The disturbing assertions and claims made by enthusiasts under the frenzied press of intense revivalism signal the presence of a false structure of belief encouraged by wanderings of illusion propagated and reinforced by the pressure of social conformity. For Edwards, religious rationalism's claim for the human capacity for moral and spiritual development engenders human power and the comfort of certainty, thus intensifying alienation.

The psychological corollary to discernment of the primary quality of resistance as solidity, as opposed to secondary qualities of what Edwards calls aspects of a "passional nature," signifies an extrapolation from his interpretation of Locke to illustrate the fallibility of the mind. As the physical world is one with divine communication, and divine ideas create atom or solidity as energetic forms of resistance, God creates an actual idea. Though matter is dependent on idea, an object or thing is really real, is as common sense imagines it. Idea instigates concretion; enriched empiricism ideally calls for the human co-creation of centers of divine energy that are embodied. Glory fulfills fact as the communication of divine being illuminates a shadow world; this leads Edwards to assert, "There is no proper substance but God Himself."[18] Here reality is proper because both fit and right, and belonging to God. Edwards's synonymy of the aesthetic and the ethical emerges from like interpretation to ground his philosophy of excellence.

The human person is thus embedded in a reality not his own, a reality awkward and lacking goodness, somehow awry. Thus the play of light and shadow that seeks an end both fitting and right as an embodiment of divine communication emerges from aesthetic perception, which is an amalgam of true and false affections that consequently demand pragmatic verification. Such play reflects a pragmatic poetics at work in which the excitement of actual ideas motivates charitable action creative of more complex beauty. With sanctification of the heart, an amplified sense apprehends an enriched empiricism through the imbrication of revelation and creation that becomes fused through aesthetic perception, symbolic language, and virtuous action pragmatically tested that makes spirit, understood as love, evermore present within the world. In the relationship between Edwards's visionary works such as the *Personal Narrative* and *Images and Shadows*, and his incipient pragmatism in *Religious Affections* and *Nature of True Virtue*, there is a textual representation of his philosophy of excellence and its pragmatically realized enriched empiricism. Thus, as with James, pragmatic interpretation does not define a metaphysical worldview, but supports its advance.

In "The Mind" #1, Edwards's view of divine excellence as it permeates the creation implicates the human capacity for both spiritual and pathological vision. Edwards is concerned with the failure to address the beauty of being due to the falling away from being towards nothingness that defines the privative notion of sin. Thus the perception of the divine actual idea present within the Creation as active energy holding all being in relation is subject to diverse forms of human misconception and manipulation. Psychological illusion and moral and spiritual corruption plague the human vocation to remake reality. This requires a creative dissent that involves the willed emptying of self-interest. Elisa New writes,

> The prehensile eye, imperial, ideological . . . is, in (Edwards's) philosophical tradition . . . restored to, and disciplined within a context that deems it an extremity of the ego. Rather than distrusting the horizon of our contact with the world . . . this tradition hews to a sense of Being as present in relation, Being quickening in poised attention, Being emergent in perceptions of a fullness anterior to any which we might entertain.[19]

The prehensile 'I' operates from the passions resultant from the fallen state of the natural man, who sees a disjointed and perplexing chaos because not quickened and deepened by truly holy affections. With the experience of sanctification, the saint imperfectly reads the Book of Nature through types both historical and ontological, as a complexly harmonious vision of divine activity in which the human is called to play a dramatic role.[20] Such reading is, in fact, the inclination to personate Christ that embodies the test of religious affection's pragmatic value for the community. In some of Edwards's earliest scientific writings we see this inclination to pursue a deep reading of nature that yet is stymied by his later struggle with the doctrine of predestination. Backsliding from such insight suggests the pitfalls of the human person's incomplete glimmer of edifying dependencies and relations such that the self alienates itself from its own true nature as a creature of an active God. The regenerate person, in belonging to the Being of God, embodies a similar energy intent on the illumination of a shadow reality with the divine light that informs the aesthetic perception that remakes the Creation.

Edwards's greatest insights on excellence are found in fragments intended for an unfinished treatise on the mind. In *Mind #1*, Edwards writes,

> One alone without reference to anymore cannot be excellent; for, in such case, there can be no manner of relation no way, and therefore no such thing as consent. Indeed, what we call 'one' may be excellent because of a consent of parts, or some consent of those in that being that are distinguished into a plurality

some way or other. But in a being that is absolutely without any plurality there cannot be excellence, for there can be no such thing as consent or agreement.[21]

Excellence cannot exist in isolation, but must be relationally patterned, and thus plural or relational, an idea Edwards draws from his interpretations of the trinity and of the Books of Nature and Scripture. The regenerate sense of the heart reads this language of the creation, which reveals the divine communication of actual ideas, in such a way as to come into relationship with the divine in the world. Nurtured by the deepening presence of God in natural symbols that reveal moral and spiritual excellence, the heart expands, feels more fully its interdependence with reality, and the absolute dependence of creature and creation upon God. Excellence is synonymous with holiness, divinity, or beauty because it bears the communicative impress of God as Being in General. The idea that parts consent implicates this divine impress that "feels" and delights in the Creation. This makes disposition central to the creative act, as Edwards asserts; how one feels and what one loves drives the springs of action.

The excellencies of the created world are so extensive that, Edwards notes, "It would be a most tedious piece of work to enumerate them." The complex beauty of flowers, of the body of man and other animals, of the branching of rivers and trees suggests the consent of parts that abound in nature. On a moral and spiritual level, the consent of being to being becomes far more complex. Edwards writes, "For being, if we examine narrowly, is nothing else but proportion." All contradiction and disproportion leads to "an approach to nothing . . . and the greatest and only evil."[22] Here Edwards underscores the privative notion of sin as a falling away from being. Excellence is an idea that informs Edwards's notion of true virtue and reinforces both the creative dimension of the sense of the heart and the need for pragmatic interpretation of religious affections.

Human knowledge of such excellence relies upon the sense of the heart to envision networks of connection and community among diverse forms of being, both intelligential and non-intelligential. This act, as New observes, "confirms being nowhere but in the experience of being," as the new sense partakes of the aesthetic perception of things and persons, and envisions their relational complexity. This occurs through the sense of the heart active through an enlivened will's exertion of attention. Within this dynamic is the crucial activity of the heart's perception of the actual ideas of divine presence within reality, operating as a type of spiritual reconstruction of self and world in which fact becomes enlivened ad infinitum.

Edwards's enriched empiricism embodies his notion of excellence, in which the divine communication of being is synonymous with love. When Edwards talks about excellence as natural, moral, and spiritual, he moves from the spiritual perception of natural phenomena in their patterned beauty to the range of ethical and spiritual actions to which such symbols point. He writes,

> When we spake of excellence in bodies we were obliged to borrow the word 'consent' from spiritual things. But excellence in and among spirits is, in its prime and proper sense, being's consent to being. There is no other proper consent but that of minds, even of their will; which when it is of minds towards minds, it is love, and when of minds towards other things, it is choice.[23]

Consent to natural types or symbols, when perceived with the sense of the heart, is consent to divine communication within a shadow existence that promises a greater fullness. Similarly,

> Bodies are but the shadow of being, therefore the consent of bodies one to another and the harmony that is among them is but the shadow of excellency. The highest excellency therefore must be the consent of spirits one to another. . . . And the sweet harmony between the various parts of the universe is only an image of mutual love.[24]

Edwards's enriched empiricism depicts an expanding harmony, proportionality, or unity in multiplicity with which he understands the overlapping realities of natural, moral, and spiritual beauty. Further, such an organic unity describes the power of religion to engage the person with the divine or, in its illusory modes, to create a falling way from being towards nothingness. Substance for Edwards is God, and objects are centers of energy, the visible beauties of the world that reflect divine creativity. When witnessed through the sanctified sense of the heart, shadow is fulfilled as divine substance reverberating to deeper, more complex relations.

Thus, in and through the created world, the regenerate self traces the sacred in nature and community. The former guides the believer much as the life of the community does, to apprehend the overflowing presence of divine communication. This arises most richly through spiritual relationships, however, and Edwards changes his terminology accordingly: "When we spake of external excellency, we said that being's consent to being must needs be agreeable to perceiving being. But now we are speaking of spiritual things, we may change the phrase and say that that mind's love to mind must needs be lovely to beholding mind."[25]

Through a convolution of spirit, the regenerate person awakens to a deepened vision of a more intimate world. One holds or excites in the mind the being to which one consents. Concentrated focus leads to awareness of the complex relation or proportion of the other such that being grows through mutual possession or love. This does not erase the fallibility of the saint in expressing benevolent consent. Edwards asserts that nature, scripture, ritual, and community "have a tendency to assist those whose hearts are under the influence of a truly virtuous temper to dispose them to the exercises of divine love, and enliven in them a sense of spiritual beauty."[26]

This is the moment of expansion from potentiality to actuality that realizes intimacy of relation to beauty in its diverse yet overlapping forms, making the saint a poet via a parallelism of charitable action and pragmatic interpretation. Edwards sees the failure to love as a deformity when not beautiful or proportional as judged by attention to God as Being in General: "a manifestation of a defect of such a love . . . shows that it is not being in general but something else that is loved, when love is not in proportion to the extensiveness and excellence of being."[27] Though there are many forms of love that contribute to the goodness of society, the only truly virtuous love is to God as Being in General pragmatically tested so as to eliminate illusory concepts of love that emerge from self-interest, even when benign.

In other words, the material world does not dissipate into spirit, but becomes ever more glorious and beautiful, and thus more clearly revelatory of divine creativity and human consent to Being in General even as it remains teleologically dynamic. Edwards writes that the discovery of new objects of perception is an invaluable advance of the knowledge of divine activity: "For to find out the reasons of things in natural philosophy is only to find out the proportion of God's acting."[28] Idea and object, spirit and matter reverberate in a way that suggests emanation and remanation, the communicative circuit traveled between divine and human love whose ends are necessarily found within the fulfillment of Being in General. To experience being through the actual ideas of the Creation is to fulfill one's destiny as a spiritually perceiving agent belonging to the divine. This is a theological resonance of James's vaguely expansive notion of religious experience as constructive of everlasting possession. Both descriptions of relationship suggest that freedom exists not apart from others, but in what for human beings can at best be a quasi-absolute dependence productive of mutual responsibility understood as aesthetic propensity.

Such apprehension is affective or experiential, and propels the self into the world as a fuller manifestation of actuality that in turn resonates proportionality to all of the encounters she has with other persons and community. As what Bruce Kuklick calls "God's will in action,"[29] the creation expands to the beholding of the actual idea by the regenerate heart in such a way that the perception of being amplifies Being in General. As New observes, "The world is not less for its dependencies, but more, the sinner not less for his consent to Being but more. Beauty inheres in development of such dependencies."[30] Such dependency is not defined by personal autonomy or hierarchical power but by relations that exert aesthetic and ethical responsiveness to being. Divine love humbles itself in its pervasive and perpetual desire for communication.

This is one reason why Edwards employs the oppositional terms image and shadow to describe the language of the divine present within the Book of Nature. Such terminology allows for an ambidextrous beholding that both actualizes and dissipates the conceptual building out of experiential affections. Edwards's enriched empiricism values both natural phenomena and intelligential being as modes representative of divine activity present in history. Relations between ideas and things form the central dimension of Edwards's dispositional ontology, for it is in the communicative continuity between ideas and things that each comes to fruition. The image casts a shadow, and the shadow suggests the potentiality for expanded relation in the processive energy of the heart bent to the poetic refashioning of self and creation. One alone cannot be excellent, and excellence is the essence of divine and human communicative dynamism and purpose. Mind and matter, idea and thing, image and shadow are circles within the circles of divine communicative activity that place human agency, when exerted charitably within the community, in the space between presence and absence, self and other. Such a space is a democratic space because open to the dispositions and transitions of intelligential fellowship that seeks a place, a home; this is the occasion for delight at the affirmative advance of one's fellow creature. It also necessitates pragmatic assessment of this public space, as the implications of dispositions and transitions for the fruitfulness of the community discriminates between that which is of value and that which diminishes affirmative advance.

Edwards's enriched empiricism depicts an expanding harmony, proportionality, or unity in multiplicity with which he understands the overlapping realities of natural, moral, and spiritual beauty. Such an organic unity describes the power of religion to engage the person with the divine or, in its illusory modes, to create a falling way from being towards nothingness. Substance for Edwards is a reflection of divine creativity, as objects are centers of energy and the visible beauties of the world. When witnessed through the sanctified sense of the heart, the actual idea is fulfilled as substance, is the thing itself, through the circling energy that awakens a deepened vision and creates a more intimate world. This is the moment of expansion from potentiality to actuality that realizes intimacy of relation to beauty in its diverse yet overlapping forms, making the saint a poet via a parallelism of charitable action and pragmatic interpretation. Such repetition mimes the divine activity, or personates Christ, deepening consent to Being in General through fellow-feeling, an affinity become sacred. The saint, in personating Christ, becomes a center of light, of divine energy manifest in the world. Edwards writes,

> If all virtue primarily consists in that affection of heart to being, which is exercised in benevolence, or an inclination to its good, then God's virtue is so extended as to include a propensity not only to being actually existing and actu-

ally beautiful, but to possible being so as to incline him to give a being beauty and happiness.[31]

The parallelism of charitable action and pragmatic interpretation suggests the ways in which the regenerate heart enriches the bare world of paltry empiricism and enlightens human blindness. Repetition is never repetitive—even a copy is never a copy—and thus the expansion of excellence through consent creates both a more intimate or glorious reality and an energetic extension of the possibility of such glory that has a gravitational pull. This happens ontologically through the spiritual sense that awakens the person to divine presence in the world of nature and in society; creatively through the consent of being to being, the affection of heart to being that affirms and advances excellence in its diverse expressions and contexts; in the poetic remaking of the world that such consent realizes when pragmatically tested; and teleologically in the inclination to possible being. Thus God's two books, Scripture and Nature, when attended to by the awakened heart, reveal and create reality anew. These two books, both defined in terms of narrative gaps of parataxis, leave out explanation in order to enable the creative activity of the perceiving heart to fill in reality or create deeper relations expressive of excellence. Thus repetition conveys relation as it unfurls to greater effect. Nature, scripture, rituals of prayer and preaching as they petition God and man, all work to the ongoing series of divine communication that, to quote Hopkins, "Kéeps gráce: thát keeps all his goings graces."[32]

We misunderstand human excellence if we take relation and agreement to mean the loss of distinctive individuality rather than the augmentation of personhood that achieves deepened social, and hence spiritual, moral, and aesthetic tendencies. These deepened relations intensify the recognition of the dignity of sentient being through the increased complexity that represents the affirmation of being in its aesthetic and ethical expression. The act of charity, while disinterested, invests Being in General with an affirmation that advances divine love. Human beings can never realize true virtue, but they can deepen their sense of dignity by the affirmation and advance of the dignity of the other, imagined as recognition of the face of the other that is the face of God. This divine communication enlivens both the natural world and the historical process, and is available to those whose heart has been sanctified, and who act in such a way as to awaken the individuals and the communities of which they are a part.

Edwards's view of the divine theatre witnesses a gracious impress upon the awakened perceiver much as God brings weight or gravity to bear upon paltry empiricism. Such weight is dynamically creative, as it coheres the parts into form reflective of the very glory from which it emanates. The creative weight of God's love conveys such power to the perceiver, transforming her vision. Thus God reveals through nature the potential for augmenting being and advancing redemptive history, a deepening of relations that traces the sacred ever forward.

The communicative God speaks infinitely and differentially to intelligential being, guiding each to his own tracings, an activity creating a more excellent reality in which glory expands through the finite repetition of the divine wheels of providence. To surpass or transcend, as the noun "excellence" suggests, requires transformation of the limitations of fallen human nature. God's presence in nature and scripture is an ongoing aid to the reflection necessary to the awakening of the heart.

Claims to being's imperfect immersion in being itself require the test of fruitfulness. The interpretation of the affections is an ongoing activity, a part of the imaginative circling of reality that mimes Ezekiel's wheels. The fact of original sin makes such an exercise not of value to the individual alone, but to the entire human community because of the desired end of glorification of God. The "infinite repeatability" of the circulation of the heart that seeks more suggests the rich retelling of reality that expands excellence, and thus intimacy, through the intensiveness and extensiveness of the imaginative cohesion of idea and thing. Repetition means to seek out again and again, to petition the divine for communication with self and world, a form of prayer that establishes the relationship between the human and the divine. As Lee notes, "Reality is a permanent process of the multiplications of actualities (relations). . . . Reality is not something that is achieved once and for all but something that is achieved again and again."[33]

Thus Edwards's notion that humanity's only real concern is excellence; all the rest is retrogression. Aesthetic perception and extension of the regenerate heart continues the "repetition in the finite mind of the eternal I AM" through virtuous love proved and expanded by pragmatic poetics. Such repetition makes the creative imagination a form of prayer, the action of the saints a form of praise always available in the "infinite repeatability" that pragmatically seeks good ground. As Richardson remarks, "The most distinctive feature of Edwards's style, both in the writings he kept as his own and in his sermons . . . is this manner of progressive repetition of certain words in their variants."[34]

Such repetition mimes the divine activity, or personates Christ, deepening consent to Being in General through fellow-feeling, an affinity become sacred through practice. As Edwards writes in "The Mind" #66, "All sorts of Ideas of things are but the repetitions of those very things over again, as well as the ideas of color, figures, solidity, tastes and smells, as the ideas of thought and mental acts." We see a similar view in *Miscellany #782* where Edwards discusses the excitation of actual ideas as a type of repetition in the finite mind garnered by concentrated attention. The inner world of experience grows in complexity and becomes excellent just as the human community arises to a richer network of relation through such excitation. The saint, in personating Christ, becomes a center of light, of divine energy manifest in the world that illuminates such ideas for which "there is very often no actual idea of those things when we are said to think of them." Too often, Edwards laments, we have no idea at all, "but only make use of the signs instead of the ideas."[35]

This is especially problematic when the confusion of sign for idea leads to widespread confusion about the true nature of religion. Edwards thus defines true virtue not in terms of divine assistance to natural principles, which can in themselves produce much good, but in the infusion of the spiritual regeneration that transforms the very foundation of heart and mind.[36] The love to Being in General is primary, and supercedes all other forms of virtue, which are all of value, but all tainted by human self-interest. The remarkable thing about true virtue is not only its purity of will towards Being in General as the true foundation of all forms of virtue, but Edwards's emphasis that true virtue has a propulsive intensity that expands the inclination to possible being. True benevolent consent thus invokes what Lee has called "the rhythm of becoming" that is "ontologically productive."[37] And because the saint can never know whether he is truly virtuous, pragmatic testing must always be the penultimate end of the aesthetic-ethical synonymy emanating from the sense of the heart. Pragmatic poetics, then, seeks an ultimate end in the glorification of God that is, as Augustine put it and Edwards echoed, an end without end. The art of expansiveness is ongoing in time, infinite repeatability necessary because of humanity's creation as image and dust. Deadening matter and individual beauty infinitely repeat in ways that endlessly trace the sacred.

The widening of the heart that brings the ideal and the empirical together is characterized by a propulsive intensity that traces the sacred. In so doing, the true virtue that Edwards celebrates is never realized anymore than the glorious end of the creation is fulfilled. There is a lure to creativity in the foundational change in the regenerate heart, and yet it is praxis that drives the process of history. True virtue aims at the expansiveness of Being in General as an expression of being's consent to being that enriches the world with a glory or light that further illuminates the path. But the tendency to "have a determination of mind to union and benevolence to a particular person, or private system . . . is but a small part of the universal system of being [and] is not of the nature of true virtue." Such "private affection . . . contains but a small part of the great system . . . is limited to so narrow a circle."[38] The private circle omits Ezekiel's wheeling manifest in the sense of the heart, and thus creates a retrospective faith that falls away from Being in General.

The lure to creativity is the result of the teleological leading implanted by God in the reconstitution of the heart. This leading speaks to the greater purpose of intelligential being to participate in the glory and happiness of God. Through infinite repeatability of the art of expansiveness that emerges from the pragmatist poetics emergent from the new sense, glory becomes. Edwards works this out in the companion to his treatise on ethics, *The Nature of True Virtue*, entitled *The End for Which God Created the World*.

The propulsive intensity of the sense of the heart's apprehension of the excellencies Edwards found everywhere—in nature, scripture, history, and the human person's physical body and intelligence—characterized religious life as just this drive forward. Edwards sees "man chilled with the vast idea" of the universe's complexity, which is but a shadow of God's glory. His language is peppered with metaphors of quantity, of "many millions of millions of little worlds" and "infinite number X infinite X infinite X infinite," a phrase repeated eight times in one sentence.[39] This speaks to his view that "as bodies are but the shadow of being, therefore the consent of bodies one to another and the harmony that is among them is but the shadow of excellency."[40] Thus the end of glory results from a cosmos of infinite divine communication reimagined through intelligential being moving away from a fallen state to intimate relation with a divine frame of millions of parts. There is an exponential dynamic at work that is a resonating organicism that implicates all of God's diverse communications—nature, scripture, the regenerate individual, human society, and religious communities—in the poetic remaking of the creation tested for its practical effect and consequently repeated or discarded. Pragmatic poetic refashioning of the creation traces the sacred through the world in the hope of writing it down, much as James sees that truth is salted down: "holiness should be as it were inscribed on everything."[41]

The diminution of being triggered by false religious affections reflects the self-delusion and suffering Edwards witnessed in his ministry. And despite reflections on the joyous fulfillment of God's glory, and the role the regenerate saint plays in it, "Edwards confessed to having little faith in the meager powers of human expression. . . . The greatness of God must always elude mortal description, words being less fitted to express things of so sublime a nature."[42]

The paradoxical demand is that in order to be fully alive one must embrace kenosis and the pain of self-emptying. Full engagement with the divine theatre overflowing with the presence of God requires a dying to the self akin to agonistic or strenuous effort that makes liminality essential to the future development of charitable community. But Edwards mistrusted human power; its inability to appreciate absolute dependence as an avenue to freedom rather than a transit away from it, undercut his own visionary hope. As New comments,

> Ego, when juxtaposed with an Edwardsean consent, is revealed as the most retentive of faculties. When consent arbitrates the eye's attentions, then the will to power is revealed to be no more than a syndrome of withheld consent, and ideological sovereignty unfree because fugitive from experience.[43]

This ideological sovereignty recalls Edwards's struggle with theological determinism in the *Personal Narrative*. The spiritual pathology of self-interest and pride haunts Edwards's work because lived out. Edwards sees the aesthetic and the ethical as synonymous because the consenting act creates beauty only within the society of being in which it takes hold as a communally recognized act of truth or meaning. Thus, when the dynamic nature of consent is understood as benevolence to Being, it intensifies the proportionality of the world as it augments worth or value in the very real locus of human suffering and need. The individual practice of beauty as truth is not for the individual even as he or she enjoys such exercise. True virtue brings to fruition the potentialities envisioned by the person through the sense of the heart. Affirming such potentialities both reveals and creates the divine idea present within material reality as an ongoing fulfillment of that idea. The delight found within such glorying reverberates to future proportionality or complex beauty, and remanates to its divine source as a type of fulfillment. This expands Being in General itself and liberates the person able to participate in returning vitality to its source. Responsibility involves responsive consent to beauty and to the good, and is at the heart of expansiveness. The saint is ontologically productive and contributes to the redemption of history as a personation of Christ. On a moral and spiritual level, consent and dissent operate as instruments of this plastic power of creativity driving human purpose much as Ezekiel's wheels symbolize the divine dynamics of redemption history.

While recognizing the bare fact of persons as individual centers of being, the sense of the heart engages in an imaginative reckoning of reality that, at its closest point of intimacy, paradoxically affirms the dignity and face of the other before its own being. Such a vision defines the very dignity of the human person who is a saint. The human purpose is to participate in this dramatic activity in the intelligential and differentiated advancement of being. Action in rhythm with divine communication not only remanates to God, but signals the person's mutual possession of and with God that transforms self-interest towards benevolence to Being in general. And this event is ongoing in time, signaling a millenial progress that Edwards deeply cherished, and that transcended the American project that he increasingly saw in terms of a private system, and not an exceptionally blessed state. Edwards's world was one of an enriched empiricism of divine activity in which he traced the sacred in search of deep beauty in a spiritual wilderness of enthusiasts and rationalists, both gaining power and both demonstrating what to Edwards was the diminution of being itself.

"Advantageous Connexion" and the Expansion of Intimacy

In *The Varieties*, James emphasizes the value of conversion and the mystic sense of hidden meaning as offering the richest of resources for tracing the sacred because of their widening of the self. He writes,

> Usually when we have a wide field we rejoice, for we then see masses of truth together, and often get glimpses of relations which we divine rather than see, for they shoot beyond the field into still remoter regions of objectivity, regions which we seem rather *about to perceive* than to perceive actually.[44]

James's language brings together joy and truth, the ecstatic and the ethical, as dynamically invoking "glimpses of relations" apprehended through the act of divining complexities that promises actual perception of "remoter regions of objectivity." Here we see the overlapping experiences of revelation and creation, linking idealism and empiricism, that pattern a field composed of present and future masses of truth propelling the promise of the self's further widening and the consequent expansion of intimacy. This represents his field theory of consciousness, which "commemorates . . . the indetermination of the margin." The margin "lies around us like a 'magnetic field,' inside of which our centre of energy turns like a compass-needle." For James, the significance of the field-theory is that "it casts light on many phenomena of religious biography. . . . The most important consequence of having a strongly developed ultra-marginal life of this sort is that one's ordinary fields of consciousness are liable to incursions from it of which the subject does not guess the source."[45]

The pragmatic poetics of making and testing relations is intensified and propulsive through a mystic sense able to see into hidden meaning, portrayed in James's thinking about the value of religious experience. In applying radical empiricism to the arena of mankind's most important function, that of religion, James establishes a complex relation illustrated by his notion of everlasting possession in Lecture 2 of *The Varieties*. Through religious feeling or experience, a relation to wider regions of being, sometimes referred to as More or as a wider spiritual environment, propels acts creative of further relations whose tendencies look ahead to transitions into evermore complex beauty, a beauty whose potential reinstates both vagueness and precision. This is a type of thinking beyond patterns, as Eugene T. Gendlin has written, and it expresses the purposive dynamic of thought essential to the views of both Edwards and James. Gendlin writes,

> The poet tries this line and that. Many lines come. Some seem good. The poet listens into what each of those lines can say. Poets constantly listen into an unexplored openness—what can this new phrasing say? A great many such lines come and are rejected. The poet reads to the end of the written lines again—and again. Each time that ..... comes.
> ....
> The blank is *vague, but it is also more precise* than the poet can as yet say. It cannot be said in common phrases.... This ..... demands and implies a new phrase that has not yet come. So the ..... is actually more precise than what has ever been said before—in the history of the world.[46]

The primacy of feeling as cognitive and creative of new lines of relation that move ever forward in complexity and potentiality reinstates the vague and its precise situation. This describes the dynamics of parallelism in the art of expansiveness as it moves from potentiality to actuality to realize intimacy of relation. This pragmatic parallelism of relations growing into other relations illustrates the infinite repeatability previously discussed as matter defying matter. The pragmatic poetics of religious experience "tries this line and that . . . into an unexplored openness" that traces the sacred.

James's pragmatic philosophy of radical empiricism germinates from his earliest philosophical reflections upon his felt helplessness and perceived loss of creative freedom in an imperiously nihilistic universe. Unlike the lived brokenness of traditional empiricism, James's radical empiricism envisions a world in which human action has creative and moral value and function. In *The Meaning of Truth* James defines radical empiricism in terms of a postulate, a statement of fact, and a generalized conclusion:

> The postulate is that the only things that shall be debatable among philosophers shall be things definable in terms drawn from experience.... The statement of fact is that the relations between things, conjunctive as well as disjunctive, are just as much matters of direct particular experience, neither more so nor less so, than the things themselves. The generalized conclusion is that therefore the parts of experience hold together from next to next by relations that are themselves parts of experience. The directly apprehended universe needs, in short, no extraneous trans-empirical connective support, but possesses in its own right a concatenated or continuous structure.[47]

The first tenet makes experience inclusive of conjunctive and disjunctive relations, excluding transcendent connectors such as God, the soul, or absolute truth. For James, rationalism and empiricism alternatively emphasize a theological or materialist determinism that in both cases leaves the person bereft of engagement. While he favors empiricism for its focus on concreteness, he bemoans its chopped up view of life, and its consequent disengagement from human activity. His radical empiricism is ultimately a critical commentary on empiricism that supports his high estimation of religion's functional value. In *Pragmatism*, James states that the quandry of contemporary life may be found in the following impasse: "You find empiricism with inhumanism and irreligion; or else you find a rationalistic philosophy that indeed may call itself religious, but that keeps out of all definite concrete facts and joys and sorrows."[48] The aesthetic pleasure of systematic philosophy is retrospective, has no responsibility to concretion, and too often manifests itself in the alienating quality of vicious intellectualism as feeling becomes ossified in conceptual systems. James notes, "It would be an obvious absurdity if such ways of taking the universe were actually true."[49] But James's apparent favoring of empiricism also leaves him cold, and he struggles to synthesize the two in an ambidextrous beholding of retrospective custom and prospective vision, of knowledge about and knowledge by acquaintance.

As illustrated by the concept of mutual possession, James favors a view of life that sees working relations opening a wide field in which joy arises in intimate relation to the massing of truths. In "A World of Pure Experience" James suggests why religious experience is "mankind's most important function":

> Relations are of different degrees of intimacy.... [The most intimate of all is] the relation experienced between terms that form states of mind, and are immediately conscious of continuing each other. The organization of the Self as a system of memories, purposes, strivings, fulfilments or disappointments, is incidental to this most intimate of all relations, the terms of which seem in many cases actually to compenetrate and suffuse each other's being.[50]

The compenetration and suffusion of the most intimate of relations suggests an aesthetic dynamic at work in the act of creative concretion that is different from that of structured rationality in suggesting a dynamically social reality. For James, reality is a relational environment analogous to a community in which the amelioration of suffering comes about through creative action that attempts to discover fulfilling terminations expansive of both vitality and possibility. Thus James sees action as "the workshop of being"; the intimacy that forms community expresses itself in acts of consent and dissent that enrich the potentialities present within such a view of reality.

In his introduction to Edwards's *Miscellany #782*, Perry Miller notes the sympathies that James's radical empiricism has with Edwards's enriched empiricism in the creative compenetration of the act of benevolent consent. Miller writes, "It is fascinating, considering how William James went deliberately back to sources which were also Edwards's, and how aware he was of the wrong turning the empirical tradition had taken between Edwards's time and his own, to find how nearly James came to restating Edwards's conclusions. Such reasoning as Edwards here exemplifies seems to have informed many of James's observations":

> Consent to the idea's undivided presence, this is effort's sole achievement. Its only function is to get this feeling of consent into the mind. And for this there is but one way. The idea to be consented to must be kept from flickering and going out. It must be held steadily before the mind until it fills the mind. Such filling of the mind by an idea, with its congruous associates, is consent to the idea and to the fact which the idea represents![51]

The "feeling with" of consent advances the building-out of the world that is so central to James's project. The mind's growth in the apprehension of "masses of truth" expands the facts present within the world, and sets them in motion to do work and find fruitful transitions or clear terminations that further expand compenetration and its successful leading. New relations are glimpsed, and novel possibility returned to the widened self as new ideas for focused concentration. Such a communicative circuit signals the consciousness as a society, as feeling within itself, and of reality as compenetration, each of which concentrically contributes to a collective pulse towards a socially dynamic universe. The result for the engaged person is,

> Your imagination is extended. You divine in the world around you matter for a little more humility on your own part, and tolerance, reverence, and love for others; and you gain a certain inner joyfulness at the increased importance of our common life. Such joyfulness is a religious inspiration and an element of spiritual health, and worth more than large amounts of that sort of technical and accurate information which we professors are supposed to be able to impart.[52]

The rejoicing noted by James resonates to the world of experience as infinite repeatability, aesthetic and ethical creativity that plays into the building out of the universe. Just as Edwards's praying aloud and hymn-singing in the *Personal Narrative* awakens the divine in the world, to rejoice in relation to the widening of the heart expands fact and reality to a new reach of creative freedom.

Critical to this engagement with concrete reality—the consenting excitement of actual ideas that awakens and advances happiness—is what James calls affectional facts. Affectional facts demonstrate the meaning of James's concept of pure experience in that they embody an ambiguity suggestive of the transactional environment realized in the "stuff" that is pure experience. Pure experience is fluctuation, with potential for selection and addition that expands relation and intensifies function; notions of consciousness, of subject and object, emerge from pure experience for functional reasons within a contextual situation. Thus continuity of consciousness exists to bridge the chasm between subject and object, just as there exists an intimacy between sensations and ideas, akin to "those cunning circular panoramas that have lately been exhibited, where the real foreground and the painted canvas join together."[53] This is an image that also suggests the relation between knowledge by acquaintance and knowledge about. Religious experience serves such a critical function because it affirms and advances life in a transitional environment, and does not simply rebound to the value of a subject relating to an object, nor does it require a transcendent force to hold everything together. In fact, the subject is dissolved and the transempirical disappears, suggesting the socially intimate nature of James's radical empiricism as it describes an organic ecology.

In the environment of pure experience, affectional facts illustrate the transactional dynamic at work in the ambiguity of inner and outer, subject and object. In some sense this reflects James's notion of the melting mood in *The Varieties*, the interaction of fields of conscious and of reality that define experience as normatively liminal, always in transit.[54] They embody feelings that are also felt in objects or things, enabling a communicative circuit that impresses upon self and world both feeling and being felt, and that allows for consideration of religious experiences as real and felt. This signifies a living religion that does not require a transempirical connective support because it travels relationally amid subject and object, like James's example of the train shooting forward while the passenger looks backwards. The thing is the sallying forth:

> Life is in the transitions as much as in the terms connected; often, indeed, it seems to be there more emphatically, as if our spurts and sallies forward were the real firing-line of the battle, were like the thin line of flame advancing across the dry autumnal field which the farmer proceeds to burn. In this line we live prospectively as well as retrospectively. It is 'of' the past, inasmuch as it comes expressly as the past's continuation; it is 'of' the future, in so far as the future, when it comes, will have continued it.[55]

Thus the art of expansiveness lies in the lines of connection between feeling and thing, affection and fact that can be made to widen self and world through poetic remaking of felt relations into facts of feeling. The irreligiousness of empiricism and the abstractedness of systematic rationality are dispelled by the migratory patterns of affectional facts aesthetically remaking and being remade by encounter with conjunctive and disjunctive relations given in the world of experience. The determinism of God and of materialism are stunted but tempting, the former because of radical empiricism's emphasis on relations rather than absolutism or paltry empiricism, and the latter because radical empiricism makes for a dangerous and unmoored life that demands responsibility to and for a wider reality. James rejects "the absolute all-witness that 'relates' things together by throwing 'categories' over them like a net."[56] The reliance upon an absolute power holding sway over all reality is repugnant to James on both epistemological and moral grounds. Beliefs, values, ideas, and persons all must operate functionally, all must work hard in an open-ended, malleable, and mysterious universe that presents us with danger whether we engage it or hide from it in retrospective custom and systematic thought.

James's thinking suggests that all felt relations and experiences be treated as essential elements within the examination of human existence and meaning, and the fact that life is intensively social and ought to be extensively social. The intensiveness and extensiveness of complex relation or proportion shapes the full fact: "a conscious field *plus* the object as felt or thought of *plus* an attitude towards the object *plus* the sense of a self to whom the attitude belongs."[57] The full fact represents the cognitive power of feeling's significance for the value of religious experience, the dignity of the person for whom it converts self and world, and for attendance to a view of reality that neither abstracts the person nor shackles him to material reality. The cognitive power of feeling carefully attended to and brought into action in the world informs the art of expansiveness.

James notes the importance of the "concrete bit of personal experience, not hollow, not a mere abstract element of experience, such as the 'object' is when taken all alone." This suggests that the full fact exists "on the line connecting real events with real events," making the individual a participant in the intimate world of experience inclusive of "the individual pinch of destiny."[58] The role of the person with his private events is here given a public role: every person counts. This recalls James's story of Crump's conversion, of which he observes, "A small man's salvation will always be a great salvation and the greatest of all facts *for him*. Who knows how much less ideal still the lives of these spiritual grubs and earthworms, these Crumps and Stigginses, might have been, if such poor grace as they have received had never touched them at all?"[59] The affectional facts of personal experience roll out into the world to make their way in concrete actuality for good or ill, truth or termination. But it is in the validation of such feeling that the world is made. Radical empiricism undergirds this point in seeing the value of such relations and their freedom from rational systems with their divine glue and paltry empiricism with its bare offerings for human interaction. The inclusiveness of relations conjunctive and disjunctive are significant for the life of the individual and her contributions to building out the world. Human dignity is at the heart of radical empiricism as a worldview that makes a place for the dignity of human creative freedom. It emphasizes the social as a critical factor in the construction of reality. In James's discussions of the ends of thought as harmony, clarity, and peace is a concern for the practical meaning of human life in community.

James's critique of philosophy in *Pragmatism* and elsewhere bears a similar disquiet with the ways in which the intellectual class easily dismissed the human problem, as with the example of Corcoran's suicide. His radical empiricism highlights a similar issue, that of the exclusion of experiences of all types from analysis. James's use of metaphors like stream or field to describe consciousness suggests the metaphysical and psychological ecosystem in which human beings grow. Those who read James as a defender of individualism have it wrong.

James's emphasis on genius and his assertion of the great man theory speak more to his concern with evolutionary progress for the sake of human cooperation and fulfillment than it does for the recommendation of egotism. James's radical empiricism esteems the poet and the genius, and the mystic sense of hidden meaning that he witnesses in their work, and its inherent social character. The widened heart in a expansive and open universe has the opportunity, challenging as it is, for the development of value both personal and communal.

This view is suggestive of Edwards's definition of excellence: "That which is beautiful with respect to the university of things has a generally extended excellence and a true beauty; and the more extended or limited its system is, the more confined or extended is its beauty."[60] Both men struggle against private systems, whether a rational system of thought, paltry empiricism, or a closed society. And like Edwards's excellence, James sees these private systems emerging from a retrospective aestheticism productive of self-interest, social custom, and rational conceptualization.

The prospective aesthetics of James's knowledge by acquaintance functions in relation to the goals of thinking, to seek detail and inclusion "represented without omission, addition, or distortion" and with "harmony, beauty, impressiveness or suggestiveness for life, of their total effect."[61] Much of James's advocacy of a melioristic religiousness seeks to put these aesthetic qualities into action as consequences of affectional facts selectively directed, poetically fashioned, and concretely tested. Such affectional facts are critical to James's prioritization of religious experience and the development of a radically empiricist worldview because they give credence to the felt and the invisible as real and active, perhaps more important to human development than anything else because spontaneous variations seeking adaptive success. The full fact is in the making in the workshop of being, the products of which the world is made and built-out. Thus rational structure operates as one element in an aesthetic-ethical dynamic that subsumes it, and forms a valuable moment in thought when brought into relation to the retrospective aesthetic that guarantees comforting limits that yet alienate one from experience. James writes,

> What can kindle feeling but the example of feeling? . . . The one *fundamental* quarrel [radical] Empiricism has with Absolutism is over this repudiation by Absolutism of the personal and the aesthetic factor in the construction of philosophy. That we all of us have feelings, [radical] Empiricism feels quite sure. That they may be as prophetic and anticipatory of truth as anything else we have, and some of them more so than others, cannot possibly be denied.[62]

The kindling of feeling, the resonating affectionality reminiscent of Edwards's notion of consciousness as "feeling within itself," makes of consciousness a society of complex relations selectively attended to so as to dispose the self to act. And the society of consciousness concentrically communes with centers of interest of other selves and with spiritual centers at work in the wider wilderness of an unfinished and malleable universe.

James observes that this is a dramatic process for the individual undergoing the birth of new belief, whether religious or not, and this explains the importance of retrospective rational structure. "New truth is always a go-between, a smoother-over of transitions," James writes. He continues, "It marries old opinion to new fact so as to ever show a minimum of jolt, a maximum of continuity. . . . To a certain degree, therefore, everything is plastic." Pragmatism reveals radical empiricism and the creation of additive beliefs to be a messy affair that again shows rationalism wanting, "a skinny outline rather than the rich thicket of reality." Thus "pragmatism may be a happy harmonizer of empiricist ways of thinking, with the more religious demands of human beings" as it brings the felt experiences of a widening universe and the new beliefs and values that emerge as a result into a state of mutual possession with concrete reality.[63] But the radical empiricist needs a base of operations that temporarily ends homelessness; rationalism provides a substitutionary environment that funds experience and furthers survival.

The religious demand offers both flight and perch, respecting the sensitivities of human beings in the traumatic experience of grafting new experiences on ancient stock. This is witnessed in the continuum in *The Varieties* from the sick soul to the divided self, and the conversion that does not discover such an end, but comes into relation with a creative lure to more work energized by a new strenuousness. The new reach of freedom that results from religious experience, as James describes it in *The Varieties*, parallels the communicative relation of Edwards's enriched empiricism as it enables alienation to end in the creativity of relationship that affirms and advances a deeper intimacy. But the unsettling marriage or mutually possessive principle is a call for more work as a relation to the More fringed with novelty, possibility, and danger to the foundations of persons, as experiments with over-beliefs always are. James's enriched empiricism is stereoscopic, as it must be, holding systematic rationality and thickening concretion as representative modes of retrospective and prospective vision, one seeing from the past, the other seeing into the future, one knowing conceptually, the other knowing by acquaintance. One claims a restful harmony that may lull the listener to sleep, the other a harmony filled with dissonance that shifts and sways and disturbs the participant in its performance.

James bolsters these views in *Pragmatism*, where he sees rationalism and empiricism as temperaments that reflect the aesthetic pleasure of systematic satisfaction that supports the interests of the thinker seeking guarantees rather than the reality of the world. James identifies the problems of both as intellectualism and sensationalism, the tender-minded and the tough-minded. His youthful dilemma of determinism echoes in his contention that "the progress of science has seemed to mean the enlargement of the material universe and the diminution of man's importance."[64] His development of radical empiricism and its pragmatic method serves as a corrective to rationalism and empiricism, and in so doing expands the reach of humanity into the penumbral and generous regions of a widened spiritual reality. He writes,

> Once admit that experience is a river which made the channel that now, in part, but only in part, confines it, and it seems to me that all sorts of realities and completenesses are possible in Philosophy, hitherto stiffened and cramped by the silly littlenesses of the upper and the lower dogmatisms alternating their petty rationalistic and materialistic idols of the shop.[65]

Here is James's "protestant reformation in philosophy," which leads to "philosophic questions . . . of a less abstractionist type . . . more scientific and individualistic in their tone yet not irreligious either. . . . The earth of things, long thrown into shadow by the glories of the upper ether, must resume its rights."[66]

James speaks for a popular audience in *Pragmatism*, and he begins and ends the lecture series with a focus upon the practical value of religion. Pragmatism values affectional facts and the quality of romance that seeks the ideal wedded to concrete reality, and thus serves radical empiricism as a method of testing the fruits of additions to the world of experience's complex relationality. Thus James see pragmatism as "first, a method; and second, a genetic theory of what is meant by truth."[67] Pragmatism in relation to religious experience traces the sacred and marks the trail as it disappears into the horizon. It serves the world of experience by working out the implications of experience for the affirmation and advance of truth as a species of good.

There is a double urgency in thinking, which James sees as a marriage function, an aesthetic experience both seeking and establishing satisfaction in an ongoing process of prospective and retrospective experience. The double urgency requires the additive power of new fact, while it also is "grafting itself then upon the ancient body of truth." There has to be an aesthetic coherence and satisfaction that is a successful addition to "earlier truths . . . and novel observations." Knowledge by acquaintance and knowledge about function together to remake reality and become true. James notes, "That new idea is truest which performs most felicitously its function of satisfying our double urgency."[68]

In Edwards's enriched empiricism we see a similar marriage function, though its partners are creator and creation, heaven and earth, as opposed to affectional fact and concrete and unfinished universe. Each seeks an end to alienation and an expansiveness of intimacy that reflects the intensiveness and extensiveness of clarity, harmony, and repose that is the goal of thinking. James, however, sees a sovereign God as too abstracted and offering unequal access to believers, and thus of limited value, even if such sovereignty is exercised as transactional communication.

Pragmatism offers more value to human survival and advance than rationality because it enters into the thicket of reality. It traces the sacred on the ground, as it functions as "a happy harmonizer of empiricist ways of thinking, with the more religious demands of human being."[69] God, from this grounded perspective, is at work in human trials and triumphs, "needed in the dust of our human trials, even more than his dignity is needed in the empyrean."[70] Pragmatism's navigation of this thicket illustrates the poetic refashioning of aesthetic facts with practical consequences through a discriminating transactional conversation that Seigfried sees as "consisting of an original synthesis of the careful description insisted on by Louis Agassiz as being the necessary requisite of the newly emerging science of natural history and of description as the 'seeing-into' at the heart of Ralph Waldo Emerson's romantic, poetic vision of the world."[71]

James's radical empiricism holds that the person is a participant, not an observer, within a world of experience in which objects, actions, relations, and disjunctions, exist within an ongoing reality of both mutual possession and the failure to cohere. Thus the self is interactively dynamic, constantly fashioning and refashioning the experiential reality of which it is a part. James writes, "Our fields of experience have no more definite boundaries than have our fields of view. Both are fringed forever by a *more* that continuously develops, and continuously supercedes them as life proceeds."[72] This communicative interaction, much like Edwards's view of the dispositional dynamics of religious affections, requires pragmatic testing that indicates fruitful transition to change the world or termination that lends insight into whether an act has cash value in the long run. In *Pragmatism*, James's theory of truth as a species of good echoes Edwards's notion of true virtue in presenting a picture of the working out of affectional fact that synthesizes the aesthetic and the ethical in the high estimation given to "actual connexion." James uses the terms "agreeable" and "fitting" in *Pragmatism* to display this synthesis and its relation to a widened social character that is democratic.[73] This is not language used to suggest the argument by design, but to emphasize promise emerging from the propulsive intensity of life lived forward in transitions and terminations.[74]

For James, the active self exists as functional consciousness moving between disposition or affectional fact, agreement, and verification. The attempt is to realize the organic integration of self, community, and social universe. James writes,

> Truth (is) essentially something bound up with the way in which one moment in our experience may lead us towards other moments which it will be worthwhile to have been led to. . . . When a moment in our experience, of any kind whatever, inspires us with a thought that is true, that means that sooner or later

we dip by that thought's guidance into the particulars of experience again and make advantageous connexion with them. This is a vague enough statement, but I beg you to retain it, for it is essential.[75]

James emphasizes that "advantageous connexion" is an idea essential to his thought, and embodies the value of vagueness as plasticity. Truth is a process arrived at through the act of pragmatic poetics, a complex and lapidary layering of agreement, proportionality, harmony, and dissonance, all aesthetic dynamics contained under the rubric "advantageous connexion." They bear the propulsive force of a dispositional psychology that, driven by a complex range of feeling and pragmatic testing, shifts the spatio-temporal locus of self and world. The fact that "truth *happens* to an idea" signals pragmatic poetics as "the ordinary agreement formula":

> Our ideas 'agree' with reality. They lead us, namely, through the acts and other ideas which they instigate, into or up to, or towards, other parts of experience with which we feel all the while—such feeling being among our potentialities—that the original idea remain in agreement. The connexions and transitions come to us from point to point as being progressive, harmonious, satisfactory. This function of agreeable leading is what we mean by an idea's verification.[76]

James's pragmatic theory of truth reveals its role as the method by which radical empiricism gains its footing. Radical empiricism reflects a reality of agreement-events that form "an aesthetic matrix rather than . . . a rational structure."[77] Such an aesthetic matrix informs the question of whether the universe is one or many, a topic that shapes James's concept of god(s). And here James supports such a matrix as a compenetration of variety and unity working together, like knowledge by acquaintance and knowledge about, to seek totality: "Acquaintance with reality's diversities is as important as understanding their connexion. The human passion of curiosity runs on all fours with the systematizing passion."[78] The animal metaphor suggests the evolutionary importance of the working of ideas in concrete reality.

As in his radical empiricism, both conjunctions and disjunctions have equal power. The "reticulated or concatenated forms which make of it [the universe] a continuous or integrated affair" is matched by the failure of connection that makes of the universe not one, but many. "The great point," James writes, is that "the oneness and the manyness are absolutely co-ordinate. . . . We now need conductors and now need non-conductors, and wisdom lies in knowing which is which at the appropriate moment." That is, we need to know when we find lines of influence that hang together, and when we find a termination that must recede into the past because of its failure to tend towards continuity and integration. "There is no species of connexion which will not fail," James adds, "if instead of choosing conductors for it, you choose non-conductors."[79] The prospective aesthetics James invokes is necessarily asymmetrical because on the way forward into a wilderness environment.

The world picture of absolute unity illustrates "the sublimest achievement of intellectualist philosophy," James finds, but because so fails to address both conjunction and disjunction of relations in the world of experience. Instead the backers of absolute unity dogmatically embrace abstractedness in a way that makes for systematic certainty and reasoned authority, but that thus rejects the value of the living experience of "the man-like God of common people." For James, "things tell a story . . . the world is full of partial stories . . . a rope of which each fibre tells a separate tale."[80]

The partial story, representative as it is of struggling human authors rather than authors of completed unities and abstractions, reflects a variety that shapes James's support of a pluralistic universe partly joined and partly disjoined, the world of experience of radical empiricism. This has significant implications for his thinking about religious experiences and the expansion of intimacy that may result. The glimmer of masses of truth is an intimation that calls for more work, and suggests that whatever god(s) arises within the tissue of experience will be a consequence of such work. Pragmatism, and the radical empiricism that it represents, "widens the field of search for God," and thus reflects James's notion that a pluralistic universe best describes his radical empiricism and its pragmatic method.[81]

This widened search for God is not a metaphysical quest for the right word, concept, or construct, as comforting as such an end might be. Rather it reflects the prospective aesthetics of pragmatic poetics. Pragmatism's "only test of probable truth is what works best in the way of leading us, what fits every part of life best and combines with the collectivity of experience's demands, nothing being omitted."[82] Thus whatever notion of god(s) or the More arises within the tissue of experience, James sees it as finite:

> The existence of such larger souls may be called a theological question, and I believe that such questions should be discussed as any other question is discussed, in all the ways which may make a decision seem probable or not. But I do not believe, picturing the whole as I do, that even if a supreme soul exists, it embraces all the details of the universe in a single absolute act either of thought or of will. In other words I disbelieve in the omniscience of the Deity, and in his omnipotence as well. The facts of struggle seem too deeply characteristic of the whole frame of things for me not to suspect that hindrance and experiment go all the way through.[83]

In "Pragmatism and Religion," the concluding lecture of *Pragmatism*, James elaborates upon the distinction between monism and pluralism that funds the rhetorical force of the book. Opposing the "rational unity of things" with their "possible empirical *unification*," James focuses not upon completion but on the possibility of ongoing process. In this process James further develops his concept of an interactive reality now understood as the workshop of being. Such interaction defines his doctrine of meliorism, which relies upon pragmatic poetics acting in concert with living options as opening the possibility of salvation; cherished ideals exist as affectional facts that motivate action. James argues, "Every such ideal realized will be one moment in the world's salvation." These are not "bare abstract possibilities," but "*live* possibilities . . . and if the complementary conditions come and add themselves, our ideals will become actual things."[84]

Thus the live option of "The Will to Believe," when conjoined with affectional facts, "will in the fullness of time, give us a chance, a gap that we can spring into, and, finally, *our act*. This is the process of salvation that James envisions, one that is "a social scheme of cooperative work genuinely to be done." The making of ideals that sally forth to be compressed as acts is ontologically productive. James writes,

> Our acts, our turning-places, where we seem to ourselves to make ourselves and grow, are the parts of the world to which we are closest, the parts of which our knowledge is the most intimate and complete. Why should we not take them at their face-value? Why may they not be the actual turning-places and growing-places which they seem to be, of the world—why not the workshop of being, where we catch fact in the making, so that nowhere may the world grow in any other way than this?[85]

Emphasizing radical empiricism's rejection of a transempirical glue, James sees the turning-place of fact in the making as "*living reason*" that only exists because "demanded . . . to give relief to no matter how small a fraction of the world's mass." In the piecemeal growth of the world, "Being grows under all sorts of resistances in this world of the many, and from compromise to compromise, only gets organized gradually into what may be called secondarily rational shape."[85] The risk and adventure of a world in the making in which salvation is a possibility is what James offers as his vision of religion's functional service to humanity. Religious affections when considered through the lens of radical empiricism cultivate an intimacy that brings relief to the incompleteness and dissonance of spectatorship that fosters foreignness. Akin to Edwards's enriched empiricism in which the true excellence of religious affections is discerned by the intimate expansion of complex relations that express an aesthetic creativity synonymous with actions aspiring to true virtue, James envisions a pluralistic universe in which the sacred trace draws forth sustained and sustaining relations before evanescing into the past.

Chapter 5
Strenuous Democracy and the Workshop of Being

Hope and promise are natural consequences of religious experience and its poetic deepening of enriched empiricism. Edwards's and James's dynamic views of reality suggest that such deepening finds a model in democracy, which is always in the making, "a moral-aesthetic aspiration . . . its achievements are properly deemed artworks that make claims to being both beautiful and good."[1] Both Edwards and James offer visions of the good society that are meaningful because they include the dynamic and vague elements necessary to the aesthetic-ethical aspirations of a democratic community. Through the lens of Edwards and of James, this requires a type of strenuousness best achieved through religious experience poetically fashioned and pragmatically tested.

Edwards and James are profoundly concerned to participate in the development of an inclusive community in which members selflessly and generously give of themselves to uplift and harmonize with those to whom systematic philosophies and retrospective visions are blind. Edwards's "holy and happy society" and James's pluralistic universe each invoke a model of an ethical republic based on concern for the neighbor.[2] Edwards does so through faith in a communicating God, while James sees "we inhabit an invisible spiritual environment from which help comes, our soul being mysteriously one with a larger soul whose instruments we are."[3]

The realization of such a society requires a strenuous democratic process in which the authentic engagement of the individual's benevolent consent to a community seeking a cooperatively made salvation is paramount, and transcends both the spiritual hypocrisy and the self-interest embodied in American exceptionalism. The good society arrives with the unfolding inclusion of different persons within the cooperative project of human salvation. James writes, "This requires the risk of engagement with a world that is dangerous because of its contingency, and because there are no certainties, no guarantees that one's best efforts will not be stymied in the attempt to find meaningful termini."[4]

This is the workshop of being where James says we catch fact in the making through the circulative efforts of the heart to impress affectional facts upon reality so as to transform experience. Like Edwards, James sees that "Being grows under all sorts of resistances in this world of the many, and, from compromise to compromise, only gets organized gradually into what may be called secondarily rational shape." Unlike Edwards, James rejects the idea of an Absolute that fulfills every need "without having to consider or placate surrounding or intermediate powers."[5] While Edwards's notion of God as Being in General suggests a plurality of agents participating in mutually consenting actions advancing the glory of the Creation, ultimately such becoming has its beginning and end in divine glory, in which the agent participates. But for James this model of God opens the door to an absolutism causing a work stoppage. His notion of the finite god or the wider self is one in which the vague is injected such that there is a more dynamic and piecemeal forward motion. Ironically, Edwards's call for practical verification of religious affections led some to foster religious illusions that sufficed as proof of salvation, leading to James's wary view of the idolatry created in the conception of an absolute God.[6]

Contesting the engagement with experience or the consent to Being in General are economies of faith in which retrospective thinking reigns. Power exerts control over those caught within the networks of exchange that define systematic determinisms found in closed societies, or drops them out of the system into myriad forms of marginalization, shades without boundary, without any fixed identity, but feeling the whole as "one pulse of life."[7] These economies of faith are concerned foremost with certainty and the maintenance of custom and tradition such that the creative freedom of the individual, who exists within overlapping and successive states of simultaneous life as "centre surrounded by a fringe that shades insensible into a subconscious more," is sacrificed at the altar of social control and coercion. Edwards's philosophy of excellence sees that the creative freedom of the individual describes dissent from nothingness that is one with consent to Being in General. In James's language, this means,

> Intellectualism's edge is broken; it can only approximate to reality, and its logic is inapplicable to our inner life, which spurns its vetoes and mocks at its impossibilities. Every bit of us at every moment is part and parcel of a wider self, it quivers along various radii like the wind-rose on a compass, and the actual in it is continuously one with possibles not yet in our present sight.[8]

Rosalind Deutsch argues that such a mode of being witnesses to persons and prospects that undercut the claim to "my possession of the world . . . totalizing vision." She continues,

> Like democracy, the ethical relationship appears when certainty disappears; when, acknowledging otherness, we lose our footing and thus, as Julia Kristeva says, become receptive to conflicts. More:

> "The capacity to be non-indifferent to the other is the essence of the reasonable human being." Non-indifference, or responsibility, means that the social world can no longer be construed as an object for the subject, for its understanding. Avowing that the world does not belong to "me" or "us" makes us reasonable. In the presence of the Other, the social world slips from the subject's grasp."[9]

The question for Edwards and for James is how best to imagine life lived forward in the risk and adventure of building out the community of being through the disinterested responsibility to reality that defines the general notion of consent, not as acquiesence to closed systems, but as the affirmative advance of other beings and of reality itself. Their rhetorical task as public intellectuals is to invoke the vague vistas from which such democratic action arises, and to encourage the type of agonistic or strenuous effort that religious experience brings to bear upon the efforts to build a synonymously aesthetic and ethical society.

The Conjunction of Opposites in "The Excellency of Christ"

As previously discussed, Edwards's system of being is a cosmos-wide theater of dignity that invokes through the regenerate heart a disposition of dissent that shapes the responsible acts of persons in community to create what Edwards calls charitable fruits. This is commensurate with Edwards's notion that one alone cannot only not be excellent (proportional, beautiful, relational) one alone cannot be at all. Edwards's notion in *Mind #1* that even the concept of oneness is a consent of parts is ineluctably social in origin. Consciousness modeled on a social analogy demonstrates the constitution of existence known in the synonymy of aesthetics and ethics. In such a philosophy of relation, language both forms and dissolves resemblance or analogy; its metaphoricity parallels the dynamism of the propulsive nature of reality. This process of symbolization or metaphoricity defines language in its most satisfactory engagement with reality not as a completion of meaning or interpretation but as the germination of ongoing communicative energy through the self-consuming dynamic of the piling up of conjunctions of opposites that overflows with a surplus of meaning. For Edwards, Christ is the perfect model for agency of this power, while for James, the notion of the genius, prophet, or holy tramp is a functional analogue to this model of Christ as the poet or artist imagined by both Emerson and Henry James, Sr.

For Edwards, language as living organ imitates the passion, and thus the excellence, of Christ. God's two books, the Bible and the Book of Nature, reveal the process of emanation and remanation in which humanity serves as both signifier and symbolic process. Edwards's concept of typology is thus horizontal

Chapter 5

and historical and yet also vertical and ontological, true to its roots in the works of the Cambridge Platonists yet radically historicized by Edwards's philosophy of history. This makes the image and action of Christ constitutive of the sense of the heart, anticipating the Romantic theory of the religious imagination in which reason is logos echoed by the poet.

This is illustrated by Edwards's notion of the saint as the personation of Christ or of the regenerate soul as "symphonizing" with Christ.[10] Typological language suggests both the telos of fulfillment historically and cosmically in such a way that opposition does not dissolve into an onto-theological center, but so as to suggest the death and resurrection of human creative habitation within a fluctuating reality, the push and pull of past and future. Ezekiel's vision that the spirit is in the wheels means that the wheel figures, disfigures, etches yet empties itself as it proceeds.

For Edwards, then, the saint is a student of the pragmatic poetry of Christ that is divine excellence. The saint studies and practices the self and its fluctuating dispositions in order to tease out the practice of charity in the community. This poetic excellence, "charity in the making," involves the ability to bring radically disparate elements together in such a way as to form complex relational patterns that serve as termini of inclusion, affirmation, and love. Edwards's sermon "The Excellency of Christ" is a lesson in living out the union of diverse opposites, a mystical marriage symbolically representative of the enriched empiricism of Edwards's philosophy of excellence.

"The Excellency of Christ" is one of Edwards's great artistic achievements, and a lesson in lifting up the divinity in other persons that aspires to a new heaven and new earth of peaceful repose. Like his famous sermons, "God Glorified in Man's Dependence" and "Sinners in the Hands of an Angry God," Edwards employs unusually powerful psychological techniques that make reality palpable to the listener. The editors of *The Sermons of Jonathan Edwards* observe,

> Edwards employed a radical rhetoric that suggests that he should be placed within a tradition of Christian writers generally identified as "metaphysical." . . . The literary preoccupation with capturing spiritual experiences in all their passionate intensity, representing *the spiritual* in concrete language implying an almost physical tangibility, distinguishes Edwards's homiletics. Edwards thus belongs to the international coterie of preachers and poets that includes the seventeenth-century John Donne and George Herbert, as well as Edwards's near contemporary Edward Taylor, though unlike Taylor's, Edwards's technique does not hearken back to an earlier age so much as extend the approach into a new dimension of psychological realism in religious rhetoric.[11]

Edwards's rhetoric of psychological realism takes the form of language vividly sensational and philosophically and theologically paradoxical such that the mind of the congregant must break from normal conventions and assumptions. Contingency, oppositionalism, the piling up of conjunctions of images, all function to break normative frames of orientation and to draw the reader into an infinite Creation in which humanly constructed systems of belief and custom are relativized by the vastness, complexity, and contingency of the universe. As Edwards writes in *Miscellany #42*, "Man is chilled by the vast idea."[12]

In "The Excellency of Christ," Edwards appeals to the listener by showing the diverse proportionality of Christ's excellencies. This demonstration attempts to welcome the congregant into a friendship with "a person of great dignity,"[13] and thus to lead her towards salvation in a way that Edwards makes appear easy and "wonderful."[14]

The conjunction of opposites structures the sermon such that the diverse excellencies of Christ suggest an intensely dynamic and processive path to follow, and not the stopping point that is sometimes claimed of the reconciliation of opposites. In this sense, Edwards's enriched empiricism, as it partakes of the model of Christ, expresses the unifying power of the consenting heart in a way that anticipates the use of oppositional conjunctions and the description of the imagination by William Blake and by Coleridge. James Engell writes, "Jesus becomes the Logos, the act of love incarnate, and for Blake, as for Coleridge and Schelling, Jesus is the imagination in divine-human form. . . . Jesus and the love that is Jesus become, for Blake, the imaginative connection of the 'One and the all'."[15] For Edwards, "The Excellency of Christ" speaks to the erasure of subject and object as substantives, and the fluid motion between the most diverse and disparate elements of reality illustrated by the agency of Christ and, to a far lesser sense, of the saint. Thus selfhood is normatively liminal, and consciousness a society of resonating feeling active in a malleable reality.

The text for Edwards's sermon is Revelation 5:5-6, but Edwards's primary use of verse is to employ the images of lion and lamb as representative of the oppositional dynamic present within Christ as diverse excellencies.[16] Edwards's premise or doctrine is "*There is an admirable conjunction of diverse excellencies in Jesus Christ*," and from this premise Edwards demonstrates these diversities, and how these manifest themselves in "Christ's acts." This is a sermon that seeks to apply these arguments to the life of the faithful. Edwards's emphasis on consenting agency is of paramount importance in his lesson.

Edwards's demonstration of Christ's excellence focuses upon the adjective "diverse." The emphasis placed on diversity speaks to the complex relational matrix that defines Being in General, of which Christ is the human paradigm. These are, Edwards tells us, "diverse from one another," and "otherwise would have seemed to us utterly incompatible in the same subject." And the beauty within this personage is that these diverse excellencies "are exercised in him towards men." These are excellencies that entail the various ways in which the divine has reached out to human beings so as to include even the most marginalized of persons in the fullness of Being in General. Edwards's social consciousness is intensely present, as he teaches lessons akin to those of the

Sermon on the Mount to his parishioners, who are given to stingy self-interestedness. He writes, employing a catalogue of scriptural texts for support,

> None are so low, or inferior, but Christ's condescension is sufficient to take gracious notice of them. . . . He condescends to such poor creatures as men; and that not only so as to take notice of princes and great men, but of those that are of meanest rank and degree, "the poor of the world" (Jas. 2:5). Such as are commonly despised by their fellow creatures, Christ does not despise. I Cor. 1:28, "Base things of the world, and things that are despised, hath God chosen." Christ condescends to take notice of beggars (Luke 16:22), and of servants, and of people of the most despised nations. . . . Yea, which is much more, his condescension is sufficient to take a gracious notice of the most unworthy, sinful creatures, those that have no good deservings, and those that have infinite ill deservings.[16]

Edwards reaches out to the diversity of spiritual experience within the congregation. He makes clear that Christ seeks to unite with them in spiritual marriage, and even was willing "to yield up himself to an ignominious death" for the "despicable and unworthy." The return of the repentant sinner to relation with God as Being in General is an act in which the glory of the Creation grows in the only way that it can. As Elisa New observes,

> Edwards makes the affective capacity of the human being—its relational aptitude (for love, hate, desire, awe et cetera)—the seat of what liberty we have. Not prior to these affections but rooted in them, the will's very freedom is paradoxically, but not illogically, located in its *susceptibility*. Thus it is no wonder that sin and its concomitant state of unregeneracy should typically be expressed in rebelliousness (and damned by it) since God's manifest face is attractiveness. Simply put: when God's Being is concatenate relation, true freedom can be nothing but consent to that relation.[17]

From this level of utter tragedy in the crucifixion, Edwards moves to a moment of unexpected levity, suggesting the resurrection of Christ and its correspondence to the comedic or redemptive. And Edwards does so in such a way as to lampoon the wealthy members of Northampton and to show his common touch with the average person. As in sermons such as "Sinners in the Hands of an Angry God" and "God Glorified in Man's Dependence," Edwards makes contingency the equalizer of all persons. Noting the admirable qualities of humility and condescension in such a supreme being, Edwards writes from ministerial experience:

> We see by manifold instances, what a tendency an (sic) high station has in men, to make them to be of quite contrary disposition. If one worm be a little exalted above another, by having more dust, or a bigger dunghill, how much does he make of himself? What a distance

does he keep from those that are below him! And a little condescension, is what he expects should be made much of, and greatly acknowledged. Christ condescends to wash our feet; but how would great men (or the bigger worms), account themselves debased by acts of far less condescension![18]

The facets of Christ's excellencies incorporate a complex proportionality of conjunctive oppositions that energize the dynamic process of benevolent consent in those who imitate it through the demand that one envision the fluid relationality between intelligential beings. Among these oppositions are infinite justice and infinite grace; and the seemingly incompatible oppositions of infinite glory and lowest humility, and of infinite majesty and transcendent meekness. The concatenation of conjunctions present within "The Excellency of Christ" recalls the conjunction of opposites present in Edwards's *Personal Narrative*, where his spiritual experiences come with the transformation of the heart and the reinterpretation of God, the Bible, and nature. Both pieces were written between 1738 and 1740, and thus complement each other in a powerful way as a method of instruction for a community still reeling from the confusion of enthusiasm and despair present in revivalism.

One of the most striking conjunctions in the *Personal Narrative* is that of majesty and meekness, which seemingly traverses the cosmos to suggest that weakness is strength, affirmation of the other an empowering act resonating to the good of all. The quality of transcendent meekness stands forth as a particularly powerful instrument for the saint to put into practice. Edwards notes,

> Meekness . . . is a virtue proper only to the creature. . . . thereby seems to be signified, a calmness and quietness of spirit arising from humility, in mutable beings, that are naturally liable to be put in a ruffle, by the assaults of a tempestuous and injurious world. . . . For there never was such an instance seen on earth of a meek behavior, under injuries and reproaches, and towards enemies; who when he was reviled, reviled not again; who was of a wonderful spirit of forgiveness, was ready to forgive his worst enemies, and prayed for them with fervent and effectual prayers.[19]

This passage reveals the depth of the philosophy of excellence because the quality of transcendent meekness suggests the divine power to be found in disinterested moral action. It is "a virtue proper only to the creature" because its ultimate power lies in giving up one's life for the other, and only the fallen human being can experience death. Transcendent meekness teaches the human how to practice dissent and resistance, and to forgive for atrocities, helping to establish a culture in which the language of reconciliation reigns.

Transcendent meekness expresses the heart's capacity to practice a type of negative capability inspired by the kenosis of Christ in which the paradox of absence instantiates sacred presence as agapic love: this is how meekness transcends. The paradoxical demand is that, in order to be fully alive one must embrace kenosis, and the pain of self-emptying experienced by the person suffering religious melancholy or godly sorrow (Edwards) or the divided self or the sick soul (James). Full engagement with the world of experience requires a dying to the self akin to agonistic or strenuous effort that makes liminality essential to the future development of charitable community. Such transcendent meekness suggests the type of affirmative augmentation of the neighbor that defines benevolence to being, which enriches the symmetry of the community in its teeming, transitional dynamic.

Particularly intriguing here is the role that prayer plays in the practice of transcendent meekness. The ability to forgive and to create reconciliation is intimately related to the power of prayer. Prayer functions as a communication with the holy such that the self is empowered to become ever more meek, creating a space for the other to emerge from shame and a sense of sinfulness so as to enter into relationship as a fully human person. Edwards's recommendation of prayer would be heartily approved by James, who writes in *The Varieties*,

> If we take (Prayer) in the wider sense as meaning every kind of inward communion or conversation with the power recognized as divine, we can easily see that scientific criticism leaves it untouched. Prayer in this very wide sense is the very soul and essence of religion.[20]

Christ embodies a divine dignity that enables benevolent action towards the very lowest creatures. Such dignity is best expressed through agonistic suffering, the strenuous mood that transforms the very language of man with the language of grace:

> The weapon with which Christ warred against the devil, and obtained a most complete victory and glorious triumph over him, was the cross, the instrument and weapon with which he thought he had overthrown Christ, and brought on him shameful destruction. Col. 2:14-15, "Blotting out the handwriting of ordinances . . . nailing it to his cross; and having spoiled principalities and powers, he made a show of them openly, triumphing over them in it."[21]

The idea that suffering changes language is at the very center of the rhetorical strategies that Edwards and James each employ. The economies of faith that embrace certainty, conformity, preparationism, retrospection, nationalism, or other closed systems of custom and tradition, structure reality through the inscription of ordinances, laws, and principles as fixed entities of social control. Because experiential religion breaks down the normative structures of the self, and expands the self in relation to Being in General or a wider spiritual environment, it erases the symbolic structures defining the self, and reinscribes the images and symbols by which one views reality.

For Edwards this means that the life of the saint is concerned with learning how to read the language of grace within the cosmos. For James this means embracing a process of thinking and a use of language that is as metaphorical or vehicular as possible in order to stream forward intensively into the world of experience. This is harmonious with Coleridge's use of his notion that the imagination dissolves and dissipates percepts in order to unify and reconcile. This is a circumscription or circumnavigation of reality that embraces the process of "knowledge by acquaintance" and "knowledge about," and that Coleridge understands in terms of the centrifugal and centripetal motion of the imagination.

Edwards details numerous facets of Christ's diverse excellencies such that the listener becomes overwhelmed with the complex relational dynamics of charity present within the character and actions of Jesus as the Christ. This represents the intensified spiritual beauty available through "closing with Christ" and receiving a renewed heart, and it immerses the listener in a world of complex and dynamic relationality without end. The key to Edwards's imaginative display of the excellencies of Christ is that the apprehension of such complex beauty has a profound transformative power that drives the person into engagement with Being in General such that the world unfurls in relational possibility on an exponential level. And in this double-barreled, germinative rhythm of becoming modeled by Christ, the operative element of conjunction is wonder.[22]

In some sense, wonder becomes the method of excellency, as it drives both an amazed apprehension and a mysterious and awe-filled approach to the overwhelmingly rich reality that Edwards describes. He builds his application of the sermon's lesson upon the desire for closing with Christ that appears so easy to do because the utter attractiveness of these conjunctions of excellence make the argument self-evident. In Christ there exists the most complex and beautiful mosaic of relations whose invisible connections remake a despairing world. Edwards describes the idea of the marriage of Christ with the believer as a "spiritual union, so close as to be fitly represented by the union of the wife to the husband, of the branch to the vine, of the member to the head, yea, so as to be one, and to be called one spirit."[23]

The question remains as to how the person can receive the sanctification of the heart, the new sense enabling the engagement with wonder. Edwards envisions this as the benevolent action of being affirmed through acts of charity. But the sermon "The Excellency of Christ" offers a way to approach such charitable action through the appreciation of the stark oppositions present within reality and the ways in which Christ acted to overcome them. The dualism of the created order may be reconciled by the capacity to read the images and shadows that exist in God's other book, Nature, and to act through the circulating powers of the heart to overcome alienation through disinterested and virtuous consent, making a democratic space for the other to enter and engage. The marriage metaphor suggests that the union is of the one and the many, and the humility and transcendent meekness shown by Christ illustrates the way in which such social space is cleared. The concatenated conjunctions of Christ's excellence suggest an ongoing process of instilling charity into the world as a dynamic process that radiates to God and other persons so as to build up a cosmos-wide community of consent. The saint, as a student of the poetry of the excellence of Christ, embodies pragmatic poetics herself, bending the heart to the work of remaking the world through charitable action that communicates the language of grace.

This is illustrated by the life of the saint. The saint "personates" Christ. Edwards describes the saintly life by building up descriptive phrases that illustrate the organic quality of his vision through biblical metaphors combining natural images and spiritual activity. These phrases underscore the capacity of language to advance human insight ontologically, historically, and socially:

> So the saints are said to live by Christ living in them (Gal. 2:20). Christ by his spirit not only is in them, but lives in them; and so that they live by his life; so is his Spirit united to them, as a principle of life in them; they don't only drink living water, but this living water becomes a well or fountain of water in the soul, springing up into spiritual and everlasting life (John 4:14), and thus becomes a principle of life in them; this living water, this Evangelist himself explains to intend the Spirit of God (ch. 7:38-7:39). The light of the Sun of Righteousness don't only shine upon them, but is so communicated to them that they shine also, and become little images of that Sun which shines upon them; the sap of the true vine is not only conveyed into them, as the sap of a tree may be conveyed into a vessel, but is conveyed as sap is from a tree into one of its living branches, where it becomes a principle of life.[24]

The saint, through the activity of the heart, embodies a principle of being able to engage with the complex system of relations that defines Being in General, though in an incomplete and imperfect way susceptible to backsliding. As a personation of Christ, the saint is an image for others to learn from, and part of that lesson is reading the shadows of divine presence so as to engage and fulfill them as images or actual ideas reverberating to make an enriched creation. Learning the poetry of excellence demands involvement in the ongoing process defined by image and shadow, actuality and potentiality, that makes for a strenuous faith.

Thus the excellence of Christ demonstrates the activity of conjoining diverse and perhaps unimaginable opposites together so as to amplify being itself. Such an action is an expression of grace that reflects rays, or transitional potentialities, to various ranges of experience. Grace is, if nothing else, a dynamic principle that ends in practice in the community, and therefore exists as the only viable sign of truly holy affections:

> True grace is not an unactive thing; there is nothing in heaven or earth of a more active nature; for 'tis life itself, and the most active kind of life, even spiritual and divine life.... There is nothing in the universe that in its nature has a greater tendency to fruit. Godliness in the heart has as direct a relation to practice, as a fountain has to a

stream, or as the luminous nature of the sun has beams sent forth, or as life has to breathing, or the beating of the pulse, or any other vital act; or as a habit or principle of action has to action; for 'tis a principle of holy action or practice. Regeneration, which is that work of God in which grace is infused, has a direct relation to practice; for 'tis the very end of it.[25]

The difficult verification of claims to religious affections resides in the problematic structures engendered by conceptual knowledge. As Edwards and James agree, the process of truth verification is very often assumed rather than carried out through the rigor of trial. It is very easy to inset personal experience into the matrix of normative assumptions and beliefs so as to claim such experience as verified because it fits into this web of custom and authority. This is a problem seen in a person's verbal assertion of election to claim a status through seemingly compelling evidence that is assented to by other members of the community without experiential verification. Such acclamation manifests a reassertion of the protective cocoon of certainty and control that makes much of social life comfortable, but that may mistake fevered imaginings or imposture for true grace.

Edwards notes that such claims to certainty mark the legal and evangelical hypocrite. Of the two, Edwards finds the evangelical hypocrite far more dangerous:

> The latter are commonly by far the most confident in their hope, and with the most difficulty brought from it: I have scarcely known the instance of such an one, in my life, that has been undeceived. The chief grounds of the confidence of many of them, are the very same kind of impulses and supposed revelations (sometimes with texts of scripture, and sometimes without), that so many of late have had concerning future events; calling these impulses about their good estate, the witness of the Spirit; entirely misunderstanding the witness of the Spirit.[26]

The evangelical hypocrite wounds revivalism in a variety of ways: he misleads other seekers, arouses delusions and hysteria in the community, and provides fodder for rationalist critics of revivalism. The pragmatic poetics of the saint, when strenuously active in the community, presents an entirely different model of Christian practice.

Saintliness is ultimately unknowable to the saint herself. However, the action of charity in the community may be the most reliable sign that someone is a saint. Edwards also sees that the saint is notable for earnestness in seeking God:

> There is an end to many persons' earnestness in seeking, after they have once obtained that which they call their conversion; or at least, after they have had those high affections, that make them fully confident of it. . . . The holy principles that actuate a true saint have a

> far more powerful influence to stir him up to earnestness in seeking God and holiness, than servile fear. Hence seeking God is spoken of as one of the distinguishing characters of the saints . . . the Scriptures everywhere represent the seeking, striving, and labor of a Christian, as being chiefly after his conversion, and his conversion as being but the beginning of his work. And almost all that is said in the New Testament of men's watching, giving earnest heed to themselves, running the race that is set before them, striving and agonizing, wrestling not with flesh and blood, but principalities and powers, fighting, putting on the whole armor of God, and standing, having done all to stand, and pressing forward, reaching forth, continuing instant in prayer, crying to God day and night . . . is spoken of, and directed to the saints.[27]

Edwards sees the Christian life as one of spiritual warfare, its weapons similar to those of Christ's diverse conjunctions carried out in earnest effort. He writes, "The kingdom of heaven is not to be taken but by violence. . . . Without a constant laboriousness, there is no stemming the swift stream in which we swim, so as ever to come to that fountain of water of life, that is at the head of it."[28] Receptive to difference and conflict in making a charitable and democratic community, the saint ever hopes for the mutual possession that affirms and advances Being in General.

Mysticism and the Strenuous Mood

The model of Christian warfare that Edwards employs finds an analogue in James's notion of "the moral equivalent of war." James writes of the demand for a fight against the mechanistic elements of nature so as to erase inequality: "That so many men, by mere accidents of birth and opportunity, should have a life of *nothing else* but toil and pain and hardness and inferiority imposed upon them, should have *no* vacation, while others natively no more deserving get no taste of this campaigning life at all – *this* is capable of arousing indignation in reflective minds."[29]

The moral equivalent of war is action within the stream of experience to stem the tide of violence and injustice that emerges from the evolutionary process. For James, to be fully human is to transcend, and thus transform, the Darwinian struggle, thus replacing it with a struggle for humanity. The most powerful force driving such transcendence of one's own animal nature and brute competitive drive is experiential religion, and it is through experiential religion that James, like Edwards, sees the human agent engage reality with freedom and compassion. Not surprisingly, James finds Puritanism to be a model for what he calls in "The Moral Philosopher and the Moral Life" the strenuous mood:

> The capacity for the strenuous mood probably lies slumbering in every man, but it has more difficulty in some than in others in waking up. It needs the wilder passions to arouse it, the big fears, loves, and indignations; or else the deeply penetrating appeal of some one of the higher fidelities, like justice, truth, or freedom. . . . All through history, in the periodical conflicts of puritanism with the don't-care temper, we see the antagonism of the strenuous and genial moods, and the contrast between the ethics of infinite and mysterious obligation from on high, and those of prudence and the satisfaction of merely finite need. . . . The capacity of the strenuous mood lies so deep down among our natural human possibilities that even if there were no metaphysical or traditional grounds for believing in a God, men would postulate one. . . . Our attitude towards concrete evils is entirely different in a world where we believe there are none but finite demanders, from what it is in one we joyously face tragedy for an infinite demander's sake. Every sort of energy and endurance, of courage and capacity for handling life's evils, is set free in those who have religious faith. For this reason the strenuous type of character will on the battlefield of human history always outwear the easy-going type, and religion will drive irreligion to the wall.[30]

The essay "On a Certain Blindness in Human Beings" portrays the poet or prophet capable of awakening the torpor of normative existence. It was intended as a popular lecture addressed to college students, but it carries the weight of William James's most deeply cherished beliefs and ideas:

> It is more than the mere piece of sentimentalism which it may seem to some readers. It connects itself with a definite view of the world and of our moral relations to the same. Those who have done me the honor of reading my volume of philosophic essays will recognize that I mean the pluralistic or individualistic philosophy. According to that philosophy, the truth is too great for any one actual mind, even though that mind be dubbed 'the Absolute,' to know the whole of it. The facts and worths of life need many cognizers to take them in. There is no point of view absolutely public and universal. Private and uncommunicable perceptions always remain over, and the worst of it is that those who look for them from the outside never know *where*.[31]

In the essay, James describes the human desire for conceptual certainty with the traditional image of blindness, which he sees profoundly affecting the structures of knowledge and the moral life. The blindness that characterizes human beings is caused by both the necessary phenomenon of conceptual thinking and the reliance upon established fact and custom that ironically cuts one off from the very world of experience that such conceptualism seeks to negotiate.

Such a constructed separation from experience, resulting from the process of conceptualization, is another instance of James's two-fold theory of knowledge. The limitations of individual lives and the circumscribed territory in which most persons live out their daily dramas vitiates the capacity to apprehend reality in a sphere wider than one's own, and makes second-hand conceptualism the major focus of attention. The human community deteriorates due to the inability of persons to attend to, and empathize with, voices and visions divergent from their own.

James supports the importance of the cognitive value of feeling for the moral life and the fundamental importance of individual creativity for the life of the human community and the advancement of truth as a species of good on which it depends. While James's posture frequently presents an intensified support of the feeling apprehended through "knowledge by acquaintance," his seeming imbalance in favor of affectional facts is an illusion created as a part of his rhetorical strategy. Feeling without subjection to practical verification and the salting-down of valuable and novel discoveries and insights makes "knowledge by acquaintance" mere subjectivism of no pragmatic value.

Citing Wordsworth, Stevenson, Tolstoy, Whitman, and Emerson, among others, James makes a strong appeal for the primary value of "pure sensorial perception" and "the mystic sense of hidden meaning," as aspects of human personality and cognition that restores vision or insight necessary for the moral life to grasp the full implications of action within a dynamic, unfinished, and pluralistic universe. Only with awakening to what James calls "the vast world of inner life beyond us" is the possibility of creative and responsible engagement with reality, understood as a complex fabric of relations, possible. James finds the recovery of vision to be intimately tied to the perception of beauty in an overwhelmingly rich world of experience, a perception that can remake the self and motivate a more profound moral life. Such beauty is synonymous with James's pragmatic concept of truth as a species of good, for it must enter into the stream of experience and the process of verification that is communal.

In various points in his writing, James repeats the belief that poetry and art exist as constructions of mystical experience. Central to this restoration of the living world of dynamic activity is the poet, prophet, or genius able to charge language with the power to break the world constructed by "rational proposition." This reinstatement of the vague is particularly powerful as a means of creating the space where "life continuous with our own" can enter and create amplifying relationship. The vague helps us to tune the mind aright.

In particular, James names Whitman as "a contemporary prophet," and cites the poet's "Crossing Brooklyn Ferry" at length. Whitman's democratic pluralism offers a vista of the dynamic and complex network of relations that informs the synonymy of aesthetics and ethics that James embraces. Such synonymy is essential to the morally creative engagement with reality of radical empiricism. For James, pragmatist aesthetics are one with the moral life. His valuation of poetic insight exemplifies a model of the pragmatist imagination, and is a heuristic device supportive of the pluralistic vision of reality that he developed as his philosophy of radical empiricism. It illustrates how the individual and the world of experience interact so as to add to the concatenated layering of relations that thicken and build out piecemeal salvation.

The problem that James confronts in addressing the blindness of certainty is that such blindness describes how the world is shaped so as to aid survival and protect the human from the chaos of reality. James writes,

> We are practical beings, each of us with limited functions and duties to perform. Each is bound to feel intensely the importance of his own duties and the significance of the situations that call these forth. But this feeling is in each of us a vital secret, for sympathy with which we vainly look to others—the others are too much absorbed in their own vital secrets to take an interest in ours. Hence the stupidity and injustice of our opinions, so far as they deal with the significance of alien lives. Hence the falsity of our judgments, so far as they presume to decide in an absolute way on the value of other persons' conditions or ideals.[32]

James paints a picture of a world of alienation in which the values and beliefs of fellow humans remain private when they should be brought into common conversation, and tested for their value as vessels of meaning. To be a spectator is "to miss the root of the matter and to possess no truth."[33] To focus only upon one's own duties, one's own joy, is a type of sin for James, a hardening of the heart towards the complex joy lying beneath the surface of things:

> Our deadness towards all but one particular kind of joy would thus be the price we inevitably have to pay for being practical creatures. Only in some pitiful dreamer, some philosopher, poet, or romancer, or when the common practical man becomes a lover, does the hard externality give way, and a gleam of insight into . . . the vast world of inner life beyond us, so different from that of outer seeming, illuminate our mind. Then the whole scheme of our customary values get confounded, then our self is riven and its narrow interests fly to pieces, then a new centre and a new perspective must be found.[34]

The singular joy or delight of the self-interested individual is transformed by a love that illuminates "the vast world of inner life beyond us." The restricted boundaries of the self are broken by the relational power of transformative love; the breaking of the self, with its personal values, follows, and transformation is set in motion. James anticipates the famous analysis of conversion in *The Varieties* with this passage's last sentence: ". . . our customary values get confounded . . . our self is riven . . . narrow interests fly to pieces . . . a new centre and a new perspective must be found." It is as if James anticipates his lectures on the healthy-minded, the sick soul, and conversion in this brief talk.

James does not arrive at a discussion of the wider self in "A Certain Blindness." James is less psychological and more evocative in his appeal to the hearts of his listeners. Like conversion,

> This higher vision of an inner significance . . . often comes over a person suddenly; and when it does so, it makes an epoch in his history. As Emerson says, there is a depth in those moments that constrains us to ascribe more reality to them than to all other experiences. The passion of love will shake one like an explosion, or some act will awaken a remorseful compunction that hangs like a cloud over all one's later day.[35]

James finds affinity with Edwards in his estimation that the beauty of nature is one of the most powerful instigators of the awakening of vision: "this mystic sense of hidden meaning starts upon us often from non-human natural things."[36] James gives illustrations to the audience "of this sense of a limitless significance in natural things. Just what this hidden presence in Nature was . . . the poet never could explain logically or in articulate conceptions."[37] James, however, offers an indirect and vague cue to which the reader can turn, and it is in the direction of an emptying of self-interest in the desire for the self-fulfillment experienced in a plunge into the divine:

> So blind and dead does the clamor of our own practical interests make us to all other things, that it seems almost as if it were necessary to become worthless as a practical being, if one is to hope to attain any breadth of insight into the impersonal world of worths as such, to have any perception of life's meaning on a large objective scale. Only your mystic, your dreamer, or your insolvent tramp or loafer, can afford so sympathetic an occupation, an occupation which will change the usual standards of human values in the twinkling of an eye, giving to foolishness a place ahead of power, and laying low in a minute the distinctions which it takes a hard-working conventional man a lifetime to build up.[38]

James points his audience to the value of disinterest that is a type of negative capability that delights in the various beauties of experience, and which is akin to Edwards's concept of true virtue as benevolent consent. Defining the mystic, the tramp, and the loafer (lover) in terms of images traditionally applied to Christ, James recommends a life of Christ-like vision to his audience, though in terms both vague and indirect. But what is most intriguing is that James employs the diverse conjunction of oppositions suggested by the model of Jesus as outsider. Worthlessness as a practical being is, in fact, supremely pragmatic for James, at least in terms of advancing the complex beauty of the experiential matrix. The mystic sense of hidden meaning overturns normative standards, as foolishness takes priority over power, and all normal distinctions of class, race, and profession are erased. This is why the homeless tramp, the mystic, prophet, or fool is the human embodiment of James's metaphysics of experience, which might also be seen as a metaphysics of homelessness:

> Truth grows up inside of all the finite experiences. They lean on each other, but the whole of them, if such a whole there be, leans on

nothing. All 'homes' are finite experience; finite experience as such is homeless. Nothing outside of the flux secures the issue of it. It can hope for salvation only from its own intrinsic promises and potencies. To rationalists, this describes a tramp and vagrant world, adrift in space, with neither elephant or tortoise to plant the sole of its foot upon. It is a set of stars hurled into heaven without even a centre of gravity to pull against.[39]

The key to escaping the deadness of practical life is to become "some pitiful dreamer, some philosopher, poet, or romancer" exulting in "a tramp and vagrant world" not by romanticizing suffering and tragedy, but by recognizing that truth and compassion are available through life understood as pilgrimage. The illumination that the liminal personality receives comes from a wider spiritual environment suggested in *The Varieties* and *A Pluralistic Universe*. Love is present in the relationality that breaks down the boundaries of normative ordinances. Such relationality is achieved through the act of love within the circling of the imagination out into a world of risk. Vagueness is a key to James's thought here also, for he neither wants to define theologically the depths of vision he points towards, nor does he want to build conceptions that will further barricade the reader behind socially sanctioned second-hand conception. Vagueness and indirection are pivotal dynamics within his rhetoric that seek to respect the individual creativity of the listener while also persuading her to turn to experience with her own ideas and values.

The major figure in James's catalogue of the outsider and the tramp is the poet. For Emerson, Jesus is a type of poet, a sayer of symbols, of living words that draw the reader into the engagement with reality that demands that he, too, become a poet remaking the world in his individual contributions of insight and novelty. For James, as for Emerson, Whitman best exemplifies the "American Bard" as a holy tramp, a type of Christ, bringing forth living and prophetic words suggestive of the overflowing world of experience. James embraces Whitman as "a contemporary prophet" in accord with James's definition of the prophet as a realist of distances reversing high and low and foolishness and power in a way similar to Edwards's notion of the excellence of Christ.[40]

This becomes particularly clear in James's choice to interpret Whitman's poetry to make his point. Given James's practical philosophical concern for those persons marginalized by the systematic philosophy of his colleagues, his own poetic taste evolves from vision garnered through nature to the illumination offered by the crowd. He notes that Whitman "felt the human crowd as rapturously as Wordsworth felt the mountains, felt it as an overpoweringly significant presence, simply to absorb one's mind in which should be business sufficient and worthy to fill the days of a serious man."

James embraces the figure and poetry of Whitman because,

> He abolishes the usual human distinctions, brings all conventionalisms into solution, and loves and celebrates hardly any human attributes save those elementary ones common to all members

of the race. For this he becomes a sort of ideal tramp, a rider on
omnibus-tops and ferry-boats, and, considered either practically or
academically, a worthless unproductive human being.[41]

The poet exemplifies the pragmatic focus upon the building-out of the malleable universe envisioned by James's radical empiricism, and here recalls James's appreciation of Whitman in "Pragmatism and Religion." And because he exists as a marginalized person, the poet as ideal tramp presents the reader with the democratic demand of inclusive conversation and consensus decision-making as part of the workshop of *democratic* being. James employs the image and person of Whitman to inculcate the political meaning of radical empiricism into his address. James Livingston writes,

> James uses metaphors of unemployment (the tramp, the loafer, the worthless practical being) to convey the contingent character of selfhood and consciousness. James invokes Whitman to illustrate his argument, and does so in a way that precludes the possibility of withdrawal from the phenomenally commercial world in the name of the truth or the integrity of the self. . . . (James) is drawing upon this popular figure ("your insolvent tramp") of the late nineteenth-century American imagination. . . . He was the workingman disinherited by capital; in the rhetoric of the social sciences, he was the collective savage, the tool of the demagogue. . . . What makes Whitman dangerous in a civilization devoted to the expansion of socially necessary labor is what makes him useful, and delightful, to James.[42]

James sees the holy tramp as a type of Christ who expresses the transcendent meekness that allows a fluidity of self and other, of idea and thing. The image manifests the width and thickness of the world of experience, James's radical empiricism, which challenges the deterministic systems in which freedom dissipates. Thus does James critically address corporate capitalism's frequent abuse of the workingman, as seen in the example of Corcoran in the first lecture of *Pragmatism*.[43] Whitman illustrates the fluid continuity between all beings and things with the image of the tramp's boundary-less existence that makes a democratic space for all. In this sense he is a living embodiment of James's metaphysics of experience in which "things are given as continuously joined." The ties between poet and reader are unraveled and rewoven through the concatenation of relationships into which the poet enters with a malleability heretofore unimagined. This creates a benevolent and delightful consent that anticipates and makes possible James's notion of intimacy as a compenetration and suffusion of "each other's being."[44]

In *A Pluralistic Universe* James expands upon this notion of compenetration or suffusion in which one shades into another, describing relation among the many:

> The difference between living against a background of foreignness and one of intimacy means the difference between a general habit of wariness and one of trust. One might call it a social difference, for after all, the common *socius* of us all is the great universe whose children we are. If materialistic, we must be suspicious of this socius, cautious, tense, on guard. If spiritualistic, we may give way, embrace, and keep no ultimate fear.[45]

Whitman is the great American poet of democracy because he is the great poet of intimacy. To immerse the reader in his vision of the pragmatist imagination's remaking of the world of experience, James inserts the first three of the nine cantos of "Crossing Brooklyn Ferry" and a letter of Whitman's exultation of the spectacle of life from the top of an omnibus, in "A Certain Blindness."[46] Whitman's 1856 poem "Crossing Brooklyn Ferry," originally titled "Sun-Down Poem," brings together the most disparate elements of the world of experience to convey knowledge "fully round" in the "living moment," the full facticity of the additive relational vagueness of experience that James so deeply cherishes as a model of a pluralistic universe based on trust and intimacy. Whitman achieves such a vision by piling up diverse conjunctions of persons, space, and time such that the surge of human agents into the stream of experience flows out into the mother-sea of reality. The twilight theme of the poem's original title suggests that the immersive mood rests not only in the poet, but characterizes the quality of reality as well.

For the auditor, the experience of hearing James read such a large amount of Whitman has the effect of making the poet's musical and imagistic fluency expressive of the essay's polyrhythmic rhetoric and intent that reflects its pluralistic inclusiveness. The beauty of the visionary qualities that James wishes to bring to the reader—the mystic sense—carries with it a moral destiny in the democratic engagement with the crowd that Whitman shares. The poem's setting is the liminal landscape of the "flood-tide" at dusk, as the poet, watching "face to face" in direct apprehension of the living reality, sees the crowds, "the hundreds and hundreds that cross, returning home." This crossing is both a daily event and the process of human life as it crosses over the river to an eternal home. Whitman expands the present moment into an unending future of human activity: "And you that shall cross from shore to shore years hence, are more to me, and more in my meditations, than you might suppose."

The complex plurality of the human crowd points to the future observations of other beings, and integrates within the thick world of experience the widest range of otherness. Whitman intones the incantatory word "others" as the subject of the next four lines. These others are projected into the future to experience the same living moment of the integration of the one and the many; all will cross at twilight, fifty years, a hundred years, "ever so many hundred years hence." The poet thus suggests the compression of the infinite in the finite that defines the living moment of intimate immersion in the stream of experience: "it avails not, neither time or place—distance avails not." The poet and the reader, the living and the dead, the individual and the wider environment suffuse each other's being in the differentiated solidarity of the one and the many as common travelers seeking to return to a home to which they have contributed their unique part.

The poet's vision of democratic beauty carries a powerful moral force of mutually consenting beings passing through life, sharing the diverse expressions of vital experience: "These, and all else, were to me the same as they are to you." The identity the poet revisits in the poem is the complex unity of being that underlies the possibility and vitality of the phenomenal world. This experience is of transition and relation that makes and remakes individual and communal life from the myriad opportunities present in such a world.

The act of crossing, the experience of the liminal, and the real loss and gain that defines it, of knowledge by acquaintance and conceptual knowledge that parallel the processive flow of the stream of experience, is the true reality available to all. But those willing to abandon or suspend the practical life in order to pay heed to the mystic sense of hidden meaning and the holiness discovered by the continual bending of the self to the world are perhaps the only ones to witness it. Human beings resist the truth James invokes; through building practical lives that secure them against the dangers of life, they are blinded to the intimacy of reality. Thus the practical man barricades himself in custom and tradition to preserve life, but in actuality creates a thinner life of paltry empiricism.

Whitman indicates that the holy tramp prophesies through the act of imagination, which is symbolized in the circling of the gulls. Recalling the blessed albatross of Coleridge's *Rime*, seeing for Whitman comes in learning from the gulls

> I watched the Twelfth-month sea-gulls—I saw them high in the air,
>   Floating with motionless wings, oscillating their bodies,
> I saw how the glistening yellow lit up parts of their bodies, and left the Rest in strong shadow,
> I saw the slow-wheeling circles, and the gradual edging toward the south.[47]

James sees Whitman's verse as "a succession of interjections on an immense scale." These utterances draw the mind in myriad directions, breaking the normative frame of orientation through a type of linguistic crossing. This is how one looks upon the panorama of life with a redeemed vision, "face to face." Paul's image of perfected humanity as expressed in 1 Corinthians 13:12 has been realized in the poet, who sees clearly the ebb and flow of the life swirling around him through the complex patterns of nature, human history, and the crowd as they permeate the experience of the tramp.

Enveloped in "the hundreds and hundreds that cross, returning home," Whitman gives poetic voice to James's radical empiricism. Life is filled with swirling motions of human struggle and human beauty, of nature's tides and turnings, and all are imbued with feelings of the individuality of every person and everything. And each participates in the living crowd, a complex unity of individual relations, *e pluribus unum*, all expressing the dignity that defines their uniqueness. Such a dynamic representation of the world of experience is filled with the activity of crossing from shore to shore, from individuality to community, from life to death, from generation to generation, of others and others and others and others. For the poet to reach out to his subject and his audience with such intense suffusion is to perform the very action of intimacy through something similar to Christ's transcendent meekness that enables the creation of a democratic space for the other. As Kerry C. Larson reads the poem,

> Whitman is quite single-minded in his determination to erase all boundaries, to overcome all distance, to create, in effect, a space in which reader and poem are one. . . . His verse craves a "life of continuous intimacy," a "laying on of hands" whose touch can allay the terrible doubt of appearances and whose reach testifies to a longing for a deepened union with others.[48]

This is an image of diverse excellencies in which every person is potentially a personation of Christ, a poet, though this higher vision can only be achieved through a type of religious experience that invokes a laying on of hands that invokes the spirit, and thus radically reorders one's life. All of life swirls and oscillates, glistens and wheels, to the eye of the poet. Such crossing speaks to the process of life in death that reflects the world of experience. Persons, ideas, nature's beauties, all things live, die, become part of the wider world of being that James came to call the mother-sea. The poet's vision incarnates the overwhelmingly dynamic picture of James's radical empiricism, with tendency, transition, fulfillment, and termination embodied by the shimmering motions of natural, human, and material objects in a complex and dynamic pattern. Such a communion of relations expresses the fluid and overlapping beauty of life understood as simultaneously a free-floating mosaic and an ethical republic, a union of the aesthetic and the ethical in the process of making truth through actual connection.

Perry quotes James's notebooks in a passage that expresses both James's appreciation of poetic vision and his method of communicating its meaning to his audience:

> According to Bergson . . . what we conceptualize statically as a certain grammatical subject . . . is an active life exhibiting always something new, new by addition and new by default. . . . Does the "active life" character pertain also to the constitution of reality?—So that no element of it could be treated as a "piece" or stable grammatical subject . . . implying at bottom that our grammatical forms . . . are inadequate. . . . The problem is to *state* the intuitive or live constitution of it without paradox. One can do so only by approximation, awakening sympathy with it rather than assuming

logically to define it; for logic makes all things static. As living, no *it* is a stark numerical unit. They all radiate and coruscate in many directions. Be the universe as much of a unit as you like, plurality has once for all broken out within it. Effectively there are centers of reference and action . . . and these centers disperse each other's rays.[49]

"Crossing Brooklyn Ferry" is central to James's cherished argument in "A Certain Blindness in Human Beings" because it puts forth this very approximation of the world of experience. The poem enables James to portray the active life so sympathetically and in communal terms as to draw the reader into ontological wonder. Such reverie enables immersion in the pluralistic and unfinished universe that, once hidden, now mysteriously presents itself through and beneath the variety and process of daily life. And relation to the complex pattern of the consenting dynamic of such a pluralistic universe enables one to envision or imagine this reality in such a way as to engage it creatively and concentrically as a "center of reference and activity, dispersing each other's rays." Such encounter affirms and advances reality through discovery of both transition and terminus that actively builds out the universe. The selective attention that motivates engagement with the world of experience destines such action for concretion or evanescence.

For James, in the inclusion of the marginalized in the human company, the attempt to commune with their spirits or "rays" through an open embrace of the otherness that breaks in on totalizing systems of thought, vision overcomes blindness. This speaks of an experience that ranges from ontological wonder to political awareness and resistance, and constitutes "the living moments" that dramatically transform our lives. Each person has a radiating power of feeling and insight that offers amendments to the human community.

But the question remains for the reader, as for the congregant attending Edwards's delivery of "The Excellency of Christ," how does one apprehend such beauty? Whitman ends "Crossing Brooklyn Ferry" with lines anticipatory of James's notion of intimate participation in a pluralistic, panpsychic universe in which each and all democratically lend their voice and vote:

> You have waited, you always wait, you dumb, beautiful ministers,
> We receive you with free sense at last, and are insatiate henceforward,
> Not you any more shall be able to foil us, or withhold yourselves from us,
> We use you and do not cast you aside—we plant you permanently within us,
> We fathom you not—we love you—there is perfection in you also,
> You furnish your parts toward eternity, Great or small, you furnish your parts toward the soul.[50]

Whitman finds the key to engagement with the phenomenal world of "dumb, beautiful ministers" to reside in the communal "we" that is discovered "with free sense at last." Each one's actions build out the unfinished universe. The "free sense" that envisions inner significance recalls Edwards's sense of the heart and James's mystic sense that "at last" bring relief from the estrangement and torpor fostered by material determinism. It makes us "insatiate," draws us into the stream of experience from whence we never wish to return to the retrospective self "stuffed with abstract conceptions, and glib with verbalities and verbosities" in which our simpler functions often dry up, and we grow stone-blind and insensible to life's more elementary and general goods and joys."[51]

For James the means to intimacy "all depend on the capacity of the soul to be grasped, to have its life-currents absorbed by what is given."[52] Because the inherited funding of existence deadens attempts at living forward, melancholy and breakdown serve to provide the means to kenosis and the realization of meekness and humility. The result, according to Whitman, is that we do not use each other as means, but as ends: "We use you, and do not cast you aside—we plant you permanently within us." And the picture Whitman lends is fully supportive of James's notion of a salvation cooperatively realized. Each works toward the building up of eternity, "Great or small, you furnish your parts towards the soul."

Ultimately for James, the power of Whitman's vision rests in the inclusion of, and communion with, the crowd, such that democracy demands a strenuous range of moods that define the panorama of persons struggling together. This openness to the crowd, with its variety, conflict, and rich potential of relation reveals several of James's most valued ideas. The marginalized need to be included in any and all attempts to take account of experience, as James holds experience to be defined by conjunctive and disjunctive relations equally. Blindness to such disjunctions is a social habit. To achieve the inclusive vision necessary to create the intimacy productive of piecemeal salvation, experiential religion and the diversity of its expression need to be recognized as live options to which the person must be receptive. The stream of experience, once entered, inducts us into a dangerous world where creative freedom operates between the systematic constructions of absolutism and materialism to wend its way through the world.

Such transit requires the use of language, but language's danger resides in the ways in which it mimes human systems. If attentive to the flow of experience, one recognizes the necessary use of language as vehicular, transitive, and intransitive so as to be able to carry ideas into action with a sense of continuity and onrushing power of investigation and discovery. The language-user must seek the form approximating the liminal crossing of past and future, of the presence and absence of meaning, such that the person is not enmeshed in abstraction and retrospection, but is forced to plunge back into the stream. James writes,

> As long as one continues *talking*, intellectualism remains in undisturbed possession of the field. The return to life can't come about by talking. It is an *act*; to make you return to life, I must set an example for your imitation, I must deafen you to talk, or to the importance of talk, by showing you as Bergson does, that the concepts we talk with are made for purposes of *practice* and not for purposes of insight.[53]

The model for imitation for both Edwards and James is the religious genius. This type of poet demonstrates what intimacy and charity are like in a world that, without them, is broken apart into fragmented communities that by necessity construct their own economies of faith for protection and certainty. Edwards's image of Christ in "The Excellency of Christ" is of a God in human form able to bring together the most diverse and disparate features of existence. The power of conjoining diversity mimes the world as a concatenated complexity of differentiating relations mutually consenting so as to amplify Being in General, its source, sustainer, and ultimate home. This conjoining, suffusing power of the imagination informs James's notion of genius:

> Geniuses are commonly believed to excel other men in their power of sustained attention. In most of them, it is to be feared, the so-called 'power' is of the passive sort. Their ideas coruscate, every subject branches infinitely before their fertile minds, and so for hours they may be rapt. *But it is their genius making them attentive, not their attention making geniuses of them.* And when we come down to the root of the matter, we see that they differ from ordinary men less in the character of their attention than in the nature of the objects upon which it is successively bestowed. In the genius, these form a concatenated series, suggesting each other mutually by some rational law.[54]

The coruscation of Christ's excellencies, of the personating saint, disperses illuminating rays of charity to the community. Whitman in "Crossing Brooklyn Ferry" is this type of poet; he exults, "diverge, fine spokes of light, from the shape of my head, or any one's head."[55]

The visionary philosophies of Edwards and of James describe engagement with the relational matrix of reality as rigorous or agonistic. Such strenuous activity defines the language, the experience, and the life of the person so engaged with the complex and concatenated reality from which and to which the saint and the poet may bring illumination and greater justice in the ongoing play of experience. Such rigor is further complicated by struggle with the written ordinances of the various forms of limited faiths and societies funded by the past. This makes religious experience particularly important as the locus of novelty in a world assumed as fixed, regulated, known, and certain. Being's workshop thus finds its energy and materials within the experiences of connection to a wider self or spiritual environment, to an invisible world of intimate contact that seeks a democracy elusive and strenuous because in the making.

Complex Ecstasies and Democratic Expansions

In Lecture 6 of *The Varieties,* "The Sick Soul," James describes the supernaturally regenerated Christian as enjoying "complex ecstasies."[56] For James, the spiritual hydraulics inherent in the process of sanctification was in reality a matter of psychodynamic processes receptive to the possibility of wider powers supportive of human endeavor. But to James, the regenerate Christian did embrace a life of arduous struggle caught between the existential depravity of original sin and the vision of glory to be awakened in the world through acts of benevolent consent to being. This was a heroic life illustrative of James's notion of the strenuous mood that, when realized in the diverse interconnections and compenetrations of Whitman's crowd, suggests a strenuous democracy.

Such a panorama of dynamic citizenry denies the religious absolutism of Edwards's bedrock faith. However, James finds bracing the religious perspective of early New England Puritans who passionately pursued the ways of God to man through scrutiny of self and world. It is with this temper of mind that strenuous democracy may come alive. In "Pragmatism and Religion" James writes,

> Those puritans who answered 'yes' to the question: Are you willing to be damned for God's glory? were in this objective and magnanimous condition of mind. The way of escape from evil on this system is *not* by getting it 'aufgehoben,' or preserved in the whole as an element essential but 'overcome.' *It is by dropping it out altogether, throwing it overboard and getting beyond it, helping to make a universe that shall forget its very place and name.* It is then perfectly possible to accept sincerely a drastic kind of a universe from which the element of 'seriousness' is not to be expelled. Whoso does so is, it seems to me, a genuine pragmatist.[57]

The puritan who is a genuine pragmatist exhibits a mind capable of "acceptance as loss unatoned for, even tho the lost element might be one's self. . . . He is willing to live on a scheme of uncertified possibilities which he trusts; willing to pay with his own person, if need be, for the realization of the ideals which he frames."[58] The puritan takes life as a strenuous adventure that confronts evil in an unfinished and pluralistic universe. When we consider Edwards's experiences with the enthusiasms corrupting New England revivalism, and his statement in *Religious Affections* that he was taking a very unpopular position between rationalists and enthusiasts that led to an incipient pragmatism, we can only wonder if Edwards was the puritan James had in mind. James's notion of religion's value in fostering the strenuous mood ontologically productive of the unfinished universe echoes Edwards's demand for the arduous scrutiny in religious life necessary to realize God's glory in the Creation.

James's perspective suggests the creative tension of his radical empiricism: "I can believe in the ideal as an ultimate, not as an origin, and as an extract, not the whole." The dynamic pulse forward realizes "the ideals which he frames." The religious affections that James values as mankind's most important function engage the workshop of being in which fact in the making brings such affections to the world for termination or transition to "disseminated and strung-along successes." As in *The Varieties*, in *Pragmatism* James bears witness to a wider self or More that disbelieves "that our human experience is the highest form of experience extant in the universe." This wider environment functions as a creative lure forward that draws the expression, testing, and transit of religious experiences, but for the individual it does so through the practice of strenuousness.[59]

James engages Edwards in debate concerning these "complex ecstasies" in his concluding discussion of conversion in *The Varieties*, where he rejects Edwards's sharp distinction between the saint and the natural man. He writes,

> Throughout Jonathan Edwards's admirably rich and delicate description of the supernaturally infused condition, in his *Treatise on Religious Affections*, there is not one decisive trait, not one mark that unmistakably parts it off from what may possibly be only an exceptionally high degree of natural goodness. In fact, one could hardly read a clearer argument than this book unwittingly offers in favor of the thesis that no chasm exists between the orders of human excellence, but that here as elsewhere, nature shows continuous differences, and generation and regeneration are matters of degree.[60]

To James, Edwards should be more than an incipient pragmatist. He cites Edwards's own problems with the phenomena common to religious enthusiasm, those of hearing voices and seeing visions, and of turning against the unregenerate, all "counterfeited by Satan." James writes,

> The real witness of the spirit to the second birth is to be found only in the disposition of the genuine child of God, the permanently patient heart, the love of self eradicated. And this, it has to be admitted, is also found in those who pass no crisis, and may even be found outside of Christianity altogether.[61]

The erasure of self-interest that pragmatically confirms holy affections as true suggests the search for intimacy and the end of alienation that informs Edwards's notion of true virtue and James's concept of advantageous connexion that is the linchpin of his theory of truth as a species of the good. Edwards's philosophy of excellence and the notion that moral and spiritual alienation has no purchase on reality—one alone without reference to another cannot be excellent, and in fact cannot be at all—resonates with James's notion of the moral life. In "The Moral Philosopher and the Moral Life," James holds that the determining quality of the moral life is purposive, as moral relations seek "the unity of a stable system, and make of the world what one may call a genuine universe." Ethical ideals thus call to the philosopher, like other affectional facts, to be made "into a certain form." Such ideals should not be reductive or dogmatic, but "existing in the world." Thus James implicitly adds the tenets of radical empiricism to the investigation of the moral life, noting, "The higher, more penetrating ideals are revolutionary. They present themselves far less in the guise of effects of past experience than in that of probable causes of future experience, factors to which the environment and the lessons it has so far taught us must learn to bend."[62] Moral relations are living responses to the complex world of experience, and when fitting and right, reflect the aesthetic agreement and ethical consent that organically define the process of pragmatist poetics. In the essay, James further advances his critique of the abstracted philosopher shackled to his ideals.

James's version of Edwards's "one alone" is a reality he calls a "moral solitude." Hillary Putnam writes of James's moral solitude that such a model cannot be true because truth is necessarily a part of a world of experience in which moral relations require verification:

> James imagined a world in which there is only one sentient being, and wrote that none of the being's beliefs could be called "true." Why not? Because "truth presupposes a standard external to the thinker." . . . Truth, then, presupposes community. But community is not enough. The "truth" of a Khomeiniist sect is not worthy of the name, according to the great pragmatists, because it is not responsive to anything except the will of the leader. A community that subjects its beliefs to test is the minimum requirement for the existence of truth. This remarkable vision of a deep connection between truth, reality, and community drives James in propounding his "melioristic religion."[63]

Like Edwards's philosophy of excellence, James's purpose is consent to others that realizes intimacy, and, in becoming intimate, demands testing within a widened community that avoids self-interested private systems. This reflects a purposive reality that is modeled after a universe that James calls an ethical republic. The individual's moral responsibility rests in "our own human hearts, as they happen to beat responsive to the claim [of living consciousness]. So far as they do feel it . . . it is life answering to life."[64] Affectional facts lead the person to respond to life lived forward so as to affirm and advance the life of the other before oneself because responding to a neighborly and ethical republic. To fail to respond relationally is to accept the alienation James speaks of in "A Certain Blindness in Human Beings." He writes,

> Our judgments concerning the worth of things, big or little, depend on the *feelings* the things arouse in us. Where we judge a thing to be

precious in consequence of the *idea* we frame of it, this is only because the idea is itself associated already with a feeling. If we were radically feelingless, and if ideas were the only things our mind could entertain, we should lose all our likes and dislikes at a stroke, and be unable to point to any one situation or experience in life more valuable or significant than any other.[65]

Thus truth verification depends upon "knowledge by acquaintance" and relational apprehension such that an aesthetic dynamic becomes the mode by which experience happens. But at the same moment, such a dynamic also invokes the verification process. Feeling arouses appreciative participation in a wider web of relations and truth-verifications that contextualize or include the former (feeling) in the growing latter (web of relations or world of experience), as the suffusing self affectionally slides into the process of change that is occurring as past flows into present and future. Thus to accept numbness or certainty due to temperament or disposition is to embrace disjunction, fracture, and meaninglessness. This suggests something akin to Edwards's notion of the falling away from being into nothingness that he defines as sin, a privation of the good.

Moral solitude best describes this state as an existence in which other persons are objects floating about alone in a disconnected reality. For James, to accept alienation from experience is to become a heartless creature well satisfied with one's portion in life such that we do not dare risk change or engagement, even to bring generosity to an other. The moral solitude engendered by one alone is the very illusion and limitation imagined by individuals who embrace private systems. Breaking the boundaries of such systems, and thus funding an expansiveness that better approximates the enriched—and enriching— empiricism that describes reality is thus to embrace a strenuous democracy.

Equality is Edwards's starting point in his philosophy of excellence. In *Mind #1* simple equality begins his analysis of the natural, moral, and spiritual beauty that shapes reality. James's argument that, in *Religious Affections*, Edwards fails to show the regenerate saint as qualitatively different from the natural man suggests the equality inherent in Edwards's philosophy of excellence. The individual and her religious experiments are what matter, but in a public, pragmatic way that rejects private systems destructive of benevolent consent. The reality of pragmatic verification and the persistent strenuousness of humility and generosity required in the act of consent to beings and to Being in General constitutes the poetic struggle to make of self and world practical, because practiced, beauty.

James's use of Edwards to support his findings that conversion requires no supernatural agency suggests the acute reading that James gave to Edwards's work, recalling Delbanco's observation that *The Varieties* was in part a response to *Religious Affections*. And this signals the fact, as Wayne Proudfoot has argued, that James's study supported the roots of religious experience in its argument for God's reality more than the fruits of such experience: "In *The*

Varieties James relies almost exclusively on introspection and a sense of felt conviction, while Edwards is increasingly skeptical of such an approach, and looks to practice to distinguish genuine religious affections from false." This shift, Proudfoot suggests, leads to an inversion of values reflective of the fate of religious experience in America.[66]

But James's overall view rests beyond the rhetoric of *The Varieties*, as his theory of affectional facts argues for a finite god in the making. This is in keeping with his concluding tenet of radical empiricism, "The directly apprehended universe needs, in short, no extraneous trans-empirical connective support,"[67] and to his less philosophical description of the overbelief, the distinct phenomena of diverse religious traditions "supposed by each to authenticate his own peculiar faith."[68] In an increasingly psychological age, James appeals to personal narratives as introspective insight intended for pragmatic testing. While James finds in the *documents humaine* of *The Varieties* repeated evidence of spiritual incursions from extramarginal regions, he navigates among the "divergencies" of "various theologies," seeking to avoid "inveterate disputes" in order to arrive at a demythologized yet inspiring understanding of religious experience.[69] James outlines a scientific approach that clarifies broadly defined empirical facts about religious experience in order to defend the evolutionary value of religion as "mankind's most important function," and to do so in a way that defends religious experience against the "prejudices of my class."[70] This requires him to disregard what he calls over-beliefs while also finding them to be "absolutely indispensable."[71] In "confining ourselves to what is common and generic," James concludes, "We have in *the fact that the person is continuous with a wider self through which saving experiences come,* a positive content of religious experience which, it seems to me, *is literally and objectively true as far as it goes.*"[72]

James here commits himself to the idea of a widened reality or More: "we belong to it in a more intimate sense than that in which we belong to the visible world, for we belong in the most intimate sense wherever our ideals belong."[73] But this only goes so far, only goes where it may compenetrate with the world of experience, where authentic intimacy witnesses suffusion into a pluralistic universe. James's insistence on the natural occurrence of diverse religious experiences overthrows the hierarchical descriptions of the regenerate saint and the natural man, repeating his desire to be inclusive and pluralistic. And yet his rhetoric suggests belief in a supernatural God that seems to undercut his pragmatic radical empiricism. The key here is James's rhetorical intention for an audience existing in a world increasingly secularized. In *The Varieties*, religion's key function was in some sense to spark an imagination dulled by dogmatics and disappointed by determinism in order to create the possibility of spiritual experience. As James's less rhetorical writing about the wider self in *Pragmatism, Essays in Radical Empiricism,* and *A Pluralistic Universe* demonstrates, quasi-theological notions find expression in various metaphors that act to lure forward the practical testing of affectional facts in an unfinished universe.

For James, god is necessarily finite, a prolific working hypothesis if it "enters into wider cosmic relations" authenticated and salted down by pragmatic testing. Neither man nor god(s) suffer absolute dependence because in mutual possession and ongoing conversation. James affirms that affectional facts have a reality beyond religion's superficial alterations and overlays ridiculed by materialists. In fact, religion creates "a *natural constitution* different at some point from that which a materialistic world would have." James declares a "pragmatic view of religion . . . taken as a matter of course by common men," and over against materialists and "transcendentalist metaphysicians."[74]

James's concluding remarks in *The Varieties* reveal a view of religious experience as ontologically productive of reality as a result of creating working hypotheses that unfurl with novel relations and ideas. Here again is where James sets up the common man as a leveling agent in the class struggle he witnesses in the world of ideas. This is a reflection of the inclusiveness and indeterminacy of both his view of reality, and of systematic philosophy's impractical application to persons as they live together socially. For James, rational systems of thought are undemocratic in ideal and practice. James sees a very different reality at work, one that seeks inclusiveness as pragmatically valuable in its aesthetic search for harmony and clarity, terms that also apply to his ethical demand for the advance of truth as a species of the good. James thus understands religion to bring the ideal and the factual together in a working relation productive of new and complex possibilities. James's radical empiricism reflects a poetic refashioning of the world that is not seen in terms of a fulfillment of providential history and the infusion of God's glory into the world of fact, as Edwards would have it. James's notion of poetic pragmatism is of a creative process in which religious overbeliefs such as "God" play a valuable role in leading to ever more fruitful transitions and relations to novel ideas and insights that are ontologically productive, or in eliminating the practical value of such overbeliefs.

This sheds light on the strenuous democracy implicit in both men's thought. Edwards's focus on practice and James's emphasis on the reality of a finite god or wider self illustrate the importance of religious experience for American culture as it moved from a focus on God to nineteenth century nationalism. According to John E. Smith, Edwards's pragmatic turn had deleterious effects. Smith writes,

> Speaking of what we must expect from the true believer, [Edwards] writes: "[We must expect] that he makes a business of such a holy practice above all things; that it be a business which he is chiefly engaged in; and devoted to, and pursues with highest earnestness and diligence: so that he may be said to make this practice of religion eminently his work and business." We should add at once that, even allowing for the very different sense in which the term "business" was used in the eighteenth century as compared with current usage, the appearance of the term was little short of prophetic. For, as religion declined in influence during the decades after Edwards's death and the "business of religion" was no longer as central in

American life as it once had been, countless thousands of people were left merely with "busyness" as the material of their diligence and the object of their devotion.[75]

James's use of the term cash-value as a metaphor for the pragmatic verification of ideas and experiences reflects an attempt to counteract the prevailing emphasis upon material wealth and class structure in his own day.

Edwards and James each struggled with the problem of moral solitude. For Edwards, the enthusiastic hypocrite came to define the citizenry of eighteenth century America in a way more destructive of religion's value than that of rationalists or Deists. And the problem of moral solitude served to influence his trenchant criticisms of the American project embedded both in his jeremiads and the criticisms to be found throughout his analysis of religious affections. After his long experience with the extravagances of the New England revivals, Edwards rejected the American exceptionalism hoped for earlier in his career. He writes late in life, and after numerous struggles with enthusiasts and rationalists alike, of the deep pain of the failure of religion in America:

> How lamentable is the moral and religious state of these American colonies? How apparently are the hearts of the people, everywhere, uncommonly shut up against all means and endeavors to awaken sinners and revive religion? . . . May not an attentive view and consideration of such a state of things well influence the people . . . to earnestness in their cries to God for a general outpouring of his Spirit, which only can be an effectual remedy for these evils?[76]

The rhetoric of sensation that Edwards used to dramatic effect shaped sermons such as "Sinners in the Hands of an Angry God" that castigated the congregation. But this rhetoric functioned to emphasize the personal affections that could bring one into pragmatic relation to a world of glory in the making or into the illusions of self-serving hypocrisy that made for a moral solitude. The introduction of the new sense and the recommendation of spiritual experiment granted to individual believers the right to follow their own intuitions. Such intuitions led to tragedies such as Hawley's suicide, but more often to a religious style free from careful scrutiny, and thus subject to aggrandizement and inevitable disappointment.

By emphasizing the pragmatic verification of religious affections, Edwards's position was "inverted and indeed perverted." The hypocrite, as John Smith notes, practiced the vicious intellectualism that confuses signs with the reality to which they point. Second-hand religion was confused with first-hand experience, something James went to great lengths to avoid in *The Varieties*. Smith writes that Edwards's emphasis on the practice of piety reached an ironic end:

> Practice as an outward and visible sign could no longer maintain its old status when belief in an inward and invisible grace was on the

wane. Piety became practice, and vice versa, or, as the common slogan expresses it, "Work is worship, labor holy." Diligence, earnestness, steadfast, industriousness, as they gradually lost their transcendent reference in the divine spirit, were transformed into a secular substitute for religion.[77]

James democratizes Edwards's regenerate saint, and claims that Edwards did the same. And in a sense Edwards did, in a way that ironically opened the door for the enthusiastic hypocrite's empowerment that, as Edwards predicted, became a most damaging blow to religion's true business, the benevolent consent to being that increasingly glorified the world and made God grow and become happy. The offer of Christ's friendship was rejected as too demanding of disinterest and the leveling of social hierarchy. Thus focus on a democracy committed to hope evolved into a national identity found not on faith, but on individual and national self-interest. As McDermott insightfully argues, Edwards's understanding of America in the end embodied a deep disappointment:

> Edwards reminded his auditors that their covenant was only the most recent in a series of such divine contracts with nations, and that it might terminate shortly. For their sins might cause God to transfer his covenantal favors to a more faithful people. Hence American exceptionalism—in the Edwardsean dispensation—could not forestall American destruction. . . . This reading of the Edwardsean national covenant places the beleaguered theologian from Northampton within the small band of influential cultural leaders whose reflections on America's religious meaning were prophetic afflictions of the comfortable.[78]

James, in his critique of American imperialism, industrialism, and the failure to address the social ills of the working poor, joins this company. This position goes far towards understanding James's criticism of his fellow academics. James, contrary to his own class, finds religion to be mankind's most important function because, in the end, it encourages the creative transformation of human life that is an affirmation of hope. Fueled by affectional facts, human creative freedom could, if pragmatically fruitful within the stream of experience, build a more spiritually fulfilling reality. Strenuous such work would be, and in need of a democratic spirit not embodied in law or authority, but in the poetic pragmatism of a people willing to work together for the possibility of salvation. James's reinstatement of the vague is ultimately a claim for an ethical republic reliant upon a democratic process of poetic pragmatism. The vague represents the humility that Edwards sees as requisite to the benevolent consent that traces the sacred through a fallen reality. Much as James was sharply critical of fellow philosophers, Edwards found in fellow ministers who whipped their enthusiastic followers into frenzied exclamations of faith the victory of certainty and self-interest, and a decline of the curiosity that shapes faith in a world of uncertainties. The insights garnered from religious experience necessitated testing in the long run, entailing a life lived in constant conversation with the vague. This point underlies Edwards's critique of revivalism and rationalism both, much as it informs James's vision of pragmatism as a "protestant reformation of philosophy." The signs of religious experiences trace the sacred in an unsure way, leading forward over the course of a life tested and tried in creative compenetration revelatory of the sense of the heart.

The call for a salvation possibly realized in the cooperative work of the variegated human community of Whitman's "Crossing Brooklyn Ferry" negates the moral solitude James imagines as the paradoxical blindness of individualism. In "Pragmatism and Religion," he calls upon Whitman again to amplify "the pluralistic way" that relies upon the malleability of life and the possibility inherent in the inclusion of all in the building of a glorious reality. The poem "To You" interpreted pluralistically,

> May mean your better possibilities phenomenally taken, or the specific redemptive effects even of your failures, upon yourself or others. It may mean your loyalty to the possibilities of others whom you admire and love, so that you are willing to accept your own poor life, for it is glory's partner.[79]

Much as Edwards sees the world's end suffused into the glory of God, James witnesses a magnetic pull towards the mother-sea of being. In each case, strenuous democracy, in which ontological wonder was a primary value that informed spiritual appreciation of the self as the other, was necessary to the building of a cooperative salvation. And such an end, following the excellencies of Christ or the wanderings of the holy tramp, did not consider national boundaries. As Delbanco tellingly notes, the American dream "has always been a global dream. . . . To be really American has always meant to see something beyond America."[80] James's pluralistic universe does not model an illusory democratic space that is unreceptive, but one that is "self-reparative through us, as getting its disconnections remedied in part by our behavior."[81]

As both Edwards and James appreciate, the new reach of creative freedom comes in intimacy and suggestiveness. The key lies in the melting mood of susceptibility that enables the enrichment of a universe imagined after a social model. The affectional facts of human experience embody the promise of creative freedom as they redirect the attention and cast out lines that remake self and world as their pragmatic destiny is realized. James sees that moral solitude offers nothing but religious illusion in such a world, and yet such illusion is a commonplace stumbling block to the democratic space requisite to the turning of a dangerous world into a home. Susceptibility requires the feeling of effort that makes matter meaningful, that dignifies the person in making feelings felt. As Edwards observes, "Private affection . . . contains but a small part of the great system . . . is limited to so narrow a circle."[82] Pragmatic poetics reshapes and enriches a fragmentary world of private systems through the inclusion of relations conjunctive and disjunctive that form a democratic space in which the strenuous mood is at work.

Notes

Chapter 1

1. VRE, 11-12.
2. See "The Millennium Probably to Dawn in America," GA, 353-358; and VRE, 287, where James writes, "The Utopian dreams of social justice in which many contemporary socialists and anarchists indulge are, in spite of their impracticability and non-adaptation to present environmental conditions, analogous to the saint's belief in an existent kingdom of heaven."
3. Edward M. Panosian, "Jonathan Edwards: America's Theologian-Preacher," in *Faith of Our Fathers: Scenes from American Church History*, ed. Mark Sidwell (Greenville, SC: BJU Press, 1991), 33-39.
4. Hannah Arendt, quoted in Michael Jackson, *Excursions* (Durham and London: Duke University Press, 2007), ix.
5. PR, 258.
6. MA, 186; VRE, 531.
7. Andrew Delbanco, *The Puritan Ordeal* (Cambridge, Massachusetts, and London, England: Harvard University Press, 1989), 39.
8. Andrew Delbanco, *The Real American Dream* (Cambridge, Massachusetts,, and London, England: Harvard University Press, 1999), 103-107.
9. Jackson, *Excursions*, 19.
10. Janice Knight, *Orthodoxies in Massachusetts,,* (Cambridge, Massachusetts, and London, England: Harvard University Press, 1994), 22-23.
11. Quoted in Knight, *Orthodoxies*, 16.
12. Delbanco, *Ordeal*, 26.
13. Knight, *Orthodoxies*, 2.
14. Knight, *Orthodoxies*, 4.
15. VRE, 26.
16. The use of the term aesthetic invokes contradiction. Noting the interpretive confusion of the word, Richardson sees the problem residing in the notion of "art for art's sake *aestheticism*" that is "literally foreign to the sense of the term." She defines the aesthetic as "feeling as a body in its environment." I employ the terms aesthetic and anesthetic to distinguish between the prospective dynamic of feeling in a world of experience. The former defines what both Edwards and James mean by the ideas of feeling, affection, experience, and/or beauty, all of which relate to the intimate relation between aesthetic-ethics as a creative expression of disinterest. Anesthetics refers to the retrospective numbing of life lived forward creatively that seeks security and comfort, and is self-interested. See Joan Richardson, *A Natural History of Pragmatism* (Cambridge: Cambridge University Press, 2007), 256-257, and fn. 25.

17. PJE, 117.

18. RA, 84.

19. Reinhold Niebuhr, *The Irony of American History* (New York: Charles Scribner's Sons, 1952), 155-156.

20. SPW, 332-338.

21. GA, 107.

22. GA, 105

23. GA, 110.

24. Delbanco, *Puritan Ordeal*, 15. Delbanco argues that the Puritan ordeal "was a paradigmatic immigrant ordeal" in which the motives for uprootedness were diluted and rationalized by succeeding generations. In the case of the Puritans, a loss of the initial purpose of religious freedom and growth in grace diminished as they came to define themselves as Americans.

25. GA, 353.

26. See Perry Miller, *Jonathan Edwards* (Amherst: The University of Massachusetts Press, 1981), p103-104, 227-228. Miller argues that Hawley's son Joseph Jr., blamed Edwards for the death of his father, and consequently became one of the instigators who worked to force Edwards from the Northampton parish. Hawley Jr. later wrote an apologetic missive to Edwards, confessing his role in the expulsion, and asking for forgiveness.

27. Thoughts of suicide were the most despairing responses to the humiliation normative within the psychological dynamic of Puritan models of conversion. See Charles Cohen, *God's Caress: The Psychology of Puritan Religious Experience* (New York and Oxford: Oxford University Press, 1986), 18-46, 207. See also Gail Thane Parker, "Jonathan Edwards and Melancholy," *New England Quarterly* 41:193-212 for an excellent discussion of both the Puritan interpretation of melancholy and Edwards's understanding of its relation to experimental religion.

28. GA, 110.

29. GA, 110.

30. The citation is from Edwards's sermon on II Samuel 20:19, and quoted in C.C. Goen, "Editor's Introduction," in GA, 42. Goen notes Edwards's unhappiness with the factual errors printed in the 1737 London edition of "A Faithful Narrative," as illustrated by his complaint on the flyleaf of the presentation copy given to Yale College. Goen writes, "As for the other 'things diverse from fact' which provoked Edwards' complaint . . . one sometimes wonders whether his notation marks a return to an original sense distorted by editorial mishandling or represents a shift in his own thinking. For example, we know that on several occasions Edwards confessed that for all his caution he had

been too hasty in pronouncing many conversions genuine." Goen notes that Edwards crossed out a line in this edition asserting his certainty as to the conversion of sixty new church members, but he adds that Benjamin Colman, who edited it before Watts received it, may have omitted this line. Goen concludes, "Did he omit it at his own discretion, or is it a gratuitous insertion by the London editors? It seems safe to give Edwards the benefit of the doubt, because his settled conviction on the point was that since conversion is a work of God directly on the human soul, no man can know with certainty the spiritual state of another." See GA, 32-46.

31. GA, 47.

32. From a letter by "J.L." published in *American Weekly Mercury*, July 16, 1741. Quoted by Goen in GA, 50.

33. See Ava Chamberlain, "The Grand Sower of the Seed: Jonathan Edwards's Critique of George Whitfield," in *The New England Quarterly*, Volume 70, Issue 3 (Sep., 1997), 368-85.

34. Chamberlain, "Grand Sower," 374. In the sermon, Edwards draws on the parable of the sower to describe the congregants as wayside hearers, thorny-ground hearers, and stony-ground hearers. Chamberlain notes on 384, "Edwards harbored a deep ambivalence about Whitefield's ministry, which was rooted theologically in his conviction that Whitefield's theatrical preaching style dangerously encouraged religious hypocrisy and, personally, in feelings of professional rivalry." Both Edwards's theological disagreements and his bruised ego suggest the bitterness that continued to envelop Edwards's relationship with the congregants of Northampton. This also suggests a move from the community orientation of Edwards's ethics to the rampant populism and individualism that would fuel the revolution and reinvoke the authority of political and legal order over communitarianism seen in the Antinomian Crisis and amongst the Spiritual Brethren.

35. GA, 495.

36. GA, 459.

37. GA, 563.

38. GA, 564.

39. GA, 565.

40. GA, 563.

41. GA, 564.

42. RA, 20. Edmund Morgan summarizes the steps as follows: "By the time Massachusetts,, was founded, two generations of Puritan writers had devoted themselves to describing the process through which God's free grace operates in the salvation of men. . . . They wished to trace the natural history of conversion in order to help men discover their prospects of salvation; and the result of their studies was to establish the morphology of conversion, in which each stage could be distinguished from the next, so that a man could check his eternal condition by a set of temporal and recognizable signs. . . . The outlines of the pattern are plain: knowledge, conviction, faith, combat, and true imperfect

assurance." See Edmund S. Morgan, *Visible Saints: The History of a Puritan Idea* (Ithaca: Cornell University Press, 1963), 66.

43. WTB, 34, 49.
44. WTB, 49.
45, WTB, 52.
46. PR, 62
47. PR, 9.
48. PR, 10.
49. PR, 10.
50. WTB, 57.
51. PR, 21.
52. PR, 31-32.
53. William James to Hugo Munsterberg, July 8, 1891 (James Papers, Houghton Library, Harvard University). Quoted in "'The Worst Kind of Melancholy': William James in 1869" in *A William James Renaissance*, Harvard Library Bulletin, Vol. 30, No. 4, October 1982, 369.
54. LWJ, 1, 152-153.
55. WTB, 57.
56. PR, p 18, 41.

Chapter 2

1. Paul Boller argues that there is a historical analogy between science and theology in the challenges presented by determinism: "Modern scientific determinism has its roots in theological predestination and originated as a metaphysical affirmation rather than as a hypothetical presupposition to guide empirical or experimental research." Paul F. Boller, Jr., *Freedom and Fate in American Thought* (Dallas: SMU Press, 1978), 20.
2. Allen C. Guelzo, "The Return of the Will: Jonathan Edwards and the Possibilities of Free Will," in *Edwards in Our Time*, ed. Sang Hyun Lee and Allen C. Guelzo (Grand Rapids/Cambridge: Wm. B. Eerdmans Publishing Co., 1999), 87-88.
3. PR, p. 141.
4. ERE, 43; VRE, 190.
5. Boller, *Freedom*, 23.
6. TCWJ, 2, p. 259.

7. The exact date of the writing of the *Personal Narrative* is uncertain, as are the reasons for its creation. George S. Claghorn argues that it was written for his future son-in-law Aaron Burr sometime between 1740 and 1741, but the fact that some of its language corresponds to that of the 1738 sermon "The Excellency of Christ" suggests the possibility of a slightly earlier date. PW, 747.

8. See Daniel Shea, *Spiritual Autobiography in Early America* (Madison: The University of Wisconsin Press, 1988). Shea makes an insightful reading of the *Personal Narrative* in light of the *Diary*, illustrating its differences in style and editorial construction, and notes the repetition of certain scenes from *A Faithful Narrative*.

9. RA, p. 84.
10. PW, p. 753
11. PW, p. 777.
12. PW, p. 791.
13. Sang Hyun Lee, *The Philosophical Theology of Jonathan Edwards* (Princeton: Princeton University Press, 1988), 47-48.
14. PW, pp. 791-792.
15. William J. Bouwsma, *John Calvin: A Sixteenth Century Portrait* (New York: Oxford University Press, 1988), 173.
16. Bouwsma, *Calvin*, 173, 181.
17. MA, 258-259. See also Cohen, *God's Caress*, 114-118 for a helpful discussion of the misinterpretation of predestination, especially by Max Weber. Cohen quotes Shepard, one of Edwards' major influences, on this topic: "Confronted with the plaint that Christ, the means of redemption, 'is not intended for all, therefore not for me,' Shepard challenged, 'how doth this follow? How dost thou know this?'" Cohen notes that the doctrine could provide comfort to the saints' sense of their salvation as persevering through time, and concludes that the doctrine "was not designed to scare them into activity."
18. MA 2, 457.
19. MA 2, 458-459.
20. MA 2, 461.
21. Perry Miller, *Errand Into the Wilderness* (New York: Harper and Row Publishers, 1964), 167-183.
22. PW, 793.
23. RA, 109.
24. SJE, 124.
25. SJE, 139-140.
26. PW, 793.
27. PW, 802.
28. PW, 796.
29. Perry Miller, *Jonathan Edwards*. Amherst: University of Massachusetts,, Press, 273.
30. EW, 432.

31. Elisa New, "Beyond the Romance Theory of American Vision: Beauty and the Qualified Will in Edwards, Jefferson, and Audubon," *American Literary History*, Vol. 7, No. 3, (Autumn, 1995), 381-414.

32. MEN, 150-155.

33. TCWJ, v.2, 495.

34. PR, 97.

35. TCWJ, v.1, 494.

36. PR, 85.

37. TCWJ, v.2, 500.

38. TT, 139.

39. TCWJ, v.2, 498-499. R. B. Perry notes that "wissen differs from kennen, as explanation from mere acquaintance," 498. James might well have dismissed the adjective 'mere,' as knowledge by acquaintance came to be a central part of his epistemological theory and his emphasis upon the value of experience. Interestingly, Perry also notes, "In general the unpublished notes differ from the published articles in their fuller and more sympathetic attention to the motives of non-empirical philosophies." James found pleasure in idealism, but rejected it on moral and epistemological grounds.

40. EP, 370.

41. TCWJ, v.1, 499-500.

42. TCWJ, v.1, 500.

43. LWJ, v.1, 147-148.

44. Ralph Waldo Emerson, Collected Works, v.3. Introduction and Notes by Joseph Slater; text established by Alfred Ferguson and Jean Ferguson Carr (Cambridge, Massachusetts,,: Harvard University Press, 1983), 48.

45. MEN, 295.

46. VRE, 46-47.

47. PR, 111-112.

Chapter 3

1. Ezek. 1:20-21, *The Holy Bible*, King James Version (New York: Meridian, 1974), 650.

2. Samuel Taylor Coleridge, "The Statesman's Manual," in *The Collected Works of Samuel Taylor Coleridge: Lay Sermons,* ed. R.J. White (London and Princeton: Princeton University Press, 1972), 29.

3. NS, 374-375. Edwards goes on to observe that with such revolution 'a further end was obtained . . . there is a progress towards a certain final issue of things." As in his philosophy of excellence, Edwards here sees a pattern of proportionality in which the concentric wheels of providence refer from the natural to the moral and spiritual, and back again such that there is an active circulation of divine communication within the sanctified heart, the actions of the saint, and the fulfillment which remanates back to the Creator, expanding Being in General, and making God happy.

4. PU, 117-118.

5. PR, 112.

6. John Dewey, *Art as Experience* (New York: Minton, Balch & Company, 1934), 58.

7. John Wild, *The Radical Empiricism of William James* (Garden City, New York: Doubleday & Company, Inc., 1969), 361.

8. ERE, 82.

9. VRE, 55.

10. PR, 56.

11. Barbara Lewalski, *Puritan Poetics and the Seventeenth-Century Religious Lyric* (Princeton: Princeton University Press, 1979), 101-102.

12. Lewalski, *Poetics*, 102-104.

13. See "Circles," in *The Essays of Ralph Waldo Emerson.* Text established by Alfred R. Ferguson and Jean Ferguson Carr, introduction by Alfred Kazin (Cambridge, Mass.: The Belknap Press of Harvard University Press, 1979), 180-181.

14. PR, 99.

15. SPW, 345.

16. ISDT, #89, 85-86; and #154, 105-108.

17. ISDT, #190, 127-128.

18. MA2, 455.

19. SPW, 332.

20. PJE, 122.

21. SJE, 124.

22. SJE, 137.

23. ISDT, #190, 127-128.

24. SJE, 140.

25. PR, 141.

26. Jill M. Kress, "Contesting Metaphors and the Discourse of Consciousness in William James," *Journal of the History of Ideas* 61.2 (2000), 263-283.

27. John Wild, *The Radical Empiricism of William James* (Garden City, New York: Doubleday & Company, Inc., 1969), 393.

28. John E. Smith, *The Spirit of American Philosophy* (Albany: State University of New York, 1983), 69.

29. D.M. Yeager, "Passion and Suspicion: Religious Affections in 'The Will to Believe,'" *The Journal of Religion* (Chicago: The University of Chicago Press, 1989), 468.

30. William James, "Is Life Worth Living?," WTB, 55.

31. VRE, 393.

32. PU, 143.

33. TCWJ, v.1, 500.

34. ERE, 83.

35. PR, 37.

36 TT, 139, VRE, 55.

37. VRE, 59.

38. This is clearly seen in James's critique of those religious persons involved in ascetic or contemplative practices that are seemingly fruitless in terms of the enrichment of society. Such inward self-absorption is a type of pathology to James, for it fails to address the social body by which such persons are funded in innumerable ways. VRE, Lectures 12-14, 210-261.

39. VRE, 23.

40. See Wayne Proudfoot, "From Theology to a Science of Religions: Jonathan Edwards and William James on Religious Affections," *Harvard Theological Review* 82:2 (1989) 149-168. Proudfoot sees "James's attempt to find a common nucleus within the varieties of religious experience" to ignore "that belief in itself is constitutive of the experience" (168). The bias of James's apologetics and his own "over-beliefs" thus cloud the complexity of the religious experience as a socially constructed event. But, as David Lamberth argues, the descriptive and philosophical projects undertaken in *The Varieties* "are complexly interrelated, with the latter set (the philosophical, spiritual, religiously apologetic) ultimately having more significance than the former. James may in fact have embarked explicitly only on the descriptive project in what we now have as *Varieties*; however, on the basis of his own distinctions, the philosophical project can never be kept wholly at bay. Conversely, we can expect that in his treatment of philosophical issues, however sparse or extended, the empirical evidence can never be far from hand. Such is the appearance of a radically empiricist world-view." See David Lamberth, *William James and the Metaphysics of Experience* (Cambridge: Cambridge University Press, 1999), 116. Thus within *The Varieties* James seeks not simply to evaluate the meaning of religious experience as a scientist of religion, but seeks to place the value of religious experience within his evolving theory of radical empiricism and the

pragmatism that undergirds it. *The Varieties*, then, serves as one constellation of ideas within James's pluralistic philosophy, and functions to construct a validation for its inclusion within James's overall vision. Intriguing within this task is the fact of establishing some kind of wider self or More that operates in relation to human communities to introduce helpful, reparative, and/or salvific elements. This recalls the fact that James describes his work as "protestant," thus suggesting that James approaches the assessment of religious experience in *The Varieties* from a scientific point of view as a secondary concern.

41. VRE, 32. James's emphasis on solitude is somewhat misleading for his overall program demands a return to the social world of experience to test ideas in relation to other ideas, values, and beliefs. James notes that religious experience concerns the development of expansive relations in the second half of his definition of religion.

42. James first defines his concept of the vague in PBC, 150.

43. Eugene Fontinell, *Self, God, and Immortality: A Jamesian Investigation* (Philadelphia: Temple University Press, 1986), 64. See also William Joseph Gavin, *William James and the Reinstatement of the Vague* (Philadelphia, Temple University Press, 1992) for an excellent study of James's uses of the vague as it relates to diverse aspects of his thought.

44. VRE, 39.

45. VRE, 42.

46. VRE, 44-45.

47. VRE, 46.

48. VRE, 46-47.

49. VRE, 400.

50. VRE, 47.

51. See PR, 40, in which James discusses the necessity of a working god who is "needed in the dust of our human trials." He discusses the notion of a cooperative salvation in the same work, 139.

52. PR, 138.

53. VRE, 51.

54. TCWJ 2, 764.

55. James writes, "The living moments . . . have somewhat of absolute that needs no lateral support. Their meaning seems to well up from out of their very centre, in a way impossible verbally to describe. If you take a disk painted with a concentric spiral pattern, and make it revolve, it will seem to be growing continuously and indefinitely, and yet to take in nothing from without, and to remain, if you pay attention to its actual size, always of the *same* size. Something as paradoxical as this lies in every present moment of life. Here or nowhere, as Emerson says, is the whole fact. The moment stands and contains & sums up all things; and all change is within it, much as the developing landscape with all its growth falls forever within the rear window-pane of the last car of a train that is speeding on its headlong way. This self-sustaining in the midst of self-removal which characterizes all reality and fact, is something absolutely foreign to the nature of language, and even to the nature of logic, commonly so

called. Something forever exceeds, escapes from statement, withdraws from definition, must be glimpsed and felt, not told." VRE, 479-480.

56. TT, 138-139. James here also attributes the description of this experience to Emerson: "As Emerson says, there is a depth to those moments that constrain to ascribe more reality to them than to all other experiences," 139.

57. VRE, p. 480.
58. WTB, 102.
59. VRE, 189.

Chapter 4

1. Ralph Waldo Emerson, *Collected Works*, 3 Vols. Introduction and Notes by Joseph Slater; text established by Alfred Ferguson and Jean Ferguson Carr (Cambridge: Massachusetts: Harvard University Press, 1983), 49.

2. NTV, 6.
3. ISDT, 137.
4. PU, 138.
5. MEN, 3.
6. VRE, 332.

7. Frank Bidart, "For the Twentieth Century," in *Dirty Music* (Louisville, Kentucky: Sarabande Books, 2002), 17.

8. Robert Pinsky, *Democracy, Culture and the Voice of Poetry* (Princeton University Press, 2002), v.

9. PR, 258.
10. PR, 125.

11. H.R Niebuhr, *The Meaning of Revelation* (Westminster John Knox Press, 2006), 74.

12. George Rupp, "The "Idealism" of Jonathan Edwards," *Harvard Theological Review* 62, 1969, 209.

13. Janice Knight, "Learning the Language of God: Jonathan Edwards and the Typology of Nature," *The William and Mary Quarterly*, Third Series, Vol. 48, No. 4, 536.

14. Perry Miller, "Jonathan Edwards on the Sense of the Heart," *Harvard Theological Review*, Vol. 41, No. 2, 126.

15. SPW, 21. See also RA, 84.
16. SPW, 39-40.
17. SPW, 203.
18. SPW, 17.

19. Elisa New, "Beyond the Romance Theory of American Vision: Beauty and the Qualified Will in Edwards, Jefferson, and Audubon," *American Literary History*, Vol. 7, No. 3 (Autumn, 1995), 387.

20. Knight, "Learning the Language of God," Jonathan Edwards and the Typology of Nature," *The William and Mary Quarterly*, Third Series, Vol. 48, No. 4 (October, 1991), 531-551.

21. SPW, 336. For Edwards, one alone is not excellent, but simply is not, cannot exist. From this description of excellence Edwards understands God to be a communicating being best described as a society or family. This indicates the highly social character of reality and the nature of divine glory as the remaking of the tissue of experience as an intimate and expansive community. Edwards notes, "The reason why equality thus pleases the mind, and inequality is unpleasing, is because disproportion or inconsistency is contrary to being. . . . When one being is inconsistent with another being, then being is contradicted. But contradiction to being is intolerable to perceiving being; and the consent to being, most pleasing." This corresponds to the process of truth verification that James sees as the result of fruitful transitions, conjunctions, and terminations that build out the unfinished universe. See PR, 98.

22. SPW, 333-336.
23. SPW, 362.
24. SPW, 337-338.
25. SPW, 362.
26. EW, 565.
27. SPW, 362.
28. SPW, 353.

29. Bruce Kuklick, *Churchmen and Philosophers: From Jonathan Edwards to John Dewey* (New Haven: Yale University Press, 1985), 29.

30. New, "Beyond the Romance Theory of American Vision," 387.

31. EW, 542.

32. Gerard Manley Hopkins, "As Kingfishers Catch Fire, Dragonflies Draw Flame," http://www.bartleby.com/122/34.html. Accessed 6-12-2008.

33. Sang Hyun Lee, *The Philosophical Theology of Jonathan Edwards* (Princeton, New Jersey: Princeton University Press, 1988), 50.

34. Joan Richardson, *A Natural History of Pragmatism* (Cambridge, England, and New York: Cambridge University Press, 2007), 52.

35. PJE, 114, 116.
36. PJE, 123-124.
37. Lee, *Philosophical Theology*, 204.
38. EW, 554.
39. PJE, pp. 238, 98.
40. SPW, 337.
41. AW, 338.
42. New, "Beyond the Romance Theory of American Vision," 389.
43. New, "Beyond the Romance Theory of American Vision," 389.
44. VRE, 189.

45. VRE, 189-191.
46. Eugene T. Gendlin, *Thinking Beyond Patterns: Body, Language, and Situations* (New York: Peter Lang, 1991), 61. Quoted in Mark Johnson, *The Meaning of the Body: Aesthetics of Human Understanding* (Chicago: University of Chicago Press, 2008), 83.
47. MT, 6-7.
48. PR, 17.
49. PR, 25.
50. ERE, 37.
51. Miller, "Sense of the Heart."
52. TT, 165.
53. ERE, 29.
54. VRE, 126, 216. James refers to the melting mood as "an exalted affection."
55. ERE, 42.
56. MT, 7
57. VRE, 393.
58. VRE, 393-394.
59. VRE, 193.
60. SPW, 344.
61. VRE, pp. 488-489.
62. ERE, 143.
63. PR, 35.
64. PR, 15.
65. EPH, 261.
66. PR, 62.
67. PR, 37.
68. PR, 36.
69. PR, 39.
70. PR, 40.
71. Charlene Haddock Seigfried, *William James's Radical Reconstruction of Philosophy* (Albany, New York: SUNY Press,1990), 16.
72. ERE, 35.
73. PR, 59.
74. See James's pragmatic reinterpretation of the argument by design, PR, 56-59.
75. PR, 98-99.
76. PR, 97.

77. Nancy Frankenberry, *Religion and Radical Empiricism* (Albany, New York: SUNY Press, 1987), 11.
78. PR, 65.
79. PR, 68.
80. PR, 69.
81. PR, 44.
82. PR, 44.
83. MEN, 5.
84. PR, 137.
85. PR, 138.
86. PR, 138.

Chapter 5

1. Yi Fu Tuan, *Passing Strange and Wonderful: Aesthetics, Nature, and Culture* (New York: Kodansha America, Inc, 1995), 183.
2. AW, 446. Quoted in Gerald McDermott, *One Holy and Happy Society*. (University Park, Pennsylvania: The Pennsylvania State University Press, 1992), 41. McDermott makes the convincing argument that "Jonathan Edwards was a world citizen. The parochialism and egoistic nationalism ascribed to him would have struck him as myopic and characteristic only of unregenerate, natural virtue," 43. On the ethical republic, see WTB, 150. In *A Pluralistic Universe*, James states, "The pluralistic world is thus more like a federal republic than like an empire or a kingdom." PU, 145.
3. PU, 145.
4. PR, 138.
5. PR, 138.
6. John E. Smith makes this cogent argument in "Jonathan Edwards: Piety and Practice in the American Character." *The Journal of Religion*, Vol. 54, No. 2 (Apr., 1974), pp. 166-180.
7. PU, 130.
8. PU, 131.
9. Rosalyn Deutsche, "Democratic Public Space," in *The Pragmatist Imagination: Thinking About "Things in the Making,"* ed. Joan Ockman (New York: Princeton Architectural Press, 2000), 78.
10. RA, 201.
11. Wilson H. Kimnach, Kenneth Minkema, and Douglas A. Sweeney, editors, *The Sermons of Jonathan Edwards: A Reader* (New Haven and London: Yale University Press, 1999), xix.
12. MA, 224.
13. SJE, 189.
14. SJE, 167 168, 169, 170, 174.

15. James Engell, *The Creative Imagination* (Cambridge, Massachusetts, and London, England: Harvard University Press, 1981), 253.
16. SJE, 164-165.
17. Elisa New, "Beyond the Romance Theory of American Vision: Beauty and the Qualified Will in Edwards, Jefferson, and Audubon," *American Literary History*, Vol. 7, No. 3 (Autumn, 1995), 381.
18. SJE, 165.
19. SJE, 167-168.
20. VRE, 365.
21. SJE, 180.
22. SJE, 183.
23. SJE, 186.
24. RA, 200-201.
25. RA, 399.
26. RA, 173. The legal hypocrite is the rationalist who claims moral assurance by following the prescribed ordinances.
27. RA, 380-382.
28. RA, 387-388.
29. ERM, 171.
30. WTB, 159-160, 161.
31. TT, 4.
32. TT, 132.
33. TT, 133.
34. TT, 138.
35. TT, 138-139.
36. TT, 139.
37. TT, 139.
38. TT, 141.
39. PR, 125.
40. TT, 141.
41. TT, 141.
42. James Livingston, *Pragmatism and the Political Economy of Cultural Revolution, 1850-1940.* (Chapel Hill and London: The University of North Carolina Press, 1997), 169.
43. PR, 21-22. James quotes the anarchist Morrison I. Swift of the suicide of John Corcoran, a clerk who lost his job due to illness, could not support his family, and, as a result, committed suicide. Swift notes, "The records of many more such cases lie before me; an encyclopedia might easily be filled with their kind."

44. ERE, 26-27.
45. PU, 19.
46. TT, 142-143
47. TT, 142.
48. Kerry C. Larson, *Whitman's Drama of Consensus* (Chicago: The University of Chicago Press, 1988), 10-11.
49. TCWJ, II, 763-764.
50. Walt Whitman, "Crossing Brooklyn Ferry," in *Whitman: Poetry and Prose*, ed. Justin Kaplan (New York: Viking Press, 1982), 313.
51. TT, 146.
52. TT, 146.
53. PU, 131.
54. PBC, 200-201.
55. Whitman, "Crossing Brooklyn Ferry," 313.
56. VRE, 122.
57. PR, 142.
58. PR, 142-143.
59. PR, 142-143.
60. VRE, 194-195.
61. VRE, 194.
62. WTB, 141-142, 144
63. Hillary Putnam, *Realism with a Human Face* (Cambridge, Massachusetts, and London, England: Harvard University Press, 1990), 231.
64. WTB,149.
65. TT, 132.
66. Wayne Proudfoot, "From Theology to a Science of Religions: Jonathan Edwards and William James on Religious Affections." *The Harvard Theological Review*, Vol. 82, No. 2 (Apr., 1989), 152-153.
67. MT, 7.
68. VRE, 404.
69. VRE, 401-402.
70. VRE, 530.
71. VRE, 405.
72. VRE, 405.
73. VRE, 406.
74. PR, 133.
75. John E. Smith, "Jonathan Edwards: Piety and Practice in the American Character." *The Journal of Religion*, Vol. 54, No. 2 (Apr., 1974), 174-175, 178.
76. Quoted in Gerald, McDermott, *One Holy and Happy Society*. (University Park, Pennsylvania: the Pennsylvania State University Press, 1992), 77.
77. Smith, "Piety and Practice," 177.
78. McDermott, *Happy Society*, 35-36.
79. PR, 133.
80. Delbanco, *American Dream*, 117.

81. PU, 148.
82. EW, 554.

Bibliography

Bidart, Frank. "For the Twentieth Century," *Dirty Music*. Louisville, Kentucky: Sarabande Books, 2002.

Bjork, Daniel W. *William James: The Center of His Vision*. New York: Columbia University Press, 1988.

Boller, Jr., Paul F. *Freedom and Fate in American Thought*. Dallas: SMU Press, 1978.

Bouwsma, William J. *John Calvin: A Sixteenth Century Portrait*. New York and Oxford: Oxford University Press, 1988.

Buell, Lawrence. *Literary Transcendentalism*. Ithaca: Cornell University Press, 1973.

———. "The Emerson Industry in the 1980's: A Survey of Trends and Achievements," *ESQ*, Vol. 30, 2nd Quarter (1984): 117-136.

Carpenter, Frederic I. "William James and Emerson." *American Literature*, vol. 11, no. 1 (March, 1939): 39-57.

Chamberlain, Ava. "The Grand Sower of the Seed: Jonathan Edwards's Critique of George Whitfield." *The New England Quarterly*, Vol. 70, Issue 3 (September, 1997): 368-385.

Cohen, Charles. *God's Caress: The Psychology of Puritan Religious Experience*. Oxford University Press: New York and Oxford, 1986.

Coleridge, Samuel Taylor. *Lay Sermons. The Collected Works*. Ed. Reginald James White. Princeton, New Jersey: Princeton University Press, 1972.

———. *Selected Poetry and Prose*. Ed. Donald A. Stauffer. New York: Random House, 1951.

Coon, Deborah J. "One Moment in the World's Salvation: Anarchism and the Radicalization of William James." *The Journal of American History*, Vol. 83, Issue 1, (June, 1996): 70-99.

Cox, James M. "R.W. Emerson: The Circle of the Eye." *Emerson: Prophecy, Metamorphosis, and Influence*, 45-60. Ed. David Levin. New York: Columbia University Press, 1985.

Delbanco, Andrew. *The Death of Satan*. New York: Farrar, Strauss and Giroux, 1995.

———. *The Puritan Ordeal*. Cambridge, Mass.: Harvard University Press, 1989.

———. *The Real American Dream*. Cambridge, Mass.: Harvard University Press, 1999.

Deutsche, Rosalyn. "Democratic Public Space." In *The Pragmatist Imagination: Thinking About "Things in the Making,"* edited by Joan Ockman, 76-82. New York: Princeton Architectural Press, 2000.

Dewey, John. *Art as Experience*. New York: Minton, Balch & Company, 1934.

Edwards, Jonathan. *Apocalyptic Writings, The Works of Jonathan Edwards*. Ed. Stephen J. Stein. New Haven and London: Yale University Press, 1978.
———. *Ethical Writings, The Works of Jonathan Edwards*. Ed. Paul Ramsey. New Haven and London: Yale University Press, 1988.
———. *The Great Awakening, The Works of Jonathan Edwards*. Ed. C.C. Goen. New Haven and London: Yale University Press, 1972.
———. *Images and Shadows of Divine Things*, ed. Perry Miller. New Haven and London: Yale University Press, 1948.
———. *The Miscellanies, a-500, The Works of Jonathan Edwards*. Ed. Thomas A. Schafer. New Haven and London: Yale University Press, 1994.
———. *The Miscellanies, 500-832, The Works of Jonathan Edwards*. Ed. Ava Chamberlain. New Haven and London: Yale University Press, 1994.
———. *Notes on Scripture, The Works of Jonathan Edwards*. Ed. Stephen J. Stein. New Haven and London: Yale University Press, 1998.
———. *The Sermons of Jonathan Edwards: A Reader*, ed. Wilson H. Kimnach, Kenneth P. Minkema, and Douglas A. Sweeney. New Haven and London: Yale University Press, 1999.
———. *Scientific and Philosophical Writings, The Works of Jonathan Edwards*. Ed. Wallace Anderson. New Haven and London: Yale University Press, 1980.
Emerson, Ralph Waldo, *Collected Works*, vol. 1. Ed. Jean Ferguson Carr and Alfred Ferguson. Introduction and notes, Joseph Slater. Cambridge, Mass.: Harvard University Press, 1983.
Engell, James. *The Creative Imagination*. Cambridge, Mass.: Harvard University Press, 1989.
Fontinell, Eugene. *Self, God, and Immortality: A Jamesian Investigation*. Philadelphia: Temple University Press, 1986.
Frankenberry, Nancy. *Religion and Radical Empiricism*. Albany, New York: SUNY Press, 1987.
Gavin, William Joseph. *William James and the Reinstatement of the Vague*. Philadelphia: Temple University Press, 1992.
Gendlin, Eugene T. *Thinking Beyond Patterns: Body, Language, and Situations*. New York: Peter Lang, 1991.
Goodman, Russell B. *American Philosophy and the Romantic Tradition*. Cambridge, New York, Port Chester, Melbourne, and Sydney: Cambridge University Press, 1990.
Guelzo, Allen C. "The Return of the Will: Jonathan Edwards and the Possibilities of Free Will." in *Edwards in Our Time*, edited by Allen C. Guelzo and Sang Hyun Lee, 87-110. Grand Rapids, MI: Wm. B. Eerdmans Publishing Co., 1999.
Hambrick-Stowe, Charles E. *The Practice of Piety: Puritan Devotional Practices in Seventeenth-Century New England*. Chapel Hill: University of North Carolina Press, 1982.

Heimert, Alan, and Delbanco, Andrew, ed. *The Puritans in America: A Narrative Anthology.* Cambridge, Mass.: Harvard University Press, 1985.

Hodder, Alan D. *Emerson's Rhetoric of Revelation: Nature, the Reader, and the Apocalypse Within.* University Park, Pa.: Pennsylvania State University Press,, 1989.

James, Sr., Henry. *A Selection of His Writings.* Ed. Giles Gunn. Chicago: American Library Association, 1974.

James, William. *Collected Essays and Reviews.* Ed. Ralph Barton Perry. London: Longmans, Green and Co., 1920.

———. *Essays in Philosophy. The Works of William James.* Gen. ed. Frederick Burkhardt. Textual ed. Fredson Bowers. Cambridge, Mass.: Harvard University Press, 1978.

———. *Letters*, 2 vols. Boston: The Atlantic Monthly Press, 1920.

———. *Manuscript Essays and Notes. The Works of William James.* Gen. ed. Frederick Burkhardt. Textual ed. Fredson Bowers. Cambridge, Mass.: Harvard University Press, 1988.

———. *The Meaning of Truth. The Works of William James.* Gen. ed. Frederick Burkhardt. Textual ed. Fredson Bowers. Cambridge, Mass.: Harvard University Press, 1975.

———. *Pragmatism. The Works of William James.* Gen. ed. Frederick Burkhardt. Textual ed. Fredson Bowers. Cambridge, Mass.: Harvard University Press, 1975.

———. *The Principles of Psychology. The Works of William James.* 3 vols. Gen. ed. Frederick Burkhardt. Textual ed. Fredson Bowers. Cambridge, Mass.: Harvard University Press, 1981.

———. *Psychology: Briefer Course. The Works of William James.* Gen. ed. Frederick Burkhardt. Textual ed. Fredson Bowers. Cambridge, Mass.: Harvard University Press, 1984.

———. *The Will to Believe. The Works of William James.* Gen. ed. Frederick Burkhardt. Textual ed. Fredson Bowers. Cambridge, Mass.: Harvard University Press, 1979.

———. *The Varieties of Religious Experience. The Works of William James.* Gen. ed. Frederick Burkhardt. Textual ed. Fredson Bowers. Cambridge, Mass.: Harvard University Press, 1985.

Johnson, Mark. *The Meaning of the Body: Aesthetics of Human Understanding.* Chicago: University of Chicago Press, 2008.

Kloppenberg, James T. *Uncertain Victory: Social Democracy and Progressivism in European and American Thought, 1870-1920.* New York and Oxford: Oxford University Press, 1986.

Knight, Janice. "Learning the Language of God: Jonathan Edwards and the Typology of Nature." *The William and Mary Quarterly*, Third Series, Vol. 48:4 (October 1991) 531-551.

———. *Orthodoxies in Massachusetts*. Cambridge, Mass.: Harvard University Press, 1994.
Kress, Jill. "Contesting Metaphors and the Discourse of Consciousness in William James." *Journal of the History of Ideas* 61.2 (2000).
Kuklick, Bruce. *Churchmen and Philosophers: From Jonathan Edwards to John Dewey*. New Haven and London: Yale University Press, 1985.
Lamberth, David. *William James and the Metaphysics of Experience*. Cambridge, New York, and Melbourne: Cambridge University Press, 1999.
Larson, Kerry C. *Whitman's Drama of Consensus*. Chicago: The University of Chicago Press, 1988.
Lee, Sang Hyun. *The Philosophical Theology of Jonathan Edwards*. Princeton: Princeton University Press, 1988.
Lee, Sang Hyun and Allen C. Guelzo, eds. *Edwards in Our Time*. Grand Rapids, MI: Wm. B. Eerdmans Publishing Co., 1999.
Lewalski, Barbara. *Puritan Poetics and the Seventeenth-Century Religious Lyric*. Princeton: Princeton University Press, 1979.
Livingston, James. *Pragmatism and the Political Economy of Cultural Revolution, 1850-1940*. Chapel Hill and London: The University of North Carolina Press, 1997.
Lopez, Michael. "De-Transcendentalizing Emerson." *ESQ*, Vol. 34, 1st and 2nd Quarters (1988): 77-139.
Marsden, George M. *Jonathan Edwards: A Life*. New Haven and London: Yale University Press, 2003.
McFarland, Thomas. *Romanticism and the Forms of Ruin: Wordsworth, Coleridge, and Modalities of Fragmentation*. Princeton: Princeton University Press, 1981.
McDermott, Gerald R. *One Holy and Happy Society: The Public Theology of Jonathan Edwards*. University Park: The Pennsylvania State University Press, 1992.
Miller, Perry. *Errand Into the Wilderness*. Cambridge, Mass.: Harvard University Press, 1958.
———. *Jonathan Edwards*. Amherst: The University of Massachusetts Press, 1981.
———. "Jonathan Edwards on the Sense of the Heart." *The Harvard Theological Review*, Vol. 41, No. 2 (April, 1948): 123-145.
Mitchell, Charles Edwards. *Individualism and Its Discontents*. Amherst: The University of Massachusetts Press, 1997.
Morgan, Edmund S. *Visible Saints: The History of a Puritan Idea*. Ithaca: Cornell University Press, 1963.
Myers, Gerald E. *William James: His Life and Thought*. New Haven and London: Yale University Press, 1986.
New, Elisa. "Beyond the Romance Theory of American Vision: Beauty and the Qualified Will in Edwards, Jefferson, and Audubon." *American Literary History*, Vol. 7, No. 3 (Autumn 1995): 381-414.

———. *The Line's Eye: Poetic Experience, American Sight.* Cambridge, Mass.: Harvard University Press, 1999

Niebuhr, H.R. *The Meaning of Revelation.* Louisville, Ky.: Westminster John Knox Press, 2006.

Niebuhr, Reinhold. *The Irony of American History.* New York: Charles Scribner's Sons, 1952.

Niebuhr, Richard R. *Experiential Religion.* New York: Harper and Row, Publishers, Inc., 1972.

———. *Streams of Grace: Studies of Jonathan Edwards, Samuel Taylor Coleridge, and William James.* Kyoto: Doshisha University Press, 1983.

———. "William James on Religious Experience." In *The Cambridge Companion to William James,* 214-236. Edited by Ruth Anna Putnam. Cambridge, England: Cambridge University Press, 1997.

Ockman, Joan, editor. *The Pragmatist Imagination: Thinking About "Things in the Making."* New York: Princeton Architectural Press, 2000.

Packer, Barbara. *Emerson's Fall.* New York: Continuum, 1982.

Parker, Gail Thain. "Jonathan Edwards and Melancholy." *New England Quarterly* 41:2 (June, 1968): 193-212.

Perry, Ralph Barton. *The Thought and Character of William James.* Boston and Toronto: Little, Brown, and Company, 1935.

Pettit, Norman. *The Heart Prepared: Grace and Conversion in Puritan Spiritual Life.* Middletown, CT.: Wesleyan University Press, 1989.

Pinsky, Robert. *Democracy, Culture and the Voice of Poetry.* Princeton: Princeton University Press, 2002.

Proudfoot, Wayne. "From Theology to a Science of Religions: Jonathan Edwards and William James on Religious Affections." *Harvard Theological Review* 82:2 (April, 1989): 149-168.

Putnam, Hillary. *Realism with a Human Face.* Cambridge, Mass.: Harvard University Press, 1990.

Richardson, Joan. *A Natural History of Pragmatism.* Cambridge, England: Cambridge University Press, 2007.

Ruf, Frederick J. *The Creation of Chaos: William James and the Stylistic Making of a Disorderly World.* Albany: State University of New York, 1991.

Rupp, George. "The "Idealism" of Jonathan Edwards," *Harvard Theological Review* 62, 1969

Seigfried, Charlene Haddock. *William James's Radical Reconstruction of Philosophy.* Albany: State University of New York, 1990.

Shea, Daniel. *Spiritual Autobiography in Early America.* Madison: The University of Wisconsin Press, 1988.

Smith, John E. *The Spirit of American Philosophy.* Albany: State University of New York, 1983.

Tuan, Yi Fu. *Passing Strange and Wonderful.* New York: Farrar, Strauss, and Giroux, 1984.

Valeri, Mark. "The Economic Thought of Jonathan Edwards." *Church History* 60, no. 1, (March 1991): 37-54.
Whicher, Stephen E. *Freedom and Fate: An Inner Life of Ralph Waldo Emerson*. Philadelphia: University of Pennsylvania Press, 1953.
Whitman, Walt. *Poetry and Prose*. Edited by Justin Kaplan. New York: Viking Press, 1982.
Wild, John. *The Radical Empiricism of William James*. Garden City, N.Y.: Doubleday & Company, Inc., 1969.
Yeager, D.M. "Passion and Suspicion: Religious Affections in 'The Will to Believe.' *The Journal of Religion*, Vol. 69, No. 4 (October, 1989): 467-483.

Index

absolutism, 79, 101, 108, 111, 134; and quarrel with empiricism, 103
affectional facts, 45, 48, 65, 68 100-102, 105, 109, 111, 123, 136, 138, 139, 141, 142
aesthetics, 54, 103, 123, 137; and "advantageous connexion," 58, 107; different from aestheticism, 144n16; and the excellence of Christ, 36, 114, 118; and God as Being in General, 36; and the moral life, 123; as natural, moral, and spiritual, 137; poetry and the perception of, 123, 131; as prospective, 103, 107-08; and radical empiricism, 107; as retrospective, 54; in synonymy with ethics, 47, 54, 95, 103, 110, 112, 130, 136. *See also* excellence; true virtue
America, 1, 2, 24, 77; American dream, 5, 142; Edwards's criticism of, 96, 140-141, 156n2; as ethical republic, 68; and exceptionalism, 77, 110, 140; influence of Puritans on, 5-8; irony of, 10; James's criticism of, 127, 141; as New Jerusalem, 2; religious declension in, 138, 139-140; religious purpose of, 4; as spiritual wilderness, 1, 3, 5, 6, 7, 8, 9; Whitman and, 126-128
Antinomianism, 1, 3, 6, 7, 26. *See also* Spiritual Brethren
Arendt, Hanna 2
Arminianism, 3, 6, 7,14, 25, 40

Bidart, Frank, 80
Boller, Paul, 26

Book of Ezekiel, 52, 53, 55, 56, 57, 58; Coleridge and, 52-3; and imagination, 52-55
Book of Jeremiah, 57
Book of Nature, 24, 35-36, 37, 38, 79, 83, 87, 91, 112, 118
Bouwsma, William J., 31

Calvin, John, 3, 19, 31. *See also* predestination
Cambridge Platonists, 3, 61, 113
Coleridge, Samuel Taylor, 46, 52, 53, 54, 55, 114, 118; and Whitman, 129
Colman, Benjamin, 12
conjunction of opposites, 36, 61-62, 70, 112-114, 116, 118, 119, 121. *See also* Jesus Christ
consciousness: and actual idea, 33, 35; as awakened, 36; as "feeling within itself," 58, 65, 100, 103; field theory of consciousness, 25, 73, 97, 102; James's metaphors for, 63; and James's ontologic sphere, 46; and moral responsibility, 136; and pure experience, 74, 100; and sense of the heart, 37, 62; as a society, 100, 103, 112, 114; as a stream, 64, 73, 102
Cotton, John 6
creativity, 24, 26, 41, 42, 47, 49, 58, 67, 73; creative freedom, 24, 26, 32, 42, 48, 50, 54, 58, 65, 67, 68, 111, 132, 141, 142 *See also*

Index

free will; imagination; sense of the heart

Darwinism, 3, 4, 42
Davenport, James, 14
Delbanco, Andrew, 4, 7, 12, 137, 142; comparison of Edwards and James, 4
democracy, 54, 110, 134; and the excellency of Christ, 118; and pluralistic universe, 110; as strenuous, 110, 134, 137, 139, 142; and Walt Whitman, 123, 127-128, 132
determinism, 3, 9, 20, 23, 24, 25, 27, 32, 35, 41, 49, 50, 55, 59, ; and alienation, 98; and closed society, 111 and feeling, 78; and James's personal crisis, 22-23; and radical empiricism, 101; and second-hand religion, 83. *See also* predestination
Deutsch, Rosalind, 111
Dewey, John, 54

Edwards, Jonathan: and the Northampton revival, 12-16, 38; personal crisis, 27-30; and sense of personal failure, 16; Uncle Joseph Hawley's suicide, 12, 13, 17, 18, 38. *See also* aesthetics; the sense of the heart; true virtue
Edwards, Timothy, 28
Emerson, Ralph Waldo 3, 7, 9, 46, 54, 57, 64, 69, 72, 74, 106, 112, 123, 125, 126; "Circles," 46, 57, 64, 66, 69; concept of whole fact in, 66; influence on *The Varieties of Religious Experience*, 66, 68-69; and transparent eyeball image, 66, 72
empiricism, 9, 45, 47, 48, 68, 76; "shadow empiricism," 77, 82. *See also* enriched empiricism, radical empiricism
Engell, James, 114
enriched empiricism, 51, 59, 77, 79, 81-96, 99, 104-105, 109, 137; and American dream, 77; and excellency of Christ, 113-114; and good society, 110; as marriage of idealism and materialism, 74; and sense of the heart, 57. *See also* radical empiricism
excellence, 4, 8, 17, 81-93, 103, 154n21; and actual connexion, 43; as beauty, 32, 36, 102-103; and Being in General, 32, 111; and Christ, 36, 70, 112-21; and consent, 89; and experimental piety, 81; God's excellency in nature, 37; and love, 88, 92; in *Mind #1*, 87; as natural, moral, and spiritual beauty, 88, 92; and pragmatic theory of truth, 72; as true religion, 84. *See also* aesthetics; beauty

Fontinell, Eugene, 71
free will, 24-25, 47, 48; and James's personal crisis, 22-23

Gendlin, Eugene T., 94
God, 24, 52, 56, 58, 59, 62, 74, 98, 101, 106; absolute dependence on, 85, 88, 95; as communicative, 37, 39, 80, 82, 84, 85, 86, 93, 110; as finite, 26, 73, 138, 139; God as Being in General, 25, 32, 36, 39, 55, 58, 59, 61, 62, 80-82, 85-92, 94, 111, 115; God's sovereignty, 25, 27, 30, 31, 32, 35, 37, 38, 39, 50, 58, 85; James's critique of traditional concepts of God, 25, 56, 59, 68, 69, 139; and Northampton revival, 11-13, 16-17; pragmatism's search for god(s), 106-108; and the sense of the heart, 32-35. *See also* grace; predestination
grace, 6, 56, 92, 102; as active, 119-120; as divine light, 36, 38; Edwards's experience of, 27, 34-41; and excellency of Christ, 116, 117, 119; and false affections, 27, 28, 29, 30; and James's personal crisis, 26, 47; and nature, 29, 36; and practice, 140-141
Guelzo, Allen C., 24

heart, 9, 17-18, 39, 53-62, 75; as imagination, 54; in James's thought, 43-45, 47, 49, 63-67, 75; in Protestant piety, 56-57; and psychology of affections, 53, 54; and Puritan model of sanctification, 56, 62; the sense of the heart, or new sense, 9, 32-37, 40, 43, 59-62, 77, 81, 82, 84, 88, 89, 96, 114, 116, 118, 119. *See also* knowledge by acquaintance

idealism, 19, 20, 42, 54, 56, 68, 73, 83, 84, 97; and "shadow idealism," 77
imagination, 24, 26, 36, 42, 44-46, 49, 51, 52-55, 65, 78-91; in "Crossing Brooklyn Ferry," 129; and false affections, 17; and genius, 133; and Jesus Christ, 114; and joy, 100. *See also* heart
intimacy, and advantageous connexion, 135; and beauty, 91, 93; and creative freedom, 142; and democracy, 130; and foreignness, 129; and excellence,135-136, James's notion of, 72, 76, 77, 81, 97-99, 104, 105, 108-109, 127, 132, 135-136; and the More, or wider self, 138; in a pluralistic universe, 127-128; and transcendent meekness, 130; in Whitman, 130
irony of religious belief, 10-11, 14, 20.

Jackson, Michael 5
James, Sr., Henry, 22
James, William: assessment of Edwards, 9, 134-135, 136; personal crisis, 21-23, 41-51
Jesus Christ, 25, 31, 32, 37, 39; and conjunction of opposites, 61, 70; and consciousness, 37; excellence of, 36, 61, 70, 112-121; Emerson's view of as poet, 125; personation of, 64, 80, 87, 91, 93, 96, 113, 119, 130, 133; and religious genius, 133; and Whitman, 125-126, 130, 131

Knight, Janice, 6, 7, 8, 84,
knowledge by acquaintance and knowledge about, 9, 46, 53, 60, 64, 67, 68, 70, 73, 75, 81, 101, 103, 105, 107, 129, 137; and Coleridge's theory of imagination, 46, 53, 118; and Emerson's essay "Circles," 46; as *wissen* and *kennen*, 45, 149n39;
Kuklick, Bruce, 88

Lee, Sang Hyun, 30, 93, 94
Lewalski, Barbara, 65-66
Livingston, James, 127

Locke, John, 3, 85
Luther, Martin, 19

materialism, 54, 101
McDermott, Gerald, 141
melancholy, 12, 13, 17, 19, 22, 29, 40, 41, 44, 49, 56, 72 ; and excellency of Christ, 117. *See also* suicide
Metaphysical Club, 42
Miller, Perry, 35, 40, 62; comparing Edwards and James, 99; and the rhetoric of sensation, 7, 35; and the sense of the heart, 83, 84, 99
moral solitude, 136-137, 140, 142
"More," 46, 56, 58, 59, 67, 72, 97, 104, 108, 135, 138; and democratic impulse, 133-134; and ontologic sphere, 46; and radical empiricism, 67; as something there, 55; as wider environment or widened reality, 25, 26, 80, 97, 101, 117, 126, 129, 135, 138; and wider self, 66, 70, 72, 73, 74, 75 111, 124 135, 138, 139
mystic sense of inner meaning, 45, 50, 55, 67, 74, 77, 97, 103, 123-125; awakening in nature, 125; in opposition to paltry empiricism, 129; and spiritual blindness, 124; and the Spiritual Brethren, 7-8. *See also* heart

New, Elisa, 41, 88, 92, 95, 115
Newton, Isaac, 3, 85
Niebuhr, H. Richard, 80
Niebuhr, Reinhold, 9

ordo salutis, 17, 27; steps of, 146n42
original sin, 3, 6, 9, 11, 15, 84; in Edwards's *Personal Narrative*, 28-30, 38-39; and sanctification, 37, 38; and sense of the heart, 34, 36

paltry empiricism, 48, 76-77, 92, 101, 129

Index

philosophy, in America 1-2; as a guide to living, 19, 102, 105; and James's personal crisis, 42-48; as quest, 21, 44, 48; role of temperament in, 19-20; as system-building, 3, 9, 18, 20, 41, 126; as trailblazing, 1; as therapeutic, 20

pluralistic universe, 67, 77, 79, 81, 108, 109, 123, 127-128, 138; as ethical republic, 110; and Whitman, 128. *See also* radical empiricism

pragmatism, 19, 20, 21 62, 97-109; and aesthetic experience, 105-106, 108; and cash-value, 4, 21; and Edwards, 84, 86, 94, 134, 135, 139-140; and God, 106, 108; and idealism, 20; as method, 105; opposed to systematic philosophy, 20, 137, 139; as "protestant reformation in philosophy," 18, 101,105; and radical empiricism, 100, 104-5, 107, 109; and religion, 101-109, 134, 139; and social cooperation, 109; and temperament, 19-21; as theory of truth, 43, 46, 49, 50, 54, 101-109. *See also* radical empiricism; true virtue

prayer, 92-93, 117

predestination, 24, 25, 26, 30-31, 37, 40, 63, 87 147n1; Shepard's influence on Edwards's view of, 148n17. *See also* Calvin; determinism

Proudfoot, Wayne, 137, 151n40

Puritanism, 4, 7; Puritan piety, 6, 14, 54, 56; James on Puritans, 134; and strenuous mood, 121-122

Putnam, Hillary, 136

radical empiricism, 3, 26, 45, 47, 48-49, 54, 57, 59, 62, 64, 67, 81, 94-100; and absolute truth, 98, 101; and aesthetics, 123, 136; defined, 95; Edwards and, 96; and finite god, 138; and the moral life, 136; and religion, 97, 136, 138, 139; and Whitman, 123, 127, 129-130. *See also* enriched empiricism

Reagan, Ronald, 5

reinstatement of the vague; 3, 9, 19, 55, 64, 67, 71-72, 77-79, 97-98, 110, 111, 112, 123, 126, 128; and ethical republic, 141; Gendlin on, 97-98;

religious affections, 76, 78-80, 81, 84, 87, 95, 120; and Edwards's critique of rationalism and enthusiasm, 3, 10, 14, 134; false affections, 3, 5, 10, 13-14; holy affections, 14; and hypocrisy, 120, 140; and illusion, 111; James's interpretation of *Treatise Concerning Religious Affections*, 9, 134-135, 137; and pragmatic verification, 8, 17, 86, 88, 106, 111, 120, 140; Proudfoot on, 137-138; and radical empiricism, 109; Smith on, 140-141. *See also* heart

Renouvier, Charles, 47, 48

Richardson, Joan, 90

Royce, Josiah, 20

Rupp, George, 84

saint, 58, 74, 82, 83, 87, 90, 93, 94, 95, 120-121; and charity, 120; discussed in "The Excellency of Christ," 113-121; and natural man, 135; as personation of Christ, 64, 91, 93, 96, 113, 119, 130, 133; and Whitman, 133

salvation, 4, 6, 10, 11, 12, 17, 83, 85; as cooperative or piecemeal, 55, 59, 62, 68, 72, 75, 81, 109, 110, 123, 132, 141-142; and false affections, 111; and finite experience, 126; and the saint, 114; and strenuous democracy, 110; Whitman's view, 132

Smith, John E., 64, 139, 140-141

Spiritual Brethren, 7, 10. *See also* Antinomianism

Stoddard, Solomon, 11, 14, 16, 17, 28

strenuous mood, 117, 119, 120, 121-122, 133, 135, 137; and Puritanism, 121-122; and religion's value, 134-135; strenuous democracy, 110, 112, 132, 134, 139, 141, 142, 143; suicide: of John Corcoran, 20; of Joseph Hawley, 12-13; suicide and revivalism, 13, 17

Tenant, Gilbert, 14

true virtue, 54, 86, 88, 89, 91, 94, 109, 116, 125, 135; and benevolence, 91, 94, 96; and James's pragmatic theory of truth, 106; opposed to private affections, 94;

Whitefield, George, 14
Whitman, Walt, 123; and "Crossing Brooklyn Ferry," 123, 128-133; 108 democracy, 127-128, 132, 134, 142; and pragmatism, 127; as prophet, 126
will to believe, 64-65,
Winthrop, John, 5, 6,
wonder, 55, 80, 83, 131, 142; and excellency of Christ, 118
Wright, Chauncey, 42
Yeager, D.M., 65

About the Author

S.T. Campagna-Pinto is assistant professor of Religious Studies at California State University, Bakersfield.